T0326556

Long-term Care in Central and South Eastern Europe

August Österle (ed.)

Long-term Care in Central and South Eastern Europe

PETER LANG

Frankfurt am Main · Berlin · Bern · Bruxelles · New York · Oxford · Wien

Bibliographic Information published by the Deutsche Nationalbibliothek
The Deutsche Nationalbibliothek lists this publication in the Deutsche Nationalbibliografie; detailed bibliographic data is available in the internet at http://dnb.d-nb.de.

Cover Design:
© Olaf Glöckler, Atelier Platen, Friedberg

ISBN 978-3-631-61689-5

© Peter Lang GmbH
Internationaler Verlag der Wissenschaften
Frankfurt am Main 2011
All rights reserved.

www.peterlang.de

Contents

Foreword

Ageing societies together with broader socio-economic developments are challenging societies in manifold ways, not least in the ways in which they are dealing with social risks. The need for long-term care, help and support and the ways in which societies respond to these needs is one of the issues that will be most seriously affected by these changes. Historically, long-term care for older people has long been widely neglected as a distinctive social risk. The bulk of care has been and still is largely organised, provided and funded within family or other informal networks. Only in the past two decades, many European countries have started to substantially extend existing programmes and to implement more comprehensive social protection schemes in long-term care. In other countries, including those in the Central Eastern and South Eastern European region, debates on the future of long-term care have intensified only in the very recent past. This is a consequence of various factors. There are strong perceptions in society placing responsibilities for long-term care in the family context. There is little lobbying that could help make long-term care a major policy concern. There is a lack of financial resources and comparatively low policy priority for long-term care. And, a broader and more focused debate on the future of long-term care is also hindered by large variations in the general understanding and conceptualisation of care.

The project "Long-Term Care in Central and South Eastern Europe" has taken up the challenge (a) to systematically collect information on the way citizens, private actors and the state deal with the issue of long-term care, (b) to study this information in a comparative perspective, and (c) to discuss major challenges and perspectives for the future of long-term care in this region. The project covers eight countries in the Central and South Eastern European region, namely Austria, Croatia, Czech Republic, Hungary, Romania, Serbia, Slovakia and Slovenia. This book brings the results of the project together. It provides an overview of common and of diverse demographic and socio-economic challenges, it presents and discusses the current situation in the organisation, provision and finance of long-term care in the eight Central and South Eastern European countries and it discusses these results in a broader comparative European perspective.

Work for this project is based on close cooperation with many experts in the Central and South Eastern European region. They have contributed their expertise as national project partners, in interviews during study visits and in the context of two international expert workshops. We are grateful to Marina Ajduković, Gojko Bezovan, Visnja Fortuna, Zorana Franjić Staničić, Romana Galic, Ljiljana Muslić, Silvia Rusac, Filipa Linda Šimunović, Vesna Širanović, Ana Štambuk, Irena Vadlja, and Nino Žganec from Croatia; Jana Barvíková, Kristyna Cermaková, Renata Dohnalová, Iva Holmerová, Barbora Kolářová, Dana Korinková, Matěj Lejsal, Olga Nešporová, and Petr Wija from the Czech Republic; Gabriella Csillik, Csaba Dózsa, Katalin Érsek, László Gulácsi, Krisztian Karpati, and Kinga Mészáros from Hungary; Nicoleta Molnar, Liviu Popa, Livia Popescu, and Narcisa Teglaş from Romania; Dragana Dinic, Sanja Jankelic, Drago Jelaca, Marija Kolin, Lidija Kozarcanin, Sanja Miloradovic, Ljubomir Pejakovic, Nadezna Sataric, Lidija Topic, and Jasminka Veselinovic from Serbia; Božena Bušová, Helena Kuvíková, Jana Štrangfeldová, Peter Tatár, Lenka Topinková, Katarína Vidličková, and Helena Woleková from Slovakia; Lidija Apohal Vučković, Davor Dominkuš, Vito Flaker, Marino Kačič, Boris Kramberger, Barbara Kresal, Uršula Jerše Jan, Mateja Nagode, Laura Perko, Kristina Podbevšec, and Cveto Uršič from Slovenia. Furthermore, we would like to thank the authors of the chapters for their contributions and for their patience during the editing process. Many thanks also to Christoph Giesinger, Kai Leichsenring and Michael Meyer as Members of the Advisory Board. Katharina Meichenitsch, and, in the final phase, Lisa Mittendrein have not only been involved in research but have also provided administrative support. Many thanks also to Gudrun Bauer, Daniela Friedl, Sandra Hinterleitner, Gertraud Steyrer and Katalin Windisch who have been involved in more specific supportive tasks at different stages of the project. We are also grateful to the publishers and to Maureen Lenhart who has done the layout of the final manuscript. The country chapters in this book have been completed in 2009. The introductory chapter and the final chapter have been finalised till 2010, in particular while staying as a research fellow at the Hanse Institute for Advanced Studies (HWK) in 2009/10. The support of the HWK during the research stay is gratefully acknowledged. Finally, many thanks go to Franz Karl Prüller from ERSTE Foundation for his continuous invaluable support for the project. The project has been made possible by the generous support of ERSTE Foundation, active in the Central and South Eastern European region since 2003 in the pro-gramme areas "Social Development", "Culture" and "Europe".

August Österle

List of Tables

List of Contributors

Marina AJDUKOVIĆ is Professor and Head of the Chair for Theory and Methodology of Social Work and the Chair for Social Gerontology at the Department of Social Work, Faculty of Law, University of Zagreb.

Jana BARVÍKOVÁ is Researcher at the Institute of Sociological Studies, Charles University Prague.

Katalin ÉRSEK is PhD student at the Health Economics and Technology Assessment Research Centre, Department of Public Policy and Management, Corvinus University Budapest.

Vito FLAKER is Professor at the Faculty for Social Work, University of Ljubljana.

László GULÁCSI is Professor and Head of the Health Economics and Technology Assessment Research Centre, Department of Public Policy and Management, Corvinus University Budapest.

Marija KOLIN is Senior Research Fellow at the Institute of Social Sciences in Belgrade, Serbia.

Barbara KRESAL is Senior Lecturer at the Faculty for Social Work, University of Ljubljana.

Helena KUVÍKOVÁ is Professor and Head of the Department of Public Economics, Faculty of Economics, Matej Bel University Banska Bystrica.

Katharina MEICHENITSCH is a former Researcher at the Institute for Social Policy, WU Vienna University of Economics and Business.

Kinga MÉSZÁROS is a former Research Assistant at the Health Economics and Technology Assessment Research Centre, Department of Public Policy and Management, Corvinus University Budapest.

Lisa MITTENDREIN is Researcher at the Institute for Social Policy, Department of Socioeconomics, WU Vienna University of Economics and Business.

Mateja NAGODE is Senior Researcher at the Social Protection Institute of the Republic of Slovenia.

August ÖSTERLE is Associate Professor at the Institute for Social Policy, Department of Socioeconomics, WU Vienna University of Economics and Business.

Livia POPESCU is Professor at the Faculty of Sociology and Social Work, Babeş-Bolyai University Cluj-Napoca.

Silvia RUSAC is Assistant Professor at the Department of Social Work, Faculty of Law, University of Zagreb.

Ana ŠTAMBUK is Assistant Professor at the Department of Social Work, Faculty of Law, University of Zagreb.

Jana ŠTRANGFELDOVÁ is Assistant Professor at the Department of Public Economics, Faculty of Economics, Matej Bel University Banska Bystrica.

Lenka TOPINKOVÁ is a former PhD student at the Department of Public Economics, Faculty of Economics, Matej Bel University Banska Bystrica

Katarína VIDLIČKOVÁ is a former PhD student at the Department of Public Economics, Faculty of Economics, Matej Bel University Banska Bystrica

Nino ŽGANEC is Associate Professor at the Department of Social Work, Faculty of Law, University of Zagreb.

1

Providing Care for Growing Needs: The Context for Long-term Care in Central and South Eastern Europe

August Österle, Lisa Mittendrein, Katharina Meichenitsch

1. Introduction

Across Europe, there is a growing awareness of long-term care as a social risk and of the profound changes in the context, the conditions and requirements for addressing the risk. Ageing societies, changes in the socio-economic context, individual needs and preferences, family and household arrangements, social policies and the economic situation have implications for the current and future need for long-term care and for the resources that can help addressing these needs. While European countries share major trends, differences in the status-quo and in the intensity of the trends as well as country-specific context variables create quite diverse challenges, not least for the countries in Central and South Eastern Europe (CSEE) which are at the centre of analysis in this book. In the past two decades, this region has been characterised by profound political, economic and social transformations and major demographic and socio-economic changes. In this process, long-term care has been a widely neglected policy area. Public spending on long-term care remained on very low levels. With growing awareness of the increase in needs and with major changes in the context of traditional family-oriented care arrangements, however, there is growing pressure to develop novel responses towards the risk of care.

Before studying long-term care systems for single countries in the CSEE region, this introductory chapter will discuss major developments framing the current and future organisation, provision and funding of long-term care. The focus of this chapter is on the situation in Central and South Eastern European countries covered in this study and brought into a broader European perspective. Comparative data is provided for the eight study countries and for selected other European countries representing different traditions and different current situations in long-term care. After this introduction, the second section will assess the demographic changes and the implications ageing has on care needs and on care arrangements. This will be followed in the third section by a discussion of family care as the still dominant approach to covering care needs in CSEE. The section will focus on the broader socio-economic context and the potential implications current developments have for the sustainability of a system largely based on informal long-term care-giving. The more specific national situations of family care-giving will then be addressed in eight country studies. With growing pressure on traditional family-oriented care systems, there will be a growing need for care arrangements that go beyond the closer family network. In the final section, the context for these developments will be very briefly addressed, not least with a view to potential implications of increasing long-term care needs on public expenditure. A detailed analysis of the developments in single countries and a comparative analysis of these developments follow in chapters 2 to 10.

2. Ageing Societies and the Growing Demand for Care

In the EU27, the population beyond 65 years of age accounts for 17.08% of total population in 2008. According to Eurostat projections, the respective proportion will reach 20.06% in 2020 and 26.85% in 2040. (see table 1.1) The proportion of those over 80 years of age will increase from 4.41% in 2008 to 8.86% in 2040. (Eurostat 2008) These developments are a European-wide trend, but with specific differences in the status-quo and the expected developments. The current proportion of the older population in Central Eastern European countries is generally lower compared to the European average. But the region will see an even more pronounced increase in the coming decades. In all

Central Eastern European countries, the proportion of those 80 years and older will more than double between 2008 and 2040 and even triplicate in Poland and Slovakia. In the South Eastern European countries, the current proportion of those 65 years of age and older is above the Central Eastern European average, but for these countries (except Slovenia) more moderate increases are projected for the decades to come. (see table 1.1)

Table 1.1: Population projection by age class, 2008–2040

	2008		2020		2040	
	65+	80+	65+	80+	65+	80+
EU 27	17.08	4.41	20.06	5.70	26.85	8.86
Austria	17.17	4.61	19.36	5.20	27.23	8.38
Croatia	16.99	2.99	19.89	4.56	24.90	7.00
Czech Rep.	14.64	3.37	20.22	4.10	26.32	8.40
Hungary	16.17	3.71	19.82	4.75	24.96	8.41
Romania	14.91	2.78	17.43	4.21	25.52	7.44
Serbia	17.49	2.69	20.23	4.98	22.99	6.73
Slovakia	11.98	2.59	16.44	3.23	25.33	7.77
Slovenia	16.08	3.52	20.42	5.41	29.08	9.87
France	16.50	5.02	20.19	6.03	25.34	9.34
Germany	20.05	4.73	22.79	7.09	31.06	10.29
Italy	20.08	5.50	22.68	7.32	30.82	9.98
Sweden	17.52	5.35	20.81	5.41	24.27	8.39
UK	16.10	4.52	18.29	4.97	22.45	7.26

(Source: Eurostat 2008; Serbian Academy of Sciences 2007; Statistical Office of Croatia 2007; data for Croatia for the year 2006/2021/2041)

While the absolute number of older people is a highly relevant indicator for estimating the future need for long-term care (see below), the relative proportion of the older people and future changes in these proportions give an indication of the level of potential support for the older population by the working age population. In the EU27 average, in 2008, the old-age dependency ratio – the number of people over 65 years of age as a share of those of working age (aged between 15 and 64 years) – was 25.39%, that is four adults of working age per person aged 65 and over. While the ratio is similar to the European average in South Eastern European countries (Croatia, Serbia and slightly lower in Slovenia), it is significantly lower in the Central Eastern European countries. But these countries will also see more substantial increases. In 2040, the old-age dependency ratio reaches 45.36% in the EU27 region. Most CSEE countries will be still below that average in 2040, with the important exception of Slovenia (49.40%). (see table 1.2) The growing relative proportion of the older population is related to two factors, the ageing of relatively strong age cohorts, and low fertility rates. Across Europe, the fertility rate, the average number of live born children per woman in her total lifetime, has been below the so-called replacement rate at which the population would remain stable (2.1). While fertility rates have been stable and even slightly increasing again in some Western European countries, fertility rates

Table 1.2: Old age dependency ratio and projections of dependent older persons

	Old age dependency ratio				Projection: Increase of dependent older persons
	2008	2020	2040	2060	2007–2060[a]
EU 27	25.39	31.05	45.36	53.47	102%
Austria	25.43	29.18	46.03	50.65	111%
Croatia	25.24	30.23	40.47	:	:
Czech Rep.	20.59	31.07	42.71	61.40	147%
Hungary	23.50	30.31	40.11	57.64	80%
Romania	21.34	25.67	40.75	65.27	114%
Serbia	26.00	31.38	37.19	:	:
Slovakia	16.58	23.85	39.98	68.49	165%
Slovenia	22.97	31.21	49.40	62.19	101%
Germany	30.29	35.28	54.73	59.08	75%
France	25.33	32.77	43.99	45.20	101%
Italy	30.47	35.47	54.07	59.32	89%
Sweden	26.66	33.69	40.78	46.71	89%
UK	24.27	28.58	36.92	42.14	99%

[a] Projection (European Commission 2009): Projections on the basis of disability rates drawn from the SHARE and the SILC survey. This scenario ("AWG reference scenario") assumes that half of projected longevity gains up to 2060 will be spent in good health and free of disability.

(Source: Eurostat 2008; European Commission 2009; Serbian Academy of Sciences 2007; Statistical Office of Croatia 2007; data for Croatia for the year 2006/2021/2041)

in Eastern Europe have been shrinking. In 2007, the average fertility rate in the EU27 countries is approximately 1.5, varying between 1.25 in Slovakia and 2 in France or Ireland. (Eurostat 2009)

Lower life expectancy in CSEE countries is the main reason for a relative smaller proportion of the older population in these countries. In the early 1990s, life expectancy at birth in Central and Eastern Europe as compared to Western Europe was about 5 years lower for woman and 7 years for man. From the early 1990s, in some countries from the mid 1990s, life expectancy has improved considerably in Central and Eastern European countries, but differences to Western Europe remain very significant. (McKee 2007; Velkova et al. 1997) In 2007, life expectancy at birth was between 69 and 71 years of age for men and between 76 and 78 years for women in Hungary, Romania, Slovakia and Serbia, compared to 79 years for men in Italy or Sweden, and compared to 83 years for women in Sweden and 84 years for women in Italy. The Czech Republic, Slovenia and Croatia are closer to Western European levels but still lacking a few years behind. (see table 1.3)

From a health and long-term care perspective, however, it is not life expectancy but healthy life expectancy or the difference between healthy life expectancy and total life expectancy that is important. A long life does not necessarily bring more years in bad health and limitations in quality of life. As with general life expectancy, a considerable gap between Eastern and Western European countries exists in terms of healthy life expectancy. But, the difference between total and healthy life expectancy at birth is relatively similar across Europe. (see table 1.3) Hence, the assumption that a lower proportion of older people or a lower old-age dependency ratio in Central Eastern Europe goes in line with a more moderate pressure in care needs is misleading. In fact, following the healthy life expectancy concept, CSEE countries face very similar pressures as other European countries. Another consequence for the provision of long-term care stems from the life expectancy gap between men and women. Higher life expectancy of women and the gendered division of care work allows a large amount of informal care-giving provided by women to older men. On the other side, older women are then more often left without informal care-giving resources, inducing a higher demand for care from outside the household or the family.

Table 1.3: Life expectancy at birth, healthy life expectancy at birth and at age 60

	Life expectancy at birth (2007)		Healthy life expectancy at birth (2007)		Healthy life expectancy at age 60 (2002)	
	Male	Female	Male	Female	Male	Female
Austria	77	83	70	74	16.2	19.3
Croatia	73	79	66	70	12.5	16.1
Czech Rep.	74	80	68	72	13.5	16.8
Hungary	69	78	62	69	12.2	15.9
Romania	70	77	63	68	12.3	14.6
Serbia	71	76	64	66	12.1	13.9
Slovakia	71	78	64	70	12.3	16.1
Slovenia	75	81	69	74	14.3	18.1
France	77	84	71	76	16.5	20.3
Germany	77	82	71	75	15.9	19.0
Italy	79	84	73	76	16.4	19.4
Sweden	79	83	72	75	17.1	19.6
UK	77	82	71	73	15.7	18.1

(Source: World Health Organization 2009; 2003)

As chronic diseases are the most influential factor for long-term care needs in old age, their assessment is crucial for research and policy development. One way of estimating the impact of chronic diseases is through self-reported health status of the population. Even if there are indications that institutional factors increase the self-reported incidence of a long-standing illness in Central and Eastern European countries and that cultural factors have an impact on self-reported health (Anderson et al. 2009; Alber, Köhler 2004), survey results at least can help identify major variations. And studies show quite some disparities across Europe, not least between the Western and the Eastern European region. According to Alber and Köhler (2004), almost 20% of the total population in the EU15, but 32% in the EU10 report a long-standing illness or disability. Among the population aged 65 and over, the respective proportion reaches one third of this age group in the EU15 and even two thirds in the EU10. The frequency of a long-term illness or disability also varies with income, even when controlled for age, gender and employment status. In the lowest income quartile, 26.9% of the population in the EU25 report a long-term illness or disability, compared to 16.3% in the highest income quartile. In the EU10, the difference is even 13.9

percentage points (35.7% in the lowest quartile compared to 21.8% in the highest quartile). (Alber, Köhler 2004) In a more recent survey, a similar level of chronic illness or health problem is reported (24% of Europeans). 26% of these are severely hampered in daily activities. More frequently, severe limitations are reported for Central Eastern EU member countries and in the lowest income quartile. (Anderson et al. 2009)

Dementia as a major age-related illness is of particular importance for the future organisation of long-term care. (Moise et al. 2004) Wancata et al. (2003) have used different models to project the number of people suffering from dementia (including the two main types Alzheimer's disease and vascular dementia). They conclude that there have been about 7.1 million prevalent cases of dementia in Europe (including Russia) in the year 2000. The number is expected to increase to about 10 million in 2020 and to 16 million in 2050. While there was 1 person with dementia per 69.4 people in the working age in 2000, the proportion will change to 21.1 in 2050. Currently, a larger proportion of the population is affected by dementia in Eastern Europe (including Russia). Relative increases until 2050 are expected to be largest in Western Europe (+150%), medium in Northern and Southern Europe (+130%) and lowest in Eastern Europe (+110%). While knowledge of the causes of dementia is still limited, correlations exist to factors like depression, alcoholism, high blood pressure and low education. These factors might at least partly explain the current differences in dementia between Western and Eastern Europe. (Wancata et al. 2003)

As life expectancy and healthy life expectancy continue to increase in most European countries, the question arises how this will affect the health status of older people, dependency levels and periods, the need for support, and, not least, public and private expenditure for long-term care in the future. The debate on the extent of future health and long-term care needs focuses on three scenarios, a compression of morbidity, an expansion of morbidity and a "dynamic equilibrium". (Lafortune et al. 2007) A compression of morbidity indicates that the health status of the older population improves with increasing life expectancy. Even though people live longer, they spend less time in ill health and need of care. An expansion of morbidity would bring increasing longevity without simultaneous improvements in the end-of-life health status. In this scenario, increasing life expectancy would go in line with prolonged periods of ill health. The third scenario is the dynamic equilibrium scenario. As life expectancy increases, it would bring an increase in light disabilities, but a reduction of severe morbidity.

Research shows that countries across Europe will face increasing numbers of people with long-standing illnesses and disabilities in old age, but that the extent strongly depends on future morbidity assumptions. (European Commission 2009; Lafortune et al. 2007; Oliveira Martins, de la Maisonneuve 2006; Comas-Herrera et al. 2006; Jacobzone et al. 1999) A recent European Commission (2009) projection works with different scenarios, ranging between a pessimistic scenario of "pure ageing" and an optimistic scenario of "constant disability". The pure ageing scenario assumes stable disability rates with no improvements in the health status of an increasing number of older people. In this case, the number of dependent older people will increase by an average of 115% in the EU27 between 2007 and 2060, the increase ranging between 44% in Bulgaria and 314% in Ireland. In many CSEE countries, the increase will be beyond European average, in particular in the Czech Republic (+168%), Slovakia (+177%) and Romania (+130%). In contrast to this scenario, the constant disability scenario assumes improvements in the future health status of older people. It projects disability rates to shift in line with life expectancy, which would result in lower future dependency rates. But even in this scenario, the number of dependent older people would still increase by 90% in the EU27, by 126% in the Czech Republic, by 153% in Slovakia or by 98% in Romania. Another scenario, assuming that half of projected longevity gains up to 2060 will be spent in good health and free of disability, projects an increase in the dependent older population by 102% in the 2007–2060 period in the EU27. In the CSEE study countries, the increase would range between 80% in Hungary and 165% in Slovakia. (see table 1.2) (European Commission 2009)

As other regions in Europe, CSEE countries will see a growing demand for long-term care among the older population. The extent of this increase, however, is highly controversial. Not least, it will be determined by the broader socio-economic context and policies addressing the developments. Attempts to reduce the need for care in old age will require multiple measures, in the medical field, in emphasising rehabilitation, in empowering frail older people or in developing and implementing technological innovations. But even when policies are successful in reducing dependency levels, all projections conclude that Europe will still face an increase in the need for long-term care. This raises the question of how this need will be covered. As will be shown in subsequent chapters, long-term care in CSEE countries largely builds on informal family care arrangements today. In the following section, the current and future potential of families to provide a huge amount of care work will be analysed.

3. Family Care and the Future Provision of Care Work

Informal care, above all family care, accounts for about 80% of care provided to frail older people in Europe. (OECD 2005) Family care, here understood as long-term care work provided to a relative in need of care, is a highly complex concept. Family care work differs in the activities carried out, in their frequency and duration, in how responsibilities are shared between informal carers or between the informal and the formal sector, it can differ in the relationship that is established between the informal carer and the person in need of care, in the way it shapes the division of responsibilities in a household, etc. It is in particular women providing long hours of care work several times a week. While men are relatively more involved when caring for a partner and after being retired, it is mostly women that also take over caring responsibilities before retirement age. Family carers providing care work over long periods of time often experience immense physical, mental and social burdens while at the same time receiving little recognition for the work provided. For those in the employment age (mostly women), the provision of family care can have additional negative implications for the carer's personal life and career. While family care has for long been taken as granted, in the more recent past, the situation of family caregivers is given growing attention, focusing on their needs, problems and strategies, but also on their potential as a source of covering growing care needs. (Anderson et al. 2009; Huber et al. 2009; Lamura et al. 2008; Timonen 2008; Mestheneos, Triantafillou 2005; Philp 2001)

The general mode and conceptualisation of care and care provision in the family context also has an impact on the perception and the measurement of family care. Hence, different empirical studies show quite some variation across countries and have therefore to be dealt with cautiously. Lower proportions of care-givers could, for example, indicate a relatively smaller role of informal care-giving, but also different perceptions of what constitutes care work or a concentration of informal care work on fewer care-givers. Despite these limitations, existing comparative data can at least allow some general conclusions. According to the Eurobarometer survey 2002 (Alber, Köhler 2004), 23% of European citizens (EU25) are looking after someone, a person with a long-term illness or an older or handicapped person in need of help. In the CSEE region, informal care-giving is on similar or slightly higher levels than this average, in particular with regard to care provided inside the household.

Table 1.4: Proportion of people providing informal care

	Total informal care-giving	Care-giving inside the household	Care-giving outside the household
EU 25	22.7	11.0	15.0
EU 15	22.1	10.0	14.9
EU 10	26.1	16.7	15.4
Austria	25.5	10.3	18.2
Czech Republic	31.9	16.3	20.1
Hungary	21.2	14.2	9.7
Romania	26.3	15.3	13.0
Slovakia	23.5	9.8	14.1
Slovenia	21.4	11.9	11.7
France	21.8	7.8	15.6
Germany	25.0	13.8	17.4
Italy	15.8	12.0	5.1
Sweden	27.0	8.3	20.9
United Kingdom	21.7	8.8	15.0

"Some people have extra family responsibilities because they look after someone who has a long-term illness, who is handicapped or elderly. Is there anyone living with you who has a long-term illness, who is handicapped or elderly, whom you look after or give special help to? And do you provide some regular service or help to such a person NOT living with you?"
(Source: Alber, Köhler 2004)

Apart from the actual care work provided, the relative importance of family care can also be derived from attitudes towards responsibilities in long-term care. Respective studies show some similarities but also considerable variations across Europe. On the one hand, there is some broad general agreement on a public responsibility for ensuring appropriate care services. According to the Eurobarometer survey 2007 (European Commission 2007), the statement "public authorities should provide appropriate home/institutional care for elderly people in need" is supported ("totally agree" or "tend to agree") by more than 85% of the population in every EU member country, with relatively stronger support in most Northern European countries. In the same survey, the statement "every individual should be obliged to contribute to an insurance scheme that will finance care if and when it is needed" is also supported by more than half of the population, with the exception of Finland. An earlier Eurobarometer survey (Alber, Köhler 2004) points at similar preferences. When asked about who should be responsible to finance care (elderly for themselves, their children, state or other public authorities, everyone equally), most countries had a majority voting for the state. In the Nordic countries, the approval

Table 1.5: Care financing preferences

	State or other public authorities	Their children	Everyone equally	Elderly themselves
EU 25	48.70	18.00	17.00	14.50
EU 15	50.30	17.80	15.40	14.70
EU 10	40.60	19.30	25.80	13.70
Austria	22.80	44.00	20.70	11.30
Czech Republic	34.40	18.10	38.00	8.90
Hungary	29.80	29.60	34.80	4.60
Romania	22.50	45.60	24.30	7.10
Slovakia	58.10	10.50	21.30	8.90
Slovenia	42.70	20.70	18.80	17.70
France	50.70	16.30	14.10	17.20
Germany	48.70	11.60	20.00	19.00
Italy	43.30	24.50	17.10	12.40
Sweden	81.00	2.50	6.80	8.90
UK	59.60	13.00	12.40	12.10

"Irrespective of your answer, who do you think should mainly pay for taking care of elderly parents? — The elderly parents themselves, their children, or the State or other public authorities (e.g. local government, Social Security, etc)."
(Source: Alber, Köhler 2004)

was close to 90% in Denmark and at 81% in Sweden. Even in many CSEE countries, with substantially larger support for the option that children should finance care, support for state or other public authorities was between 20% and 60%. (see table 1.5)

While there is considerable expectation towards the state, the surveys also point at the importance of the family in long-term care and the perception of family responsibilities, particularly strong in the CSEE region. When asked about the care arrangement in case one would become dependent, 45% of Europeans assume that it would be most likely to be looked after in the own home by a relative. Except for Slovenia, all study countries in the CSEE region are above this average. When asked about the preferred option to be looked after, it is again 45% of Europeans that support the option of being cared for in the own home by a relative. In CSEE countries support for this option is again above the European average. (European Commission 2007)

With regard to the best option for a care arrangement in case an elderly father or mother could no longer manage to live without regular help because of his or her physical or mental health condition, 30% of Europeans state that they should live with one of their children, 24% that one of their children should regularly visit, in order to provide them with the necessary care. (see table 1.6) When looking at the outcome for different countries and regions in Europe, the picture is similar to that just drawn. While Northern and Western European countries are below this average, countries in the CSEE region (except for Slovenia) are beyond this average. 56% of Romanians, 48% of Croatians and 47% of Slovakians state that an older parent in need of regular care and help should live with children. In the Czech Republic and in Hungary the respective proportion is 36%. On the other hand, it is just 4% of the Swedes, 17% of the Austrians, 18% of the French or 20% of the British supporting this statement. (European Commission 2007)

The aforementioned and other studies show both a picture of strong filial norms and family obligations, but also an expectation towards public authorities being responsible for funding and ensuring appropriate services for those in need. (e.g. European Commission 2007; Alber, Köhler 2004; Daatland, Herlofson 2003) In CSEE, the perception of family responsibilities and the actual care work provided by families is particularly strong in a European comparative

Table 1.6: Best option for an older parent in need for regular care and help

	Should live with children	Should be supported by service providers at home	Children should visit to provide care	Should move to a nursing home	Other[a]
EU 27	30%	27%	24%	10%	9%
Austria	17%	28%	30%	9%	16%
Croatia	48%	11%	18%	21%	2%
Czech Rep.	36%	11%	30%	13%	10%
Hungary	36%	12%	35%	11%	6%
Romania	56%	10%	23%	5%	6%
Slovakia	47%	11%	28%	8%	6%
Slovenia	29%	16%	17%	32%	6%
France	18%	46%	18%	12%	6%
Germany	25%	27%	30%	8%	10%
Italy	28%	30%	22%	7%	13%
Sweden	4%	60%	13%	20%	3%
UK	20%	34%	23%	10%	13%

"Imagine an elderly father or mother who lives alone and can no longer manage to live without regular help because of her or his physical or mental health condition. In your opinion, what would be the best option for people in this situation?"

[a] Other include spontaneous answers: "It depends", "None of these", "Don't know" (Source: European Commission 2007)

perspective. A number of factors, however, might lead to a situation where it becomes increasingly difficult for many family members to continue providing long hours of care. Increasing employment participation, an increase in retirement age, urbanisation, changing family and household structures but also changing perceptions of gender and family roles will put traditional informal care arrangements under increasing pressure.

In 2008, employment rates among women in the EU27 ranged between 47.2% in Italy and 74.3% in Denmark. In most CSEE study countries the respective rate is below the EU27 average of 59.1%. But, there is a much larger proportion of full-time employed women in the CSEE region. While part time employment rate is below 12% for women in the CSEE study region, it is about 31% in the EU27 average. (see table 1.7) Given that informal carers are often in their 50s or 60s, employment participation among older persons is of particular interest. According to Eurostat (2009) statistics, employment participation of older persons (employed persons aged 55 to 64 as proportion of the general population of that age) is 36.9% in the EU average, and between 21.1% and 34.4% in the CSEE study countries. (see table 1.7) These lower rates can be caused by limited access to the formal labour market, by discrimination against older workers, but also by more generous early retirement schemes or lower regular retirement age. (Brugiavini et al. 2005)

Increasing employment participation, not least among women and older workers, is one of the main objectives of European Commission and EU member countries employment and social policies. While there are strong arguments in favour of such policies, they can put traditional arrangements for providing care under enormous pressure, in particular where there is little alternative to informal family care-giving. Long-term care-giving to a large extent is provided by women in their 50s and 60s. Given strong perceptions of family obligations and a lack of social care infrastructure in CSEE countries, increasing pressure for formal employment will create enormous burdens for these carers. According to the Eurobarometer 2007 survey, 5% of Europeans stated that they had to give up formal employment or to switch from full-time to part-time employment in order to take care for an older person, 8% expect that this will be the case in the future. (European Commission 2007) Such behaviour is a response to a mix of factors, the perception of care-giving as a family obligation, the lack of alternative provisions or the lack of financial means to pay for services, but might also be induced by policies providing incentives for family care. For carers, giving up gainful employment or switching to part-time employment has negative consequences in terms of income, pension security coverage and career perspectives. (Lamura et al. 2008; Mestheneos, Triantafillou 2005)

Another factor that might reduce the potential for informal care-giving is changes in retirement age. The average exit age from the labour force is 61.2 years in 2007 in the EU27 average. In most CSEE countries, on average, it is two years earlier. In a current wave of pension policy initiatives, proposals have been made to increase not just real average exit age from the labour force but also the regular retirement age. While such a step would have a major expenditure containment effect for pension systems, it would also impact on the po-

Table 1.7: Employment participation and average exit age from the labour force, 2008

	Employment rate		Part time employment rate		Employment rate older persons		Average exit age from labour force
	Female	Male	Female	Male	Female	Male	Total (2007)
EU 27	59.1	72.8	31.1	7.9	36.9	55.0	61.2
EU 15	60.4	74.2	36.6	8.5	39.0	56.2	61.5
Austria	65.8	78.5	41.5	8.1	30.8	51.8	60.9
Croatia	50.7	64.9	11.5	6.7	25.6	49.0	58.6
Czech Rep.	57.6	75.4	8.5	2.2	34.4	61.9	60.7
Hungary	50.6	63.0	6.2	3.3	25.7	38.5	59.8**
Romania	52.5	65.7	10.8	9.1	34.4	53.0	64.3*
Slovakia	54.6	70.0	4.2	1.4	24.2	56.7	58.7
Slovenia	64.2	72.7	11.4	7.1	21.1	44.7	59.8*
France	60.7	69.8	29.4	5.8	36.1	40.6	59.4
Germany	65.4	75.9	45.4	9.4	46.1	61.8	62.0
Italy	47.2	70.3	27.9	5.3	24.0	45.5	60.4
Sweden	71.8	76.7	41.4	13.3	66.7	73.4	63.9
UK	65.8	77.3	41.8	11.3	49.0	67.3	62.6

(Source: Eurostat 2009; * data for 2006, ** data for 2005)

tential of informal care-giving. The more individuals extend their employment career into older age, the more they will have to reduce their contributions to informal care-giving or to take on an enormous double burden of care-giving and gainful employment. A third factor having an impact on the potential of informal care-giving is living arrangements. Across Europe, approximately one third of all single households are households of people aged 65 and over. In some CSEE countries, namely Hungary, Slovenia and Romania, this age group accounts for almost half of all single households. (Eurostat 2009) Migration from rural towards urban areas and migration from Eastern European countries towards Western Europe can separate generations on larger distances and lead to situations where the older population is left on their own.

Assuming increasing employment participation, a postponement in the exit age from the labour market, a further trend towards single households, and changes in the perceptions of family and public responsibilities, a compression of the potential of informal care-giving seems a very likely trend. This is particularly true for the CSEE region, where the aforementioned trends might be even stronger given the current levels of employment participation and retirement age, but also because family care currently covers the largest part of the necessary care. On the one hand, the compression of the informal care-giver pool will increase the likelihood for a person to become responsible for providing care at some point in her or his lifetime. (Evers 2003) On the other hand, pressure on traditional informal care-giving will induce a growing demand in societies for alternative modes of long-term care provision. The ways in which informal care is organised, can take very different forms. Changes outlined above will not erase the willingness to provide informal care, but will most likely lead to changes in the form, the content and the extent of care provided. Even when being fully employed, when living on a longer distance or even across borders, family members can still become engaged in tasks of organisation and coordination, but less so in the practical day-to-day tasks of care work.

As will be shown in detail in chapters 3 to 10, the role of social security systems and even more so of private sector systems so far is largely limited and often highly fragmented in CSEE and hence not prepared to fill a gap if families are no longer in a position to provide the same amount of care work. The context for new public responses towards the risk of long-term care will be briefly addressed in the following section, before specific policy approaches in the public and in the private sector in the study region will be discussed in the upcoming chapters.

4. Towards a Stronger Public Role in Long-term Care?

To adequately deal with the aforementioned challenges, long-term care policies will have to respond on different levels, with regard to future long-term care needs, in terms of ensuring that the necessary care is provided to meet these needs, and on the level of funding the care provided. Whether there will be a compression or an expansion of morbidity in the coming decades will have the most significant impact on the amount of care that will be needed. Policies towards healthy ageing, therefore, are a key component of long-term care policies. (Oxley 2009) Where care services are needed, a pluralisation of approaches and policies is necessary. In CSEE, as will be shown in more detail in the following chapters, family care still is the dominant and often only option to ensure care for a frail older person.

In the past two decades, long-term care policies have seen major changes across Europe. (Österle, Rothgang 2010; see chapter 10) While nursing homes have historically often been the major public response, policies in the past two to three decades have started to emphasize care in the community and the development of housing arrangements that combine independent living with regular support systems in that context. (e.g. Doyle, Timonen 2008; Burau et al. 2007) Another prominent long-term care approach of the past two decades is the introduction of cash for care, personal budget or voucher systems. While these policies all aim at choice and autonomy, there is varying emphasis of the development of care markets, the creation of employment or guaranteeing specific qualities of care. (e.g. Ungerson, Yeandle 2007; Glendinning, Kemp 2006) Most recently, approaches providing help and support for families or other informal networks providing care received more recognition in long-term care policies. These policies have been driven by the aim to support informal carers, but also as measures helping to sustain or re-activate this major source of care provision. (Lamura et al. 2008; Mestheneos, Triantafillou 2005) While the respective approaches in CSEE will be discussed in detail in the following country chapters and in a comparative analysis of these approaches in chapter 10, this section will briefly outline potential implications of increasing needs for public long-term care expenditure.

In 2007, public social expenditure as a proportion of GDP amounted to 26.2% in the EU27, ranging between 11% in Latvia and 30.5% in France. Expenditure ratios in the CSEE study countries range between 12.8% in Romania and 22.3% in Hungary. (see table 1.8) Health care and pension systems on average account for more than two thirds of total social expenditure in most European countries. As will be discussed in more detail in the concluding chapter 10, information on long-term care expenditure and its comparability is very limited. Existing comparative data shows that – with the exception of the Nordic countries – public long-term care expenditure today only makes a relative small proportion of total social expenditure, but with considerable variation between countries. Spending levels range between more than 2% of GDP on long-term care (in Sweden and Denmark) and less than 0.5%. According to most of the available information, public long-term care expenditure in CSEE countries currently falls into this latter group. (Eurostat 2009; OECD 2009; Huber et al. 2009; chapters 3 to 10)

Table 1.8: Social protection expenditure and long-term care expenditure projections

	Social protection expenditure 2007		Public long-term care expenditure projections[a]		
			Level 2007 %	public expenditure increase 2007–2060 % points of GDP		
	As % of GDP	PPP per capita		pure demographic scenario	shift from informal to formal care scenario	AWG scenario
EU 27	26.2[p]	6,521.8[p]	1.2	1.3	1.6	1.1
EU 15	26.9[p]	7,464.3[p]	1.3	1.3	1.7	1.2
Austria	28.0	8,640.2	1.3	1.3	1.5	1.2
Czech Republic	18.6	3,717.8	0.2	0.5	0.6	0.4
Hungary	22.3	3,477.8	0.3	0.4	0.7	0.4
Romania	12.8	1,352.2	0.0	0.0	0.1	0.0
Slovakia	16.0[p]	2,675.1[p]	0.2	0.4	0.5	0.4
Slovenia	21.4[p]	4,760.5[p]	1.1	1.8	2.2	1.8
France	30.5[p]	8,264.3[p]	1.4	0.9	1.1	0.8
Germany	27.7[p]	7,943.1[p]	0.9	1.5	1.8	1.4
Italy	26.7[p]	6,773.3[p]	1.7	1.4	2.2	1.3
Sweden	29.7[p]	9,028.0[p]	3.5	2.6	3.1	2.3
UK	25.3[p]	7,455.1[p]	0.8	0.5	0.6	0.5

[p] provisional value

[a] Pure demographic scenario: The impact of future numbers of elderly people on public long-term care expenditure. The probability of receiving informal / formal care remains constant. Disability rates by age are constant.
Shift from informal to formal care scenario: During the first 10 years of the projection, a yearly shift into the formal sector of care of 1% of disabled older people who so far received only informal care. Half move to home care and half to institutions.
AWG reference scenario: Half of projected longevity gains up to 2060 will be spent in good health and free of disability.

(Source: Eurostat 2009; European Commission 2009)

The future development in public long-term care expenditure levels will depend on a number of factors already addressed in earlier sections. With regard to future needs, life expectancy and the development of morbidity in old age are important factors to be considered. With regard to the ways in which societies are going to meet these (growing) needs for long-term care, family and household structures, fertility rates and migration trends, values and the perception of family obligations, but also the way in which societies respond to long-term care needs through systems of solidarity or the growth of private markets are factors that will have an impact on future long-term care funding.

A report on the financial implications of ageing societies in the European Union (European Commission 2009) uses different scenarios in projecting the increase in public long-term care expenditure between 2007 and 2060. The scenarios cover demographic change, dependency and disability trends, policy developments, shifts between informal and formal care arrangements and between institutional and home care provision as well as developments in unit costs. The pure demographic scenario with constant disability rates by age and with no policy change, projects an increase of public expenditure by 161% between 2007 and 2060. Long-term care expenditure as % of GDP, in this scenario, will increase from 1.2% in 2007 to 2.5% in 2060. Increases in the CSEE study countries will be between less than 0.1 and 0.5 percentage points, with the exception of Slovenia where an increase by 1.8 percentage points is projected. Another scenario assumes a yearly shift of 1% of disabled older people who so far received only informal care into the formal care sector, with half moving to home care and half moving to institutions. In this scenario, long-term care expenditure in the EU27 would increase by 131%, long-term care expenditure as % of GDP by 1.6 percentage points. Increases in most CSEE countries are between 0.1 and 0.7 percentage points, but at 2.2 percentage points in Slovenia. The AWG (Ageing Working Group) reference scenario assumes a moderate improvement in dependency, expecting that about half of the increase in life expectancy will be spent in good health. The scenario predicts public expenditure on long-term care as % of GDP to increase by 1.1 percentage points in the EU27. For single countries, projected expenditure increases vary between just 0.1 percentage points or less in Romania, Estonia or Portugal, 0.4 percentage points in the Czech Republic, Hungary and Slovakia, and more than 2 percentage points in Sweden, Greece or the Netherlands. (European Commission 2009)

These developments, however, rest on the assumption that there will be no or very little change in long-term care policy patterns. Hence, countries with currently very low levels of publicly co-funded care provision will experience only moderate expenditure increases. This is the case for most countries in the CSEE region. It is highly questionable, however, whether these countries will be able to rely mainly on informal care when the number of older people in need grows. If they start to expand publicly co-funded care, expenditure levels converging towards a European average is a much more likely development.

This perspective is more strongly recognised in OECD projections of long-term care expenditure till 2050. (Oliveira Martins, de la Maisonneuve 2006) The OECD results show the same trend, but indicate even larger increases in long-term care expenditure as compared to European Commission (2009) projections. In general, increases are most pronounced in countries with a rapidly ageing population or with a changing population structure (e.g. Italy, Spain or Slovakia) and in countries with increasing employment participation which might hinder informal long-term care arrangements (e.g. Austria and Ireland). On the contrary, countries with already high levels of public spending rates and/or with less demographic pressure will be less affected. Only considering the demographic effect, long-term care expenditure as % of GDP would increase from 1.1% in 2005 to 2.3% in the OECD average. In the CSEE countries covered in this study, long-term care expenditure in 2050 would be close to the OECD average, characterised by steep increases from currently low levels. The projected increase for the Czech Republic is from 0.4% of GDP in 2005 to 2.0% in 2050, in Hungary from 0.3% to 1.5%, and in Slovakia from 0.3% to 2.6%. Assuming a compression of morbidity, projected long-term care expenditure as % of GDP would be about 0.5 percentage points lower. With other scenarios assuming an expansion of morbidity, an increase in dependency or substantially reduced informal care-giving, spending could even reach 4% of GDP in the OECD average.

While there is consensus across the CSEE region that more comprehensive systems towards the risk of long-term care are needed, it is not least the economic implications of such developments that hinder the implementation of novel and more universal programmes. In the following chapters, long-term care policies in eight Central and South Eastern European countries will be analysed in detail. These chapters will firstly provide some more specific information on the context for long-term care in the respective country. Then, chapters examine the status-quo and the developments in the role of the public sector, the private sector and of families in providing and funding long-term care. In the conclusions, challenges, perspectives and current policy developments will be discussed.

Bibliography

Alber, Jens; Köhler, Ulrich (2004) Health and care in an enlarged Europe. Dublin: European Foundation for the Improvement of Living and Working Conditions.

Anderson, Robert; Mikulič, Branislav; Vermeylen, Greet; Lyly-Yrjanainen, Maija; Zigante, Valentina (2005) Second European quality of life survey. Overview. Dublin: European Foundation for the Improvement of Living and Working Conditions.

Burau, Viola; Theobald, Hildegard; Blank, Robert H. (2007) Governing home care. A cross-national comparison. Cheltenham: Edward Elgar.

Comas-Herrera, Adelina; Wittenberg, Raphael; Costa-Font, Joan; Gori, Cristiano; di Maio, Alessandra; Patxot, Concepció; Pickard, Linda; Pozzi, Alessandro; Rothgang, Heinz (2006) Future long-term care expenditure in Germany, Spain, Italy and the United Kingdom. In: Ageing & Society, Vol. 26, No. 2, 285–302.

Daatland, Svein Olav; Herlofson, Katharina (2003) 'Lost solidarity' or 'changed solidarity': A comparative European view of normative family solidarity. In: Ageing and Society, Vol. 23, No. 5, 537–560.

Doyle, Martha; Timonen, Virpi (2008) Home care for ageing populations: A comparative analysis of domiciliary care in Denmark, Germany and the United States. Cheltenham: Edward Elgar.

European Commission (2009): The 2009 ageing report: Economic and budgetary projections for the EU-27 Member States (2008–2060). Joint Report prepared by European Commission (DG ECFIN) and the Economic Policy Committee (AWG). European Economy 2/2009. Brussels: European Commission.

European Commission (2007) Health and long-term care in the European Union. Report. Special Eurobarometer 283 / Wave 67.3. Brussels: European Commission.

Eurostat (2009) Eurostat Statistics. http://epp.eurostat.ec.europa.eu (1 December 2009).

Eurostat (2008) Ageing characterises the demographic perspectives of the European societies. Statistics in Focus 72/2008. Brussels: European Commission.

Evers, Adalbert (2003) Public financing for long-term care. Beyond residualism and full-coverage universalism. In: Kovács, János Mátyás (ed) Small transformations. The politics of welfare reform – East and West. Münster: Lit Verlag.

Glendinning, Caroline; Kemp, Peter (eds) (2006) Cash and care: Policy challenges in the welfare state. Bristol: The Policy Press.

Huber, Manfred; Rodrigues, Ricardo; Hoffmann, Frédérique; Gasior, Katrin; Marin, Bernd (2009) Facts and figures on long-term care – Europe and North America. Vienna: European Centre for Social Welfare Policy and Research.

Jacobzone, Stephane; Cambois, Emmanuelle; Robine, Jean-Marie (1999) The health of older persons in OECD countries: Is it improving fast enough to compensate for population ageing? OECD Labour Market and Social Policy Occasional Papers No. 37. Paris: OECD.

Lafortune, Gaétan; Balestat, Gaëlle and the Disability Study Expert Group Members (2007) Trends in severe disability among elderly people. Assessing the evidence in 12 OECD countries and the future implications. OECD Health Working Papers No. 26. Paris: OECD.

Lamura, Giovanni; Döhner, Hanneli; Kofahl Christopher on behalf of the EUROFAM-CARE Consortium (eds) (2008) Family carers of older people in Europe. A six-country comparative study. Hamburg: LIT Verlag.

McKee, Martin (2004) Winners and losers: The consequences of transition for health. In: Figueras, Josep; McKee, Martin; Cain, Jennifer; Lessof, Suszy (eds) (2004) Health systems in transition: Learning from experience. Copenhagen: European Observatory on Health Systems and Policies.

Mestheneos, Elizabeth; Triantafillou, Judy (2005) Supporting family carers of older people in Europe. The pan-European background report. Münster: LIT Verlag.

Moise, Pierre; Schwarzinger, Michael; Um, Myung-Yong and the Dementia Experts' Group (2004) Dementia care in 9 OECD countries: A comparative analysis. OECD Health Working Papers No. 13. Paris: OECD.

OECD (2009) OECD Health Data 2009. Paris: OECD.

OECD (2005) Long-term care policies for older people. Paris: OECD.

Oliveira Martins, Joaquim; de la Maisonneuve, Christine (2006) The drivers of public expenditure on health and long-term care: An integrated approach. OECD Economic Studies No. 43, 2006/2. Paris: OECD.

Österle, August; Rothgang, Heinz (2010) Long-term care. In: Castles, Francis G.; Leibfried, Stephan; Lewis, Jane; Obinger, Herbert; Pierson, Christopher (eds) The Oxford handbook of the welfare state. Oxford: Oxford University Press.

Oxley, Howard (2009) Policies for healthy ageing. An overview. OECD Health Working Papers No. 42. Paris: OECD.

Philp, Ian (ed) (2001) Family care of older people in Europe. Amsterdam: IOS Press.

Timonen, Virpi (2008) Ageing societies. A comparative introduction. Maidenhead: Open University Press.

Ungerson, Clare; Yeandle, Sue (eds) (2007) Cash for care in developed welfare states. Basingstoke: Palgrave Macmillan.

Velkova Angelika; Wolleswinkel-Van den Bosch, Judith H.; Mackenbach, Johan P. (1997) The East-West life expectancy gap: Differences in mortality from conditions amenable to medical intervention. In: International Journal of Epidemiology, Vol. 26, 75–84.

Wancata, Johannes; Musalek, Michael; Alexandrowicz, Rainer; Krautgartner, Monika (2003) Number of dementia sufferers in Europe between the years 2000 and 2050. In: European Psychiatry, Vol.18, No.6, 306–313.

World Health Organization (2009) World health statistics report 2009. Geneva: World Health Organization.

World Health Organization (2003) The world health report 2003. Shaping the future. Geneva: World Health Organization.

2

Long-term Care in Austria: Between Family Orientation, Cash for Care and Service Provision

August Österle, Katharina Meichenitsch, Lisa Mittendrein

1. Introduction

Historically, long-term care has been primarily a family responsibility in Austria, as in many other European countries. Public support was secondary and following social assistance principles. 1993 then marks a major turning point in the development of the Austrian long-term care system. In that year, a novel care allowance system was introduced. In addition, a federal-provincial treaty confirms provincial responsibility in service provision and the need to develop an appropriate infrastructure of residential, semi-residential and community care provisions. To date, this reform shapes the Austrian long-term care system. It is characterised by the three pillars of family care, strong cash-orientation and publicly co-funded social services. In addition, from the 1990s, migrant carers mostly from neighbouring Central Eastern European countries were increasingly employed in private households. In 2007, a regulatory framework was introduced to transfer this previously grey economy of care into a new element of the Austrian care regime. While the past two decades have brought major changes to the Austrian long-term care system, it is widely acknowledged that demographic and broader socio-economic developments will require further steps. At the same time, calls for cost-containment and references to budgetary constraints have intensified and limited room for extensions.

As throughout Europe, the number of older people in Austria will increase significantly over the coming four decades, both in absolute numbers and in relative terms. In 2008, the total Austrian population was 8.3 million, of which 17.1% were over 65 years of age and 4.6% were 80 years and older. According to Eurostat projections, respective proportions will increase to 20.1% (65+) and 5.5% (80+) in 2020, and to 29.3% (65+) and 9.2% (80+) in 2040. (Eurostat 2009) Following the definition of the Austrian care allowance scheme (see section 3.1), by the end of 2008, 422,000 individuals or 5% of total population are in need of long-term care exceeding 50 hours per month. About 80% of those receiving a care allowance are above 60 years of age, almost half are above 80 years of age. Among the total Austrian population over 60 years of age, about 18% are in need of care, among those over 80 years of age, it is about half. (BMASK 2009a)

Demographic trends have various implications for societies, not least for the organisation and funding of their social security systems. (European Commission 2009) There is broad consensus that the growing number and proportion of older people will lead to further increases in long-term care needs. The extent of this increase, however, is contested. A number of international studies have shown how different the implications for long-term care needs and long-term care costs can be, depending not only on a society's age structure, but also on the development of morbidity. An increase in healthy ageing with a future compression of morbidity in old age would substantially curb the increase in long-term care needs. If an expansion of morbidity occurred, however, this would lead to a steep increase in future long-term care needs. In a detailed study on future long-term care needs and related costs, Badelt et al. (1996) analyzed the implications of three different future health and morbidity scenarios in Austria. In a "status quo scenario", the number of those in need of care will increase by approximately 60% between 1992 and 2030. This increase would be just about 30% in a "better health scenario", but almost 100% in a "long life scenario", a scenario where an increase in life expectancy leads to additional years in chronic ill health. Streissler (2004) combines estimations on care needs, care arrangements and the costs of care and arrives at similar conclusions. With the assumption of unchanged incidence, the number of those in need of care will increase by approximately 65% from 2003 until 2030. In this moderate base scenario with constant levels of social service provision, public expenditure on long-term care would increase from 1.39% of GDP in 2003 to 1.7% in 2030. A recent projection of future long-term care costs – taking into account demographic developments, different scenarios for morbidity, the demand for social services and future service costs – estimates that long-term care expenditure will increase by between 66% and 207% until 2030. In the upper-bound scenario, long-term care expenditure would then account for 2.31% of GDP in 2030. (Mühlberger et al. 2008)

The development of long-term care needs and long-term care costs is closely linked to the amount of care work that is provided by informal networks and especially by families. Given numerous changes in the broader socio-economic context, it is unlikely that informal networks will be able to provide the same large amount of informal and unpaid care this sector has been providing in the past. Since the 1950s, the proportion of single-person households has increased from 17.5% in 1951 to 33.5% in 2001. At the same time, the average number of household members decreased from 3.11 in 1951 to 2.38 in 2001, and – according to forecasts – will further decrease to only 2.15 in 2050. It is expected that up to 41.5% of the population will be living in single households in 2050. (Statistik Austria 2008) Given that the extent of informal care-giving is largely determined by cohabitation or the distance between the home of the person in need and that of potential informal carers, these developments will limit opportunities to provide extensive hours of informal care work. At the same time, the provision of informal care is also influenced by changing employment patterns and the increase in employment rates among women, which rose from 58.8% in 1998 to 65.8% in 2008 in Austria. (Eurostat 2009) Moreover, aspirations to further increase retirement age will put more pressure on traditional informal care arrangements. In the following sections, the authors will discuss how individuals, families and society deal with the risk of long-term care in Austria and whether existing approaches are an adequate response to the challenges just briefly outlined.

2. Long-term Care in the Welfare State Context

The Austrian welfare system has been classified as a corporatist, conservative, continental, Bismarck type or male breadwinner welfare model. It is characterized by social insurance against major social risks and by strong corporatist structures. Compulsory social insurance for health, accidents at work, pensions and unemployment is complemented by universal state benefits (e.g. family benefits) and by means-tested social assistance. The family orientation of the welfare model becomes especially visible in the importance of family-related criteria in access to provisions and certain explicit family obligations. (Österle, Heitzmann 2009) Up until the 1990s, long-term care was considered to be a family responsibility, to be complemented mostly with social assistance oriented public support. A more comprehensive care system was introduced in 1993. With the new approach, the country did not follow the tradition of social insurance, but has established a tax-funded scheme with a new type of care allowance.

2.1. Historical Roots of Long-term Care Provision in Austria

Until the 1980s, the major public response to long-term care needs was the provision and/or co-funding of places in residential care settings and cash benefits as an income supplement. Private non-profit organisations were active as providers of nursing homes and community services in some regions and were funded by different combinations of user contributions, social assistance payments, public subsidisation, charity, and co-operative arrangements. Different social assistance schemes (*Sozialhilfe*) in the nine Austrian provinces, replacing earlier old poverty relief programmes from the 1970s, served as the major source of public co-funding for care services. (Melinz 2008) Overall, the level of public coverage was limited, characterised by fragmentation and large differences across the country. Long-term care provision, outside residential care, was dominated by informal care work, provided mainly by women for close family members.

During the 1980s, debates about the future of long-term care, ideas of a re-orientation towards community care and calls for more comprehensive schemes intensified. In these debates, the representatives of people with disabilities were particularly active and called for schemes allowing for empowerment and autonomy in managing care arrangements. After three provinces had earlier introduced cash for care schemes, the uniform federal care allowance scheme was finally established in 1993. The regulation is based on a Federal Care Allowance Act (*Bundespflegegeldgesetz*) and nine Provincial Care Allowance Acts following the same provisions as the federal act. Accordingly, people with care needs exceeding 50 hours per month are eligible for the care allowance (*Pflegegeld*), which is paid in seven different levels. (see section 3.1) The major objectives of this scheme are to provide a contribution to care-related expenses, to enable chronically ill people to stay in their private homes, to promote free choice of care arrangements, to support people in informal care settings and to create incentives for community care development. (Pfeil 1996) In addition to the cash for care scheme, a federal agreement defined provincial responsibility for the development of adequate residential, semi-residential and community care infrastructure. (see sections 3.2 and 3.3) Since 1993, the system has not changed in its basic characteristics, but there have been extensions in social service provision, cost-containment measures, programmes to support informal carers, responses to the emergence of migrant care and a new benefit supporting 24-hour home care. Current debates are increasingly concerned with the economic sustainability of the system. (see section 6)

2.2. Main Characteristics of the Current System

The aforementioned 1993 reform redefined the boundaries of public and private responsibilities in the organisation and provision of long-term care in several ways. (see section 3) In terms of regulation, long-term care is split between different governmental levels. While administration of the care allowance is shared national and provincial responsibility, service provision (residential care and community care) is provincial and local responsibility. In terms of funding, there are different divisions between public and private contributions for different types of services and between provinces. This leads to considerable variations in the extent and in the availability of services across the country. Furthermore, it leads to variations in funding arrangements, not least in the extent to which users or family members have to contribute to the costs. (see section 3)

Apart from the attribution of responsibilities to different federal levels, the provision of long-term care is organised in different welfare sectors, most importantly in health and social care. Health sector responsibilities are strictly limited to medical nursing care and can only be provided for a certain time span, unless medical assessments define the necessity to provide further care. Beyond the formal definition of health sector responsibilities, the provision of long-term care for chronically ill people in acute care settings is still an issue when a lack of community care services limits an early return to the private home while waiting lists often hinder access to residential care settings on short notice. This duplication is addressed, not least as a major potential source for cost containment in the health sector, but has not yet been satisfactorily resolved.

Overall, the 1993 reform extended and clarified public responsibilities in long-term care. Nevertheless, the informal care sector remains heavily involved in the provision and funding of long-term care as the majority of care work is still provided within family networks, in particular by women. (see section 5) Moreover, those in need of care and their family members still have to bear considerable costs when using services in the residential care sector or in the community care sector.

2.3. Long-term Care Expenditure

Austrian public social protection expenditure amounted to € 73.26 billion or 28.5% of GDP in 2006. In a European comparative perspective, this is beyond EU average (26.9%), lower than in some of the Nordic countries, but considerably larger than in the neighbouring Central and Eastern European countries. After increases in the early 1990s, expenditure levels have been relatively stable ever since, and have even been decreasing slightly in the more recent past. About two thirds of all social protection expenditure is funded from social insurance contributions, while one third is funded from taxes. This reflects the previous characterisation of the Austrian welfare state as following a social insurance model. Almost half of total expenditure (48.6%) is for pensions, followed by another quarter spent on health care (25.5%). (Eurostat 2009)

Expenditure for long-term care accounts for a relatively small proportion of total social protection expenditure. In 2008, public spending for care allowances amounted to € 2.1 billion. (BMASK 2009a) Due to large variations in provincial regulations and in defining underlying concepts, but also due to a lack of systematic data collection, availability and quality of quantitative information on long-term care services is still limited. According to the annual report on long-term care in Austria (BMASK 2009a), net public spending on residential care amounts to € 1.178 billion in 2008, expenditure on social care services to € 0.648 billion. Other sources report smaller net long-term care expenditure on residential care and on social services. At least partly this is caused by a neglect of long-term care expenditure by local authorities. (Pratscher 2009) Taking the upper expenditure estimate, total public long-term care expenditure amounts to € 3.9 billion or 1.39% of GDP in 2008.

3. The Main Pillars of the Public Long-term Care System

The 1993 long-term care reform placed the Austrian welfare state approach on two main pillars: the provision of a universal care allowance and the regulation, co-funding and provision of residential care and community care. (Österle 2001) With the introduction of the care allowance scheme, Austria did not follow the traditional social insurance principle but established a new type of tax-funded benefit. The 1993 reform also defined that service provision in residences and in the community sector has to be extended and adjusted in order to meet the requirements of an ageing society. However, no legal entitlement has been established to ensure that people in need of care have access to specific services. In 2007, new regulations on home care were passed with the aim to legalize the employment of migrant carers in private households. Along with these regulations, a new means-tested benefit was introduced to support the affordability of these 24-hour care arrangements.

3.1. The Care Allowance Scheme

The Austrian care allowance scheme was introduced in 1993 and constitutes the core element of the Austrian long-term-care system. It is intended to allow people in need of care to make more autonomous decisions about care arrangements, to support care in private households and to stimulate the development in the social service sector. The care allowance (*Pflegegeld*) is paid to people with chronic illnesses or disabilities of all age groups, who are in need of more than 50 hours of care per month. The assessment of care needs is based on a medical examination following standardised procedures that cover medical, personal and household requirements. The assessment of dependency levels takes place during an early contact between the person in need and a physician. Any already existing care documentation, for example when staying in a nursing home or when provided with nursing care, has to be consulted. Also, a family member can be consulted in the assessment process. The allowance scheme is organised in seven levels, with benefits ranging between € 154.20 in level 1 and € 1,655.80 in level 7 per month in 2010. (see table 2.1) The benefit is not means-tested and paid tax-free to care recipients 12 times a year. In contrast to other European cash for care programmes (see e.g. Ungerson, Yeandle 2007), beneficiaries are free to make their own decision in using the money. It is only in the case of residential care, when the benefit – up to some small pocket money – is transferred directly to the nursing home. In general, the care allowance is designed as a contribution to care-related costs and is not intended to cover the full expenses of professional care.

By the end of 2008, care allowances were paid to over 422,000 recipients or 5% of the total population. This makes personal coverage in the Austrian care allowance scheme substantially more extensive than in most other European cash for care programmes. Total expenditure amounted to € 2.10 billion in 2008, compared to € 1.55 billion in 2000. In the same period, the number of beneficiaries increased by 32%. In 2008, 55% of all beneficiaries received an allowance in benefit levels I and II, 88% were granted an allowance in benefit levels I to IV. 12% of beneficiaries, who are in need of extensive care for over 180 hours per month, have been paid benefits between € 902.30 and € 1,655.80 per month. (see table 2.1)

By the end of 2008, more than 80% of beneficiaries were above 60 years of age, almost 50% beyond 80 years of age. Below 60 years of age, more men than women are among care allowance recipients, while above 60 years of age two thirds of beneficiaries are women. Among 203,000 care allowance recipients beyond 80 years of age, 159,000 are women. (see table 2.2)

From the outset of the new scheme, the budgetary implications of the universal care allowance scheme have been a regular concern and various cost

Table 2.1: The Austrian long-term care allowance scheme

	Care needs per month	Allowance in € /month, 2010	Recipients 31 December 2008	As % of total
1	>50 hours	154.20	91,499	21.67
2	>75 hours	284.30	141,918	33.61
3	>120 hours	442.90	70,748	16.76
4	>160 hours	664.30	62,820	14.88
5	>180 hours of intensive care	902.30	33,243	7.87
6	>180 hours of constant attendance	1,242.00	13,693	3.24
7	>180 hours of care, complete immobility	1,655.80	8,303	1.97
			422,224	100.00

(Source: BMASK 2009a)

containment proposals have been made. Income data shows that the vast majority of beneficiaries have low pensions. According to 2007 income statistics, approximately 55% of beneficiaries received gross pension benefits below € 860. Only 2.5% of recipients have a net pension income of more than € 2,860 per month. (BMASK 2009a) Hence, while means-testing would substantially increase administrative burdens, it would not have a major impact on total care allowance expenditure. Others have proposed to more strictly link cash benefit receipt with service consumption or to even replace cash by services. These suggestions have been widely disapproved because of their limitations for

Table 2.2: Care allowance recipients by age and sex, 2008

Age	Women		Men		Total	
	Number	In %	Number	In %	Number[a]	As % of total
0-20	5,189	41.20	7,497	58.80	12,596	2.98
21-40	8,467	43.43	11,029	56.57	19,496	4.62
41-60	22,308	48.74	23,457	51.26	45,765	10.84
61-80	88,423	62.37	53,357	37.63	141,780	33.58
81+	158,745	78.38	43,791	21.62	202,536	47.98
Total	283,132	67.07	139,041	32.93	422,173	100.00

[a] Age information is missing for 51 cases.

(Source: BMASK 2009a)

autonomy and self-determination but also for reasons of increased budgetary pressures when establishing a right to receive services. A more subtle process, however, has been quite effective in terms of cost-containment. The care allowance has been adjusted to price inflation only rarely and has therefore lost almost 20% of its value between 1993 and 2008. Despite a recent adjustment in 2009, the allowance does not reach its historical value today.

3.2. Residential Care

In Austria, residential care is a decentralised responsibility, with regulatory competence at the provincial level. By the end of 2008, residential care facilities provided a total of 72,358 places, which amounts to an average of 116 (2006) places per 1,000 inhabitants aged over 75 years. (BMSK 2008) There are, however, considerable variations in coverage not least reflecting different historical policy approaches in the nine provinces. While bed density is about 150 (2006) in Vienna and Salzburg (places per 1,000 inhabitants aged 75 and more), it is just 67 (2006) in Burgenland. While many provincial development plans recognise a need for further expanding capacities, the major perspective for the coming years is to replace old infrastructure, to adapt facilities to new requirements and quality standards, and to extend semi-residential or short-term residence options.

This reorientation in residential care has already started. On the one hand, the institutions focus on a more diverse clientele. They offer a broader range of services for people with different types of needs and they start to provide beds for short-term stays or semi-residential services. And, residential care settings increasingly focus on people with more extensive care needs. It is estimated that approximately 80% of beds in residential institutions are nursing beds, whereas only 20% are residential beds. (ÖBIG 2004) This trend towards nursing homes rather than residential homes is partly a consequence of the introduction of the care allowance scheme which enables people in better health to search for non-residential options to arrange for the necessary care. But it is also the explicit focus of the homes on the more needy population that has contributed to the shift towards nursing homes. This trend also had consequences for the employed personnel. While the total number of people aged over 75 increased by about 13% between the mid 1990s and 2002, the number of beds in residential care settings only increased by 4.3%. In the same period, staff numbers in residential care grew by almost 60%, or 7,760 full-time equivalent employees. (ÖBIG 2004) It is estimated that the self-defined objectives in provincial development plans will require a further increase in staff numbers by about 3,860 full-time equivalents till 2010. (ÖBIG 2006)

In terms of the welfare mix, local communities are the major providers of residential care in Austria (with almost 50% of beds). Non-profit providers account for 30% of the institutions and for 37% of beds. For-profit homes tend to be smaller. They represent 22% of the homes, but only 14% of beds. (see table 2.3) Overall, over the past two decades, there has been a slight trend towards the private sector, either by outsourcing former public residential care provision or by a growth of contracted private sector provisions.

Table 2.3: Providers of residential care by sector, 2008

Residential care provider	Institutions	Beds/places	Beds as % of total
Public sector	388	35,289	48.8
Non-profit sector	240	26,832	37.1
For-profit sector	178	10,237	14.1
Total	806	72,358	100.0

(Source: BMSK 2008; authors' calculations)

Access to residential care settings generally requires registration with the respective institution, but does not follow a common nationwide assessment or allocation procedure. Funding of places, except for cases of full private funding, is a combination of public and private sources. First of all, residents have to use their regular income or their pension and the care allowance, which is – up to some pocket money – transferred directly to the residential home. If this does not fully cover the respective costs, the public sector covers the difference between the private contribution and the agreed daily or monthly tariff. The arrangements follow social assistance principles, but the specific regulations and practices vary across the nine provinces in particular with regard to (partly) recovering these public expenses. While residents' assets are still used for recovering public expenses, the option of recourse to the income of children was abolished in 2009. Spouses, however, can still be held liable for some of the expenses in most provinces. In general, the costs for places in nursing homes can vary largely. The tariffs usually depend on the level of need of the resident and various structural criteria, such as the age of the institution, the number of beds per room and the quality of services and infrastructure. In practice, fees may range between € 1,000 and € 6,000 per month. (Schneider et al. 2006) While there is no systematic research into the implications that regulations on public co-funding have on residential care consumption, anecdotic evidence clearly indicates such implications. For example, it is reported that the recent abolition of recourse regulations has increased the demand for places in residences.

3.3. Community Care

Community care services in Austria have a long tradition in some specific regional contexts. Early developments are going back to the late 19th and early 20th century. However, overall, levels of community care provision remained very low until the 1980s, and have not been available in large parts of the country. With increasing emphasis on community care, attempts were also made to develop new service models and to strengthen or to coordinate existing provisions. It is seen as a more adequate approach to specific individual needs, while at the same time allowing for autonomous and self-determined living. Not least, community care is also supported for cost-containment concerns over residential care. The 1993 reform agreement made provinces explicitly responsible for developing an adequate level of social services, including home nursing, personal care, home help and meals on wheels. Apart from improving the availability of services, development plans have to consider the quality of services and the qualification of staff. (ÖBIG 2004) There is, however, no obligation to meet specific nation-wide criteria in terms of social service density, and there are no sanctions in case self-defined goals are not achieved.

In the year 2008, 13,7 million hours of community care services were provided in Austria, including home nursing, personal help, consultation and other services. Compared to the year 2000, this is an increase of about 30%. Total public expenditure for community care services has increased by 46% in the same period. (BMASK 2009a) It is estimated that about 80,000 care allowance recipients use community care services, even if to very different extent. In terms of full-time equivalents, staff numbers have increased by 51% between the mid 1990s and 2002. While the proportion of qualified nurses doubled in that period, increases have been smaller for staff with less specific qualification. As in residential care, provincial responsibilities and a lack of national framework legislation causes considerable variations in community service provision. In 2002, on average, there were 13.4 care workers (full-time equivalents; including nurses, personal carers and home carers) per 1,000 inhabitants aged over 75. The respective number ranged between 21 in the province of Vienna and 6.1 in the province of Upper Austria. Similarly, there are considerable variations across qualifications. Nurse density (the number of full-time equivalent nurses in community care per 1,000 aged 75 and over) ranged between 6.2 in Vorarlberg and 1.9 in Upper Austria. (ÖBIG 2004)

The expansion of community services in the past 15 years has not only been the consequence of provincial development plans and respective activities, but was also driven by the introduction of the care allowance scheme in 1993. The availability of cash for care improved purchasing power among those in need of care and increased the awareness of the option to "buy" qualified services. At the same time, however, an increase in co-payments for these services limited their actual consumption. Despite the considerable expansion of community care provision in the past 20 years, availability and accessibility remain limited which, not least, has made migrant care arrangements an attractive alternative to social services where long hours of care or supervision are needed. (Da Roit et al. 2007; Österle, Hammer 2006; for details see section 4.3)

The organisation of community care services and their funding arrangements differ even more across the country than in the residential care sector. About half of all community care providers are non-profit organisations. The public sector and the private for-profit sector each account for about a quarter of service providers. (BMASK 2009b, own calculations) Many non-profit providers have been and still are pioneers in the development of community care services. The five main service providers acting across Austria, with substantial variations in regional market shares, are *Caritas Österreich, Diakonie Österreich, Hilfswerk Austria, Volkshilfe Österreich* and *Österreichisches Rotes Kreuz.*

Other providers focus on certain regions and/or specific target groups. As in the residential care sector, community care is characterized by the principle of public-private co-funding. Public funding is largely based on contractual relationships between regional and local public bodies and providers or provider organisations. In the case of Vienna, e.g., service providers have to present their social service plans to the respective public body (*Fonds Soziales Wien*). During the contract period, the public body covers the expenses of the service provider according to their regular progress reports. (BMASK 2009a) User co-payment regulations again vary across the country. In general, co-payments are calculated by taking the care allowance and any regular income into consideration.

4. Private Sector Roles in Long-term Care

It is widely acknowledged that the risk of long-term care requires a balanced response, including a comprehensive welfare state approach, an involvement of informal networks and various forms of private sector activity. The latter can include non-profit and for-profit organisations, active as providers, financiers or as agents or lobbyists. In this section, three issues will be discussed in some more detail: the role of formal private actors in the provision of care in Austria, the growing migrant care sector in this country and a regional community care approach that has been following a co-operative idea for 110 years.

4.1. Formal Private Service Provision

Non-profit organizations play an important role in social security in Austria, both in a provider role and in an advocacy role. (Heitzmann 2010; Österle, Heitzmann 2009; Heitzmann, Simsa 2004) In the private long-term care sector, historically, mostly church-related non-profit organisations have been major providers and innovators of care services on a charitable basis. Today, non-profit organisations provide more than one third of beds in the residential care sector and about half of services in the community care sector. In addition, non-profit organisations play a strong role in agency and lobbying. Non-profit organisations act on national, regional, or local levels. Some organisations concentrate on certain types of long-term care support, while others cover a broad range of social services. With regard to historical roots and organisational forms, at least four types of non-profit organisations exist: non-profit organisations with a church-related background, non-profit organisations with links to political parties, non-profit organisations based on co-operative approaches and non-profit organisations that are organised as associations or clubs. (Schneider et al. 2007; Heitzmann, Simsa 2004)

The provision of long-term care services by non-profit organisations is usually based on funding arrangements that include user contributions, public funding and, in some cases, charity. While subsidisation or block grants were the major sources of public co-funding in the past, there has recently been a clear trend towards contracting arrangements. In the case of residential care, public funding is provided for infrastructure development and for service provision, in the latter case based on daily or monthly tariffs. In the case of community care, funding is usually linked to the number of service units provided. (BMASK 2009a)

For-profit providers still have a smaller market share in the provision of long-term care than non-profit organisations, but it has steadily and slowly increased. While for-profit providers account for about 20% of residential care settings and about 25% of community care providers, they tend to be much smaller in terms of service volumes compared to public and non-profit providers. In terms of paying for their services, for-profit organisations either provide to users who are in a position to privately cover all the related costs or they work on a contractual basis with public authorities.

4.2. Migrant Care and 24-Hour Support

From the 1990ies, Austria has seen a growing number of migrant care workers providing "24-hour care" in private households. Most of the arrangements have been in a grey economy of care, outside labour and social security regulations. Only in 2006, employment of migrant carers in private households became a major media-driven political issue, which subsequently led to a new regulatory context for 24-hour care work provided in private households and to the introduction of a new financial support scheme. Most migrant carers in Austria are from neighbouring Central and Eastern European countries. Arrangements are usually with two carers sharing one care situation in biweekly shifts, where each of them provides 24-hour care for two weeks and is then replaced by the other. Contacts between those seeking and those providing care is mostly arranged via agencies, but also via informal networks or individual search. (Österle, Hammer 2006)

The substantial increase in this type of care provision from the 1990ies was caused by a variety of reasons. The introduction of the care allowance scheme in 1993 has increased purchasing power in the hands of the users and it has emphasised the concept of autonomy and choice. At the same time, a lack of service capacities, increasing user fees and limitations to the amount of publicly co-funded services made it difficult for care allowance recipients to buy care work provided by social service organisations for long hours of care. Migrant care offered an affordable alternative to cover the need for extended support, in particular when a permanent live-in arrangement was sought. However, the option requires substantial disposable income and is not affordable for people with low or lower middle income. With a daily cost roughly ranging between € 40 and € 60 a day, the monthly cost of paid 24-hour care (outside labour and social security regulations) was between € 1,200 and € 1,800. From the migrant carer's perspective, working in Western European countries was attractive due to large differences in wages and economic perspectives. The geographical proximity presents an additional incentive to work in Austria allowing migrant carers to spend biweekly breaks at home without extended travel. (Da Roit et al. 2007; Österle, Hammer 2006)

After the issue of migrant care gained huge interest in public and mass media debates during the election campaign in summer 2006, a new legal act on the regularisation of these arrangements came into force in 2008. Accordingly, three types of regular employment in the private home are possible: (a) self-employed care work, (b) employment by those in need or their relatives, (c) employment by a long-term care provider. As regular employment of a carer presents a considerable financial burden to people in need of care, an additional cash benefit was introduced to support the newly regularized care arrangements. All care allowance recipients in dependency levels V to VII, those in need of 24-hour support in levels III and IV (to be confirmed by an expert) and dementia patients in levels I and II are eligible. Benefits are means-tested and only granted up to a net income of € 2,500 per month. The monthly benefit amounts to € 275 for one self-employed carer or € 550 for two self-employed carers and to € 550 or € 1,100 for one or two employed carers. Because of minimum wage and work regulations for employer-employee relationships, hiring a self-employed carer presents the cheaper option, even when considering the different benefit levels, and has become the dominant form of regularised 24-hour care.

Before the reform, it was estimated, that between 8,000 and 10,000 families used this type of migrant care services in Austria. This estimate would have accounted for about 16,000 to 20,000 migrant carers in the grey market, although media reports suggested that up to 40,000 migrant carers might have been working in this sector. After the introduction of the new scheme in January 2008, almost 9,000 self-employed care workers have been registered within the first six months. (Rupp, Schmid 2008) By June 2010, about 27,600 individuals have been registered as self-employed care workers. Financial support was applied for in about 4,200 cases in 2009.

4.3. The Co-operative Approach to Social Service Provision in Vorarlberg

In Vorarlberg, the most Western province of Austria, a unique system of community care provision for frail older and disabled people has been in use since 1899. Back then, home nursing co-operatives (*Hauskrankenpflegevereine*) were founded in many regions to improve the social situation of the population. These co-operatives are organised in small associations, mostly on the level of local communities, and are characterised by three features: (a) individual or family membership, (b) voluntary work of the management, and (c) cooperation of every member. By paying the membership fee, every citizen can join one of the co-operatives – an aspect in which they resemble the old concept of co-operative and voluntary insurance. In 2008, 66 such co-operatives provided the opportunity for membership, with about 42% of the total population being a member. About 300 care workers (86% qualified nurses) provided services to about 7,500 clients in more than 370,000 client contacts. In addition to nursing as the main task of these co-operatives, they increasingly provide guidance and counselling to informal carers as an integral part of the work package. (Landesverband Hauskrankenpflege 2009)

Almost 41% of the total costs of the co-operatives (including wages, operating costs and investments) are covered from membership fees, donations and voluntary co-payments. 60% of total costs are financed by the provincial and by local governments and by statutory social health insurance funds. An umbrella organisation of the co-operatives, established in 1975, negotiates the respective financial support schemes. The annual membership fees for the cooperatives range between € 22 and € 33 and entitle the person to receive services offered by the co-operative. With growing financial pressure, however, additional out-of-pocket payments are increasingly used at the point of use. (Landesverband Hauskrankenpflege 2009)

In recent years, membership in these co-operatives has stagnated – a development that is attributed to urbanisation processes and a decline in the perception of community solidarity. Moreover, increasing care needs made the financial situation of the co-operatives more difficult. But despite these challenges, nursing care co-operatives continue to play a key role in social service provision in Vorarlberg. Over the past 110 years, the co-operative idea has proved to be a sustainable approach to meet specific needs for care and support on the community level.

5. Long-term Care and the Family

Despite the increase in welfare provisions and private alternatives to family care, families are still at the centre of most long-term care arrangements, with family members, and above all female kin, providing large amounts of care work. And there are also strong perceptions regarding long-term care as a family responsibility in Austria. According to a Eurobarometer survey, 44% of the population support the idea that children should co-finance care for parents in need of care, a level of approval only shared by Turkey and Romania, while it just amounts to 18% in the EU average. About 50% of Austrians regard moving in together or moving to a common neighbourhood as the best setting to care for an older parent. (Alber, Köhler 2004)

Most family carers are daughters, daughters-in-law or partners. The amount and type of care work that is provided informally differs significantly by personal and social background and by gender. (Hörl 2009) Women still provide the major part of informal care work. They provide longer hours of care and serve as main care-giver in about 80% of all long-term care situations dominated by informal care provision. (Badelt et al. 1997) Statistik Austria (2003) reports 281,900 women and 144,000 men aged over 17 years of age who take care of relatives or friends (including short-term and long-term care activities). These self-declared carers represent 6.7% of the total population, the respective proportion among women being 8.5%. A more specific look at the type and amount of care work shows that men are more involved in short-term support activities of up to five hours a week, while many women provide care beyond five hours per week. This difference in the amount of care work also relates to a difference in the type of care activities performed. While personal care (eating, personal hygiene, dressing, cleaning etc.) constitutes an important part of female care work, much of the help provided by men is services like buying medicaments, fetching the mail or doing administrative work. (Statistik Austria 2003; Badelt et al. 1997) Finally, female and male carers also differ in their age. While most male family carers are retired, more than half of women providing informal care are between 40 and 60 years of age. Hence, this group faces the additional challenge and burden of whether and how to combine care work and regular employment. (Hörl 2008; ÖBIG 2004; Badelt et al. 1997)

The provision of long hours of care involves physical, mental and financial burdens. Informal carers who provide full-time care and those who combine the provision of care with gainful employment find themselves in very difficult situations. A recent study found significant differences in socio-economic characteristics and work arrangements between informal carers and persons without care obligations. (Trukeschitz et al. 2009) Informal carers who are also engaged in paid employment are characterized by lower incomes and lower levels of education compared to those not providing informal care. The results suggest that those in better income positions have more options to organize the necessary care for their relatives in need. They can reduce the double burden by paying for professional care or by giving up formal employment to provide full-time care. In contrast, persons with lower income may have no alternative to taking up the double burden, as they can neither afford professional care, nor do without their earned income. The study also found that informal care workers are more often found in flexible work arrangements and self-employment, which indicates that these are more practicable conditions for providing informal care.

Many informal carers regard the availability of the care allowance (which is paid to the person in need of care) as recognition of the help they provide. (Badelt et al. 1997) However, the benefit does usually not relieve them of the multiple burdens involved, as support directly aimed at informal carers is still scarce. (Kreimer, Schiffbänker 2005) An area where substantial progress has recently been achieved is social security coverage. From 1998, there has been an option – to those providing care to a close relative in benefit levels III to VII – for subsidised insurance coverage (in cases where carers have given up formal employment) and for self-insurance in the social pension insurance scheme at a reduced rate. As take-up remained low, from September 2009, pension insurance coverage is free for family carers.

Public support in the actual provision of informal care work, beyond the option of using social services, remains limited. Several proposals have been put forward and pilot projects have been introduced in recent years, but have not yet been established on a country wide level. (BMASK 2009a; Österle, Hammer 2004) Many informal carers provide care for months and even years without having regular contact to professional organisations that could provide advice or respite care. The programme "Consultation Cheque – Professional Advice for People in Need and Their Relatives" attempted to improve this situation. A project evaluation, however, indicates that just 1.5% to 2% of all those contacted with an invitation letter asked for consultation. But this small group was highly satisfied with the offer and responded very positively. Those who did not take up the advisory services believed to already be well informed, most often because the intense information phase at the beginning of an informal care arrangement was already over. (Schober et al. 2007) Another pilot programme offers leave and recreation for family carers combined with training and education. During the stay, information, counselling and legal advice are provided by qualified nurses. The pilot programme called "Support for People with Dementia in Need of Care and their Caring Relatives" offers financial support to cover respite care services for periods of holidays or sickness of the main informal carer. (BMASK 2009a) Besides that, residential care settings and social care providers intensify their attempts in addressing informal carers. All these programmes, however, lack a systematic approach that would provide access to the respective offers across the country on a sustainable basis. A more universal adoption of support schemes has so far been hindered, not least with reference to a lack of resources. A major recent development is the establishment of an informal carers' organisation in early 2010. While there have previously been other groups or organisations of relatives and carers, they have usually focused on specific chronic illnesses. The development of the carer organisation could help to build a stronger voice of informal carers in the policy process.

6. Conclusions and Perspectives

With the 1993 reform, long-term care was increasingly understood as a distinctive welfare sector and became a prominent social policy concern in this country. Three aspects that have been of major importance in the development of the Austrian system and that will also be at the core of future developments are picked up in this concluding section.

The relation between the strong cash orientation in the Austrian long-term care system and the provision and consumption of social services has continuously received some attention in the debates in this country. The cash orientation has been subject to various criticisms, in particular with regard to hindering professionalization and extension of community care services and herewith quality assurance in care arrangements, but also in terms of the incentives it creates for female family members in their traditional roles as carers. While these concerns are recognised, there has never been any major attempt to transform the existing cash benefit scheme into an in-kind scheme. Major reasons put forward are objectives of choice, autonomy and empowerment, but also the financial implications of an in-kind system. Nevertheless, there is some agreement that the link between the cash system and the consumption of services has to be improved. There has in fact been a substantial increase in the provision and consumption of community care services. At the same time, limited volumes of publicly co-funded services, co-payments and limited ability or willingness of users to pay for long hours of professional care work limit the use of community care services.

While the challenges of demographic and broader socio-economic changes and the need for adequate responses are widely recognised, broader public debates in recent years have largely focused on the regularisation of migrant care and on issues of financial sustainability. As outlined above, a lack of social service provision and co-payments for community care services have made migrant care an increasingly attractive alternative to these services, in particular where families were searching for options that ensure the provision of long hours of support and attendance in the private environment of the person in need. After illegal migrant care became a major political issue during an election campaign in 2006, a regularisation of this 24-hour care arrangement was introduced along with a financial support scheme. In that period, long-term care has been a major political issue for months. It has helped to bring long-term care back into a wider public debate, but the debates were almost exclusively focused on cost-effective regularisation and did not lead to a more thorough discussion of structural issues or unmet needs. The debates have not contributed much to highlight broader issues of quality and professionalization, of case management or the specific requirements of attendance when caring for people with dementia.

Debates in the past few years have shown that the need for further reform is recognized. But, any proposals for more substantial and systematic attempts are often hindered for budgetary constraints, and because of conflicting interests between different governmental levels. Different from the four branches of social insurance (pensions, health, accidents at work, unemployment), long-term care is not funded from social insurance but from general tax funds. This makes long-term care provisions more vulnerable to short-term budget cuts. Hence, at least rhetorically, there is broad agreement on the necessity for a new funding arrangement. Currently, the preferred option is the establishment of a long-term care fund, similar to one existing for family policies. More narrow conceptions of the long-term care fund would pool financial means for care allowances, while more extensive conceptions would include both care allowances and services. In the latter case, the federal structure of the long-term care system – with competences for the care allowance on the national but also on provincial levels and with responsibility for service provision on provincial and local levels – creates considerable challenges in establishing a single long-term care fund. Stakeholders need to start from the complex division of responsibilities between government levels and to work out not only the source of the funds to be pooled but also the allocation of the resources. Resolving these issues is a major reform project, but it can lead to a system that is better equipped to face the manifold challenges discussed earlier in this chapter.

Bibliography

Alber, Jens; Köhler, Ulrich (2004) Health and care in an enlarged Europe. Luxembourg: European Foundation for the Improvement of Living and Working Conditions.

Badelt, Christoph; Holzmann, Andrea; Matul, Christian; Österle, August (1996) Kosten der Pflegesicherung. Strukturen und Entwicklungstrends der Altenbetreuung *(Long-term care costs. Structures and trends in long-term care for older people).* Wien: Böhlau.

Badelt, Christoph; Holzmann-Jenkins, Andrea; Matul, Christian; Österle, August (1997) Analyse der Auswirkungen des Pflegevorsorgesystems *(An analysis of the impact of the Austrian long-term care system).* Wien: Bundesministerium für Arbeit, Gesundheit und Soziales.

BMASK (2009a) Österreichischer Pflegevorsorgebericht 2008 *(Austrian report on long-term care).* Wien: Bundesministerium für Arbeit, Soziales und Konsumentenschutz.

BMASK (2009b) Mobile Soziale Dienste in Österreich, Ost, Mitte, West *(Mobile social services. East, Centre, West).* Wien: Bundesministerium für Arbeit, Soziales und Konsumentenschutz.

BMSK (2008) Altenheime und Pflegeheime in Österreich. Ost, Mitte, West *(Residential care in Austria. East, Centre, West).* Wien: Bundesministerium für Soziales und Konsumentenschutz.

Da Roit, Barbara; Le Bihan, Blanche; Österle, August (2007) Long-term care policies in Italy, Austria and France: Variations in cash-for-care schemes. In: Social Policy & Administration, Vol. 41, No. 6, 653–671.

European Commission (2009) The 2009 ageing report: Economic and budgetary projections for the EU-27 Member States (2008–2060). Joint Report prepared by European Commission (DG ECFIN) and the Economic Policy Committee (AWG). European Economy 2/2009. Brussels: European Commission.

Eurostat (2009) Eurostat Database. http://epp.eurostat.ec.europa.eu (30 December 2009).

Heitzmann, Karin (2010) Poverty relief in a mixed economy. Theory of and evidence for the (changing) role of public and nonprofit actors in coping with income poverty. Frankfurt: Peter Lang Verlag.

Heitzmann, Karin; Simsa, Ruth (2004) From corporist security to civil society creativity: The nonprofit sector in Austria. In: Zimmer, Annette; Priller, Eckhard (eds) Future of civil society. Making Central European nonprofit-organizations work. Wiesbaden: VS Verlag für Sozialwissenschaften.

Hörl, Josef (2009) Pflege und Betreuung I: Informelle Pflege (*Long-term care: Informal care*). In: BMASK (ed) (2009) Hochaltrigkeit in Österreich. Eine Bestandsaufnahme (*The oldest old in Austria. A review of the situation*). Wien: Bundesministerium für Arbeit, Soziales und Konsumentenschutz.

Kreimer, Margareta; Schiffbänker, Helene (2005) Informal family-based care work in the Austrian care arrangement. In: Pfau-Effinger, Birgit; Geissler, Birgit (eds) (2005) Care and social integration in European societies. Bristol: Policy Press.

Landesverband Hauskrankenpflege (2009) Hauskrankenpflege Vorarlberg. Jahresbericht 2008 *(Home nursing Vorarlberg. Annual report 2008)*. Dornbirn: Landesverband Hauskrankenpflege.

Melinz, Gerhard (2008) Vom "Almosen" zum "Richtsatz". Etappen österreichischer Armenfürsorge-/Sozialhilfe(politik) – 1863 bis zur Gegenwart *(From „alms" to „standard rates". Stages of Austrian poor relief / social assistance (policy) – 1863 to date)*. In: Dimmel, Nikolaus; Heitzmann, Karin; Schenk, Martin (eds) Handbuch Armut in Österreich *(Handbook poverty in Austria)*. Innsbruck: Studienverlag.

Mühlberger, Ulrike; Knittler, Käthe; Guger, Alois (2008) Mittel- und langfristige Finanzierung der Pflegevorsorge. *(Medium- and long-term financing of long-term care)*. Wien: Österreichisches Institut für Wirtschaftsforschung.

ÖBIG (2006) Österreichischer Pflegebericht. Endbericht *(Care report Austria. Final report)*. Wien: Österreichisches Bundesinstitut für Gesundheitswesen.

ÖBIG (2004) Ausbau der Dienste und Einrichtungen für pflegebedürftige Menschen in Österreich. Zwischenbilanz *(Extending services for people in need of care in Austria. Interim results)*. Wien: Bundesministerium für soziale Sicherheit, Generationen und Konsumentenschutz.

Österle, August (2001) Equity choices and long-term care policies in Europe. Allocating resources and burdens in Austria, Italy, the Netherlands and the United Kingdom. Aldershot: Ashgate.

Österle, August; Hammer, Elisabeth (2004) Zur zukünftigen Betreuung und Pflege älterer Menschen. Rahmenbedingungen, Politikansätze, Entwicklungsperspektiven *(On the future of long-term care for older people: Context, policy approaches, perspectives)*. Wien: Kardinal König Akademie, Caritas Austria.

Österle, August; Hammer, Elisabeth (2006) The formalisation of informal care work. The case of Austria. In: Ungerson, Clare; Yeandle, Sue (eds) Cash for care in developed welfare states. Basingstoke: Palgrave Macmillan.

Österle, August; Heitzmann, Karin (2009) Welfare state development in Austria: Strong traditions meet new challenges. In: Schubert, Klaus; Hegelich, Simon; Bazant, Ursula (eds) The handbook of European welfare systems. London: Routledge.

Pfeil, Walter (1996) Bundespflegegeldgesetz und landesgesetzliche Pflegegeldregelungen. Gesetze und Kommentare *(Federal long-term care allowance act and provincial regulations. Laws and comments)*. Wien: ÖGB Verlag.

Pratscher, Kurt (2009) Sozialhilfe, Behindertenhilfe und Pflegegeld der Bundesländer im Jahr 2007 und in der Entwicklung seit 1997 *(Provincial social assistance, disability benefits and care allowances in 2007 and their development since 1997)*. In: Statistische Nachrichten, Vol. 64, No. 12, 1117–1132.

Rupp, Bernhard; Schmid Tom (2008) Die Förderung nach § 21b BPGG. Ergebnisse einer ersten Evaluierung. *(Financial support according to § 21b BPGG. Results of a first evaluation)*. Wien: Sozialökonomische Forschungsstelle.

Schober, Doris; Schober, Christian; Kabas, Jakob (2007) Evaluierungsstudie über das Pilotprojekt "Beratungsscheck – Fachliche Erstberatung für Pflegebedürftige und ihre Angehörige" *(Evaluation of the pilot project „Consultation cheque – Professional advice for people in need of care and their relatives")*. Wien: Institut für interdisziplinäre Nonprofit Forschung an der Wirtschaftsuniversität Wien.

Schneider, Ulrike; Badelt, Christoph; Hagleitner, Joachim (2007) Der Nonprofit Sektor in Österreich *(The nonprofit sector in Austria)*. In: Badelt, Christoph; Meyer, Michael; Simsa, Ruth (eds) Handbuch der Nonprofit Organisation. Strukturen und Management *(Handbook of nonprofit organisations. Structures and management)*. Stuttgart: Schäffer Poeschl.

Schneider, Ulrike; Österle, August; Schober, Doris; Schober, Christian (2006) Die Kosten der Pflege in Österreich. Ausgabenstrukturen und Finanzierung (*Long-term care costs in Austria. Expenditure structure and funding*). Wien: Institut für Sozialpolitik an der Wirtschaftsuniversität Wien.

Statistik Austria (2003) Haushaltsführung, Kinderbetreuung, Pflege. Ergebnisse des Mikrozensus September 2002 *(Housekeeping, child care, long-term care. Results of the microcensus September 2002)*. Wien: Statistik Austria.

Statistik Austria (2008) Statistisches Jahrbuch Österreichs 2008 (*Statistical yearbook Austria 2008)*. Wien: Verlag Österreich GmbH.

Streissler, Agnes (2004) Geriatrische Langzeitpflege. Eine Analyse aus österreichischer Sicht (*Geriatric long-term care. An analysis of the Austrian situation*). In: Wirtschaft und Gesellschaft, Vol. 30, No. 2, 247–271.

Trukeschitz, Birgit; Mühlmann, Richard; Schneider, Ulrike; Ponocny, Ivo; Österle, August (2009) Arbeitsplätze und Tätigkeitsmerkmale berufstätiger pflegender Angehöriger. Befunde aus der Wiener Studie zur informellen Pflege und Betreuung älterer Menschen 2008 (VIC2008). *(Workplace environment and work arrangements of em-*

ployed informal family carers. Results of the Vienna study on informal care and support for older people 2008). Wien: Forschungsbericht 2/2009 des Forschungsinstituts für Altersökonomie der Wirtschaftsuniversität Wien.

Ungerson, Clare; Yeandle, Sue (eds) (2007) Cash for care in developed welfare states. Basingstoke: Palgrave Macmillan.

3
Long-term Care for Older People in Croatia

Silvia Rusac, Ana Štambuk, Nino Žganec, Marina Ajduković

1. Introduction

The Republic of Croatia declared its independence in the year 1991, at that time being one of the most developed countries of the former Yugoslavia. It entered the war in the same year, leading to an economic downfall and a sharp increase in poverty. Industrial production and the gross domestic product (GDP) of Croatia plummeted in the 1990s. In 1999, total GDP only amounted to 78% of the GDP recorded in 1989. In 2002, GDP growth reached 5.6%, indicating a mild recovery in the economy compared with the previous period. In 2005, the GDP per capita (in purchasing power standards) amounted to 47% of the EU25 – a level comparable to that of Poland, the Baltic States and Slovakia, but exceeding that of Bulgaria, Romania and Turkey. (Ministry of Health and Social Welfare 2007) In terms of social protection expenditure as a proportion of GDP, Croatia spends more than the average of the new EU member states. In 2003 and 2004, social protection expenditure accounted for about 23.5% of GDP, about 4% below the EU25 average (28% of GDP in 2003). (Eurostat 2005; ILO 2005) If expenditure on war veterans, refugees and IDPs (Internally Displaced Persons) are added, the total share even exceeds 26%. Given that pension and health care expenditure account for about 80% of total social protection expenditure (Ministry of Health and Social Welfare 2007; Ministry of

Finance 2007), demographic developments have become a major challenge to the future of social protection. (Jurlina-Alibegović et al. 2006)

Similar to other European countries, the Republic of Croatia faces an ageing society, a trend that becomes most evident in low birth-rates and the growing proportion of the elderly in the population. The proportion of those 65 years and over has increased from 13.1% in 1991 to 15.7% in 2001. (Croatian Bureau of Statistics 2001) In 2004, the share of young people (under 14 years of age) and that of older people (65+) was practically identical. Demographic forecasts indicate that population ageing will continue: by 2031, the share of older people in Croatia could range from 21.8% (best-case scenario) to as much as 25.4% (worst-case scenario). (Mrđen 2005) Hence, in a comparative perspective, Croatia will be no exception in the growing need for developing a care infrastructure that can adequately cover long-term care needs of frail elderly people.

2. Social Protection and the Law on Social Welfare

After declaring independence, Croatian social policy went through major transitions in the past two decades. After the war period and the deep economic crisis in the 1990s, the first decade of the new millennium was characterised by complex processes of social policy transition and social policy development. (Stubbs, Zrinščak 2009) Poverty, labour market policies and pension policies have been major reform areas. Long-term care instead was not addressed as a specific social risk, but was covered in the broader context of means-tested social welfare policies. For reasons of rationalisation, the simplification of procedures and the call for social justice, several traditional forms of social welfare were replaced with novel approaches. (Šućur 2003; Jurčević 1999) As a major step against poverty, including poverty among the elderly population, the Law on Social Welfare came into force on January 1st 1998. Even though not specifically focused on long-term care, it is the main approach to support individuals and families in case of dependency. The law opened a new chapter in the development of the social welfare system, which slowly started to incorporate the principles of subsidiarity, decentralisation, privatisation and a general diversification of social services. Before 1998, for example, the state had been the only provider of social welfare homes. With the introduction of the new law, these homes could also be established by units of local and regional governments, by religious communities, companies, associations and other domestic and foreign legal and natural persons. This enabled the development of the private sector in the social welfare field. Even though this process is relatively slow and not fully defined, private initiatives became relatively well developed in this area. The main institutional structure for administering social welfare services are the Centres for Social Welfare, responsible for managing social assistance applications, managing placements in residential settings and community care services. (Jurlina-Alibegović et al. 2006)

One of the main characteristics of the Law on Social Welfare, which is specified by its general provisions, is the definition of the individual's personal responsibility for its own and its family members' social welfare. More specifically, everyone is responsible for their own and their families' social security through their work, income and property. In cases where this is not possible, the help of the state is ensured. In 2004, 5.8% of the population were beneficiaries of various forms of social welfare, while 2.7% were beneficiaries of permanent financial help. Almost half of all households which received permanent support were single households, a proportion significantly larger than their share among all households (20.8% according to the 2001 census). Almost 30% of all unmarried persons and families receive help for five to ten years and 94% of them have no other income besides the help of the social welfare system. Around 45% of all beneficiaries of permanent help are unemployed. (Negotiating Team for the Accession of the Republic of Croatia to the EU 2006)

If an elderly person lives in a family or alone, and does not have enough resources as defined by the Law on Social Welfare, s/he can apply for support through the social welfare system. Provisions include the right to counselling, the right to support for temporary difficulties, a social support allowance, or a supplement for help and care. The level of financial support is linked to a basic help rate (HRK 400/€ 55), which is determined by the government in accordance with the Law on Social Welfare. The social support allowance is a means-tested benefit that is paid to people without sufficient means to sustain themselves. The level of support depends on the living and household circumstances, income and the ability to work. If an elderly person lives with a family that does not have enough resources to support the elderly person, the allowance can be given up to 110% of the base rate (HRK 440/€ 59). For elderly persons living alone, the respective support level is 150% or HRK 600 (€ 81). According to data from the Ministry of Health and Social Welfare, the social support allowance has been paid to 119,470 recipients in 2005. About 10% (12,692 recipients) were 65 years of age and older. The respective number declined in 2006 (112,508 persons) and in 2007 (102,953 recipients).

A second major financial support scheme is the help and care allowance (*Doplatak za pomoć i njegu*). The allowance is provided if an elderly person cannot satisfy her or his basic needs because of age or permanent changes in health status and if the income per family member does not exceed a certain amount. The help and care allowance is provided in full (100%, which is HRK 400 or € 55) or at a decreased amount (70%, being HRK 280 or € 37), depending on the respective need. In 2007, the benefit was paid to 74,897 individuals, of which 43,741 were over 65 years of age. Another benefit defined by the Law on Social Welfare, assistance and care at home (*Pomoć i njega u kući*), can be granted to a person who needs support by another person due to age, permanent changes in health status or a physical or mental disability. The benefit can be provided to a person that cannot get such help from any other source and if the income per family member does not exceed HRK 1,200 (€ 165).

Similarly to other beneficiaries of social welfare, the elderly exercise their rights through so-called Centres for Social Welfare. These centres have the status of public institutions that, among other responsibilities, decide on the rights related to social welfare. The 80 centres in the Republic of Croatia have been established by one or more municipalities in the same county and usually can have several branch offices. A lack of personnel and a fragmented and one-dimensional approach to poverty and social exclusion has caused poor collaboration between different institutions responsible for social welfare and to low take up among the needy population. (Bayley, Gorančić-Lazetić 2006; Jurčević 2005)

3. Social Services for People in Need of Long-term Care

3.1. Residential Care

According to the Law on Social Welfare, care outside the family can include different types of residential care provided by public social welfare institutions, religious groups, associations, companies, and domestic or foreign legal or natural persons. Care and support can be organised as permanent residence, weekly or other temporary accommodation, full day and half day care centres. Residential care is provided on request and is based on a decision by the Centre for Social Welfare. Homes for the elderly and helpless are the most important residential care infrastructure. In 2007, 47 of these homes were run by units of regional governments, 74 homes by other institutions. (Ministry of Health and Social Welfare 2007) These homes offer residential services, food, personal hygiene, health and personal care, working activities and use of free time. The number of beds is limited to 200 per building. The number of homes has increased from 57 in 1990, to 63 in 2000 and 121 in 2007, while the increase in the number of places was more moderate (14,168 in 2007 compared to 13,613 in 2000). (see table 3.1) By the end of 2007, the number of accommodation requests (31,607) was twice as high as the number of available places (14,930). Due to the insufficient number of places, accommodation for elderly is increasingly offered by non-public providers with whom the state signed mutual benefit contracts.

Table 3.1: Residential care facilities and number of beds, 1990–2007

	Number of facilities	Number of beds/places
1990	57	11,961
1995	54+2[a]	12,227
2000	63	13,613
2005	108	13,827
2007	121	14,168

[a] Two homes were situated on a temporarily occupied Croatian territory, in the area which was under the temporary administration for reintegration of Croatian Podunavlje from 1996.

(Source: Ministarstvo zdravstva isocijalne skrbi website 2007)

In addition to the traditional residential care settings, family homes as a new kind of residential institution attempt to provide beneficiaries with care that is close to family conditions. According to the law, the number of beneficiaries ranges between six and 20 per family home. According to the Ministry of Health and Social Welfare, there are 52 family homes for adults and elderly and one for children, with an overall capacity of approximately 1,000 residents. (Ministarstvo zdravstva isocijalne skrbi website 2007) In the recent past, these family-type homes became an important and successful addition to the traditional homes.

Funding of residential care combines user contributions and public funding. If an elderly person has a sufficient income, s/he has to cover the expenses for accommodation. If the income is not sufficient or if the resident does not have an income at all, expenses are supplemented or fully covered by the state. In this process, the participation of family members obliged to support the elderly person is also taken into consideration. For public sector homes (former state level homes that have been decentralised to the county level after 2001), the public funding part combines contributions by the county level and by the state level. Private homes are either funded on the basis of agreements between the respective provider and the county and municipality level or are financed by resident fees or other resources of the provider.

3.2. Community Care

The development of community care is still in an early stage and remains rather fragmented. It is, however, widely recognised that strong networks of all local resources – public, and private, for-profit and non-profit – are needed to satisfy the numerous individual needs of frail elderly people. (Havelka 2001; Havelka et al. 2000) The beginning of community care services for the elderly in Croatia is marked by organizing different forms of help at home. This was done by new (but still rare) centres for rehabilitation and care at home, by different providers offering various kinds of services and by further extending programmes with volunteers. Home care for the elderly is often organised and provided by the so-called centres for help and care. According to the Law on Social Welfare, the services these centres are offering include the provision of food, domestic work, personal hygiene and other needs. According to data from the Ministry of Health and Social Welfare, in 2005, 1,884 people have been provided with services. Apart from the centres of help and care, care and related services in private homes are also offered by homes for the elderly and by religious communities, companies, associations, or domestic and foreign persons that have signed an agreement with the Centres for Social Welfare.

In order to further develop care outside institutions, the Ministry of Health and Social Welfare has recently published a call for innovative projects in the area of social welfare. Examples of projects established through this call include novel "alarm systems" providing 24-hour assistance for people living alone, or the "Third Age Centre" programme realised by the association *"Mi"* in Split. This project offers an innovative solution by connecting already existing forms of care for the elderly outside institutions and by providing a wide range of social services.

In addition to the Ministry of Health and Social Welfare, the Ministry of Family, Veterans' Affairs and Intergenerational Solidarity provides care for elderly citizens through programmes of intergenerational solidarity and through collaboration with civil sector organisations. Altogether, in 2005, these programmes reached more than 7,500 elderly people. (Government of the Republic of Croatia 2007) About 5,000 elderly in 31 projects in twelve Croatian counties have been provided with care at home through the programmes "Daily Stay and Home Help for Elderly People" and "Home Help for Elderly People". The Ministry financed the implementation of these projects that emphasise local cooperation of local and regional public institutions and NGOs working in the health and social sector. Another 2,500 elderly people have been reached in "Volunteers in institutions for elderly people". In these programmes, in cooperation with local and regional administrative units, nongovernmental organisations develop volunteering in the elderly care sector.

Another approach to community care is gerontological centres for the elderly, an approach that was set up by the health system in cooperation with different public institutions. The centres are financed by the municipalities and are situated in homes for the elderly, but work independently on programmes for monitoring, studying, evaluating, reporting, supervising and planning care and health needs of the elderly. Their primary task is to ensure daily help, care and rehabilitation for elderly people. The gerontological teams cover about 30,000 people over 65 years of age. (Tomek Roksandić 2008)

3.3. Foster Care

Foster care is a distinctive approach situated between residential care, community care and family care. Elderly people in need of care are living in foster families where they are provided with accommodation, food and – depending on respective needs - personal care, health care, education and other services. The objective of fostering is to support and protect an elderly person who is incapable of independent living and in need of permanent help by another person. While the system of fostering care has a long tradition in the country, in July 2007, the Croatian parliament passed the Law on Fostering replacing earlier special provisions in the Law on Social Welfare. The Law on Fostering prescribes stricter conditions for obtaining a fostering license, but also gives wider professional and financial support to the foster families. For the first time, they do not only receive the basic help funds for beneficiaries, but also a compensation for their work. With the law, the necessary training qualifications were defined and special teams were established to support foster families. Finally, the number of beneficiaries per family has been decreased to a maximum of 4 adult persons. By the end of 1998, 3,622 persons were accommodated in foster families, of which 1,509 were adults and elderly people. Within a decade the number of adults has increased to 3,439 in 2007. (Ministry of Health and Social Welfare 2007)

4. Civil Society and Care of the Elderly

More than 27,000 organisations, or 630 organizations per 100,000 inhabitants, are registered as civil society organisations in Croatia. (Bežovan, Zrinščak 2007) Although citizens have a positive attitude towards civil society organizations and even though counties and towns financially support the work of civil society organisations, participation in their work and volunteerism is not very developed in Croatia. The level of development of civil society in the regions reflects the difference in living standards and is concentrated in the four largest cities. However, a greater participation among the younger and more educated population is seen as a sign that the role of civil society organisations will grow. (Bežovan et al. 2005; Barić 2000)

In long-term care, civil society organisations started to have a more prominent role in the past decade. It is estimated that about 3–5% of the elderly population in Croatia receives care and support from state institutions or civil society organisations. (Government of the Republic of Croatia 2007) In the 1990ies, respective provisions used to be highly centralised with only very few NGOs being active in the social services. After legal amendments in 2001, decentralisation started (primarily for services aimed at elderly and disabled people) and the sector was opened to private profit and non-profit organisations. The Croatian Foundation for Civil Society Development specifically intends to encourage nongovernmental organisations to provide services. With this development, growing attention has been paid to the development of partnerships between local authorities and civil society organisations. This was also supported through the establishment of a government office for NGOs, the National Foundation for Civil Society Development, the Council for Civil Society Development and through legal changes affecting the role of civil society.

Although numerous non-governmental programmes for elderly care were implemented and financially supported by the state level and by county or municipality levels, the position and prospect of civil society organisations often remains precarious. The system of project funding has helped to develop and establish novel programmes, but without ensuring its sustainability through longer term contracts. This causes insecurity among professionals, has negative effects on the motivation of staff and creates uncertainty for the future of projects.

5. The Role of Family in Long-term Care

Family responsibilities play a highly important role in long-term care in Croatia. This significance can be seen from the actual provision of care, in people's opinions and expectations, and in the legal context. Article 213 of the Family Law declares adult children responsible to support their parents if they are not capable of work and do not have adequate resources to sustain themselves. According to research, 70–80% of all practical support for dependent elderly is provided by the family. In most cases, spouses and children offer extensive non-formal support, while siblings and wider family members mainly provide emotional support. (Babić et al. 2004; Podgorelec 2004)

According to the Eurobarometer Survey (Special Eurobarometer 283 2007), almost half of the Croatian respondents (48%) believe that moving in with a child is the best option for an elderly parent who becomes dependent. This level of approval is much higher than the EU average (30%), but quite in the range of other CEE countries. Interestingly, the legal obligation for children to financially support their parents seems to strongly influence the public understanding of family responsibilities. The large majority (88%) agrees that children should pay for their parents' care if their income is not sufficient. This is the highest rate of approval of all EU27 countries (and Turkey) and it is almost twice as high as the EU27 average of 48%. It might be concluded that while the provision of personal care by family members is considered important, children even more recognise the financial responsibility for their parents.

Another notable point is the difference between expectations and preferences on long-term care. In the case of dependency, people consider it to be most likely to be looked after by family members in their own home (70%). This is again a higher proportion than in any EU country and only lower than that of Turkey. However, the picture changes if people are asked for their preference on how they would like to be cared for in case of dependency. Being cared for by family members in their own home is still the most preferred option (48%). But, preferences for other forms of informal or professional care are stronger than what they expect. It also seems that the high level of family responsibility is considered problematic, as 75% of respondents believe that dependent people have to rely too much on their relatives. This level of approval is slightly above EU average, but lower than in most new EU Member States in Central Eastern Europe that share Croatia's high level of family responsibility. Despite the strong family orientation, care for the elderly is also perceived to be a public responsibility. Almost all interviewees (94%) agree that the state should provide appropriate home and institutional care for the elderly. An equally large share (93%) believes that the state should pay some remuneration or income to family carers.

An example that further highlights the importance of family care is described by a study on the situation of the elderly living on the islands in the Zadar area. (Babić et al. 2004) The research shows that care and support for dependent elderly is mostly provided by their children (56.85%), elderly family members, their spouses, and their brothers or sisters with whom they live (21.6%). Respondents emphasise the intergenerational solidarity of island families. For almost one third of respondents (female and male) the responsibility to care for their parents is among the most significant reasons why they did not leave the islands during their youth. Elderly women from the islands still expect support and help from their children, even though they rarely live with them. Only 4.7% of the interviewed rely on the organised social welfare system. A similar number of them expect help from their friends and neighbours. (Babić et al. 2004)

6. Conclusion

Demographic and socio-economic changes make long-term care one of the key challenges for the future of social protection in Croatia. Apart from growing long-term care needs, poverty is an issue closely related to these developments. Elderly people (especially elderly women) are exposed to a higher risk of poverty than the average population. It is estimated that about 14% of the population over 64 years of age do not receive a pension. According to a World Bank Study on poverty, at least 62% of the elderly over 65 without a pension are subject to poverty, compared to 19% of the same age group with a pension. (Ministry of Health and Social Welfare 2007; Government of the Republic of Croatia, Ministry of Health and Social Welfare 2007)

Long-term care is not established as a distinctive welfare sector in Croatia. The core provisions are organised in the context of social welfare, a system following social assistance principles. Cash benefits and in-kind services are funded through state and local budgets and means-tested contributions by users. From 2001, the social welfare system that defines long-term care provisions has seen important and ongoing reforms. The objective is to improve the quality of services, to facilitate accessibility and to develop alternative types of care. In this process, particular emphasis is given to care in the community, to decentralisation and to broadening the welfare mix. There is broad consensus that deinstitutionalisation of social services is a major step in making services more accessible and more consumer-oriented. But the extension of community oriented services will only be possible through intensified cooperation between the government and the non-governmental sector. And it requires a funding scheme that creates incentives for such cooperation. In this context, decentralisation is regarded as another necessary step, despite existing obstacles. Many local governments still do not have sufficient human and economic resources and cannot respond to the complex challenges of decentralisation. Changes in territorial units or the development of mechanisms to cooperate in the creation and implementation of programmes could help to overcome these difficulties. Giving users the right to choose among alternative provisions or to combine them (e.g. via a voucher system) would be another approach to strengthen the welfare mix. Finally, it will be important to not only invest in the development of new services and improving their quality but also in developing preventive programmes. While the challenges of an ageing society are widely recognised in Croatia and while the social welfare system has seen many important reform steps in the past decade, a broader public debate on the implementation of a comprehensive and integrated long-term care system has not yet begun in Croatia.

Bibliography

Babić, Dragutin; Lajić, Ivan; Podgorelec, Sonja (2004) Islands of two generations. Zagreb: Institute for Migrations and Ethnicity.

Barić, Sanja (2000) Legal system of cooperation between non-profit organisations and government and units of local (regional) self-government in the Republic of Croatia. Zagreb: B.a.B.e.

Bayley, Deborah; Gorančić-Lazetić, Helena (2006) Without a net. Faces of social exclusions in Croatia. Zagreb: UN Programme for Development (UNDP) on Croatia.

Bežovan, Gojko; Zrinščak, Siniša; Vugec, Marina (2005) Civil society in the process of acquiring trust in Croatia and building partnerships with the state and other stakeholders. Zagreb: CERANEO, CIVICUS.

Bežovan, Gojko; Zrinščak, Siniša (2007) Postaje li civilno društvo u Hrvatskoj čimbenikom (*Is civil society in Croatia becoming a force for social change?*). In: Journal of Social Policy, Vol. 14, No. 1, 1–27.

Croatian Bureau of Statistics (2001) Census. Zagreb: Croatian Bureau of Statistics.

Eurostat (2005) Social protection in the European Union, Statistics in Focus, 14/2005.

Government of the Republic of Croatia (2007) Development programme of services for the elderly in the system of intergenerational solidarity from 2008 to 2011. Zagreb: Government of the Republic of Croatia.

Government of the Republic of Croatia, Ministry of Health and Social Welfare (2007) Joint memorandum on social inclusion of the Republic of Croatia. Zagreb: Government of the Republic of Croatia, Ministry of Health and Social Welfare.

Havelka, Mladen; Despot Lučanin, Jasminka; Lučanin, Damir (2000) Potrebe starijih osoba za cjelovitim uslugama skrbi u lokalnoj zajednici (*The needs of elderly persons for comprehensive community care services*). In: Journal of Social Policy, Vol. 7, No. 1, 19–27.

Havelka, Mladen (2001) Skrb za starije ljude u Hrvatskoj – potreba uvođenja novog modela (*Care for elderly people in Croatia – a new model needs to be introduced*). In: Journal for General Social Issues, Vol. 1–2, No. 63–64, 225–245.

ILO (2005) Social security spending in South Eastern Europe: A comparative review. Budapest: International Labour Office.

Jurčević, Živko (1999) Socijalna skrb u Hrvatskoj 1998. godine (*Social welfare in Croatia in 1998*). In: Journal of Social Policy, Vol. 13, No. 3–4, 133–146.

Jurčević, Živko (2005) Socijalna skrb u Hrvatskoj od 2000. Do 2004. Analiza pokazatelja stanja i razvoja (*Social welfare system in Croatia from 2000 to 2004. An analysis of the indicators of the situation and development*). In: Journal of Social Policy, Vol. 12, No. 3–4, 345–375.

Jurlina-Alibegović, Dubravka; Mastilica, Miroslav; Nestić, Danijel; Stubbs, Paul; Babić, Zdenko; Vončina, Luka (2006) Social protection and social inclusion in Croatia. Final Report for the European Commission. Zagreb: The Institute of Economics Zagreb. http://ec.europa.eu/employment_social/social_inclusion/docs/2006/study_croatia_en.pdf (30 December 2009).

Ministarstvo zdravstva isocijalne skrbi website (2007) Website of the Ministry of Health and Social Welfare. http://www.mzss.hr (30 December 2009).

Ministry of Finance (2007) Statistical reports. Zagreb: Ministry of Finance.

Ministry of Health and Social Welfare (2007) Statistical reports. Zagreb: Ministry of Health and Social Welfare.

Mrđen, Snježana (2005) Projekcije stanovništva Hrvatske do 2031. Godine (*Projection of Population up to 2031*). In: Živić, Dražen; Pokos, Nenad; Mišetić, Anka (eds) Stanovništvo Hrvatske. Dosadašnji razvoj i perspektive (*Population of Croatia. Current development and perspectives*). Zagreb: Institute of Social Science.

Negotiating Team for the Accession of the Republic of Croatia to the EU (2006) Working Group for Chapter 19, Social Policies and Employment. Brussels, 6–8 March 2006.

Podgorelec, Sonja (2004) The quality of life of the elderly population in isolated areas. The example of the Croatian islands. PhD Work, Zagreb: Faculty of Philosophy.

Puljiz, Vlado (2001) Reforme sustava socijalne politike u Hrvatskoj (*The reform of the social policy system in Croatia*). In: Journal of Social Policy, Vol. 8, No. 2, 159–180.

Special Eurobarometer 283 (2007) Health and long-term care in the European Union. Directorate-General for Employment, Social Affairs and Equal Opportunities.

Stubbs, Paul, Zrinščak, Siniša (2009) Croatian social policy: The legacy of war, statebuilding and late Europeanization. In: Social Policy and Administration, Vol. 43, No. 2, 121–135.

Šućur, Zoran (2003) Razvoj socijalne pomoći i socijalne skrbi u Hrvatskoj nakon Drugoga svjetskog rata (*The development of social assistance and social welfare in Croatia after world war II*). In: Journal of Social Policy, Vol. 10, No. 1, 1–22.

The Family Law, National Gazette 116/03.

The Law on Social Welfare, National Gazette 73/97, 27/00, 51/00, 82/01, 103/03.

The Law on Fostering, National Gazette.79/07.

Tomek Roksandić, Spomenka (2008) Zdravlje i stariji. Registar oboljelih od Alzheimerove bolesti i ostalih psihičkih poremećaja u starijih osoba. (*Health and the elderly. Register of elderly patients with Alzheimer's disease and other mental disorders.*) http://www.hcjz.hr/pr.php?id=13046&rnd (30 December 2009).

4
Long-term Care in the Czech Republic: On the Threshold of Reform

Jana Barvíková

1. Introduction

The demographic development in the Czech Republic displays a tendency to-wards an increase in life expectancy and a stagnation in fertility at a low level. The increasing life expectancy is a positive consequence of improved health status of the population. (MoLSA 2006b) However, it is anticipated that with continuing population ageing, the number of potential long-term care system clients will increase, as will the importance of social policy focusing on assist-ance for senior citizens.

Reliable statistics are not available, but it is estimated that 80–90% of the population over 65 years of age are independent or manage with the help of their family and those closest to them, while 13% need assistance in the house-hold, 7–8% regularly need domiciliary care and around 2% require institutional care. (Kopecká 2002) Although elderly people are seen as a vulnerable group at risk of poverty and social exclusion in the Czech Republic where the real value of the average pension did not reach its value of the year 1989 until 2003 (MoLSA 2006c), long-term care for frail elderly is discussed rather as a social programme than as an issue of poverty reduction. In the year 2005, about 5.3% of the population aged 65 and over has been living in residential care settings, 7.7% have received some kind of social services. Long-term care expenditure accounts for about 0.55% of GDP in 2005, with the largest proportion (93%)

Jana Barvíková

Table 4.1: Basic long-term care data, 1990–2005

	1990	1995	2000	2005
No. of persons receiving long-term care	118,854	147,977	184,367	190,592
No. of persons in residential care[a]	51,811	61,776	70,840	77,665
No. of persons in community care[b]	67,043	86,201	113,528	112,927
Total population 65+[c]	1,008,548	1,356,232	1,423,003	1,456,391
Persons in residential care as % of total population 65+	5.14	4.55	4.98	5.33
Recipients of community care as % of total population 65+	6.65	6.36	7.98	7.75
Total spending on ltc as % of GDP	–	0.52	0.54	0.55
Spending on ltc in mio € (CZK)	–	446.49 (11,492)	580.91 (14,955)	631.18 (16,249)
on residential care (% of total spending)	–	92.08	92.41	92.76
on community care (% of total spending)	–	7.92	7.59	7.24

[a] Total number of persons (clients) in institutional care, 31 December of the stated year (statistical statement MoLSA V-01).
[b] Number of persons receiving community home care services including meals on wheels (statistical statement MoLSA V10-01)
[c] Statistická Ročenka ČSÚ, situation to the year-end
(Source: Ministry of Labour and Social Affairs)

spent on residential care. (see table 4.1) With the introduction of a novel care allowance scheme in 2007, however, expenditure levels have substantially increased and shifted towards spending on cash benefits in recent years. (see section 3.3)

2. Introduction to the Long-term Care System

The term "long-term care" is not used in Czech legislation. However, the Ministry of Labour and Social Affairs (*Ministerstvo práce a sociálních věcí*) defines the term in a document the following way: "We consider as long-term care those services which are provided with no time limit to persons dependent on help for basic Activities of Daily Living (ADL criteria). The provision of personal assistance is combined with basic medical services. In the Czech Republic we also include institutional services where social care (help in self-care activities) and health care (nursing care) are provided as long-term care. In the home environment, providers of social services and health care and, to varying degrees, informal care-givers (family members, friends and other volunteers) contribute to this care." (MoLSA 2006b)

The provision of long-term care in the Czech Republic is not organised in a single system. While the Ministry of Labour and Social Affairs takes the responsibility for the social services sector, health care for senior citizens is a part of the health care sector for which the Ministry of Health is responsible. Each of these systems has its own legal regulations, independent criteria for accessibility and quality, and a different method of financing. But, social care is primarily the responsibility of the closest family and relatives, public responsibility starts where this help is not accessible. With the introduction of a cash benefit scheme from 2007, however, a new element has been added which – together with the Social Services Act – is substantially changing the context for social care provision and funding in the Czech Republic.

2.1. Developments in the Legislative Framework of Long-term Care

Legislation covering social care services valid till 31 December 2006 was based on laws passed in the late 1980s. At that time, social policy and social services were seen in a substantially different manner, particularly with regard to the individual's freedom to make decisions and the democratic principles involved in the operation of public administration. Since 1990, the practical provision of social services has been modernised to a certain extent without the required legislative support: Social services (e.g. personal care, early care, contact centres, respite services), which typically conform more to social integration principles than "traditional" services (institutional care or community care service), had no legislative support. There was no clear, equal system for financing social services and there were no quality inspection procedures. This basically put a brake on the required developments in social services and did not ensure the provision of these services at the required standard and their availability to all potential users. (MoLSA 2005b)

This legislation could not be changed in any fundamental way before 2006 but only underwent patchwork repairs by amendments. The adoption and promulgation of Act No. 108/2006 Coll. on Social Services has then brought deep systematic changes in social care since January 2007. Apart from other radical changes (equal conditions in financing social services from the state budget, registration duty and inspection of social services, providing social services on a contractual basis, establishment of standards for the quality of social services, redefining existing services and legal grounding of some new services, etc.), a new instrument of direct payments to users of social care services was intro-duced. The level of this care allowance is tailored to the extent of dependence and enables people to pay for the required assistance and support, provided by family members, other informal carers or by professional social care service providers. The proportion that care receivers have to contribute from their own resources is regulated by maximum limits that providers can claim from cli-ents. The new concept of social services aims to ensure the provision of a wider supply of services in households, to enable clients to lead an independent life and co-decide the amount and type of services they receive.

2.2. Overview of the Current Long-term Care System

Although the distinction between health care and social care is blurred in prac-tice, professional providers have to separate services and their workers accord-ing to different resources for the payment of their costs. Health care is paid for by public health insurance while social care is paid for by state and local budgets and by contributions from clients. (see table 4.2) (MoLSA 2006b)

Table 4.2: Multi-source financing of long-term care in the Czech Republic

Source	Health care	Social services
Public health insurance	payment for medical proce-dures, flat rate, number of treatment days	
Public budgets	grants (e.g. reconstruction of health care facilities, equip-ment, preventive programmes)	grants to service providers, care allowances paid according to degree of dependence
Individuals' own income		payments from service clients for accommodation, meals, care and optional extras

(Source: MoLSA 2006b)

Long-term care (social care) is provided predominantly within the framework of social services, the social assistance system. The adoption of the new Act on Social Services clarified formerly blurred competences on national, regional and local levels of responsibility. Municipalities (*obce*) and regions (*kraje*) have to establish the appropriate conditions for the development of social services, particularly by assessing people's actual needs and the necessary resources to meet them, but also by setting up organisations to provide services themselves. The main task of the Ministry of Labour and Social Affairs is to systematically develop long-term care policies and the appropriate legal regulations and to support the quality development of social services provided.

In the public sector, the regions mainly founded residential facilities for persons with disabilities, while municipalities primarily established residential and community services for senior citizens. Increasingly, social services are also provided by non-governmental organisations which have the form of civic associations, special-purpose church facilities or beneficiary associations. Non-governmental organisations often focus on specialised residential health care services (e.g. for people suffering from Alzheimer's/dementia), on home care agencies and hospices. Finally, for-profit companies and individuals can act as providers of social services. (MoLSA 2006b)

The Act on Social Services covers a wide range of social care services and social prevention services. In the field of long-term care, these include residential social services facilities (homes for the elderly and persons with disabilities, special homes as for mentally ill or people with Alzheimer's/dementia, week-day care centres, etc.), outpatient services (daily short stay hospitals, day service centres, respite services, etc.) and home services (home help, personal assistance, emergency care, etc.). (MoLSA 2006b)

In the health care sector, it is mainly two types of services that address the need for long-term care. After-care health care facilities include long-term treatment facilities, rehabilitation centres or mental hospitals. Special outpatient facilities include home care, home care agencies providing expert and palliative care, and hospices. Hospices are a recent development and still rare in the Czech Republic. They were all established after the political transformation in 1989 by NGOs with support by the Ministry of Health and the Ministry of Labour and Social Affairs. (MoLSA 2006b)

The gaps between the health and social system, the lack of communication and continuity between these two departments, a lack of coordination of strategies and the legislative process, as well as practical obstacles in providing care were discussed in the Czech Republic for a long time. (Holmerová 2006) The separation of the health and the social care system creates several problems. One example is the case of rehabilitation and nursing care which is covered by public health insurance if provided in health care facilities, but not paid for if provided by social services in residential care facilities. Another problem is caused when patients in a relatively stabilised state receive social care in institutional health care facilities while outpatient health care would have been sufficient, just because the necessary assistance could not be ensured through family or professional social services. (MoLSA 2006b) In connection with the preparation and implementation of the new Act on Social Services the situation is currently improving.

3. Residential Care – Community Care – Payments for Care

After 1990, social services developed not only in quantitative, but also in qualitative terms, in particular with regard to improving the quality of care, accommodation and equipment. And social services providers came to include not only the state, the regions and municipalities, but also churches, civic associations, other NGOs and natural persons. From a general perspective, developments in social services reflect the trend away from institutional care towards care in the community, in line with the idea of individualising care and coming close to ordinary life in a domestic environment. This places an emphasis on an individual approach towards users and their human rights. With the introduction of care allowances directed at care users, the emphasis of individual autonomy was further strengthened. (MoLSA 2005c)

3.1. Residential Care
Up to the end of 2006, within the framework of institutional social care for senior citizens, social care services were basically provided at two types of facilities: in "pensioners' houses" (*domovy důchodců*), where comprehensive care was provided and in "pensioners' lodging houses" (*domovy-pensiony pro*

důchodce), where only some services were provided, depending on the state of health of its residents. Current legislative changes and strategic documents support the reassessment of the target groups for institutional and home care and it is believed that this will contribute to the sustainability of the system for long-term care. Through a gradual transformation of institutional social care, residential social services should be provided for persons with a greater need of assistance in daily activities and a higher level of care, especially nursing care. In contrast, people with a lower need for assistance in daily living, shall be supported within their natural social environment and in connection to family and local community resources. (MoLSA 2006b) To a significant extent, because of a lack of residential care settings, community social services or personal care, health care facilities provide services to persons that do not require in-patient health care but are unable to live on their own without assistance.

The new Act on Social Services does not state both previous types of residential care facilities mentioned above, but it defines so called "homes for the elderly" (*domovy pro seniory*), which correspond to "nursing homes" in international terminology. In homes for the elderly, in-patient services shall be provided to persons with reduced self-sufficiency, in particular due to their age, whose situation requires the regular assistance of someone else. The services provided shall include basic activities like the provision of accommodation and food, assistance with handling common self-care acts, assistance with personal hygiene or arranging for personal hygiene conditions, mediating contacts with the social environment, social therapeutic activities, activation activities, assistance with asserting rights, justified interests and looking after personal matters.

Regions and municipalities are the main providers of residential care, accounting for almost 94% of beds. (see table 4.3) According to a Ministry of Labour and Social Affairs recommendation, facilities with more than 80 places are mostly established by the regions, while other facilities are dominated by municipalities and NGOs. (MoLSA 2005c) Residential care provided on a commercial basis is still rare and privatisation of public residential care facilities is currently not an issue.

Table 4.3: Residential care by different sectors and number of places, 2006

Residential care provider	Number of places	As % of total
Public sector	47,881	93.79
Churches	2,073	4.06
Other	1,095	2.14
Total	51,049	100.00

(Source: MoLSA 2007b)

Till the end of 2006, citizens were accepted into residential care according to their applications. If a vacancy arose and the applicant met the conditions for the provision of the service, the municipality or region as the service provider made an administrative decision on the provision of the service. In the case of private residential care providers, the future service user entered into an agreement on the extent, coverage and payment of services. The Act on Social Services introduced a general contractual basis for the provision of services. Since January 2007, citizens are taken into residential care (and other types of services) according to an agreement with the provider on the extent and the coverage of services, together with a determination of the payment to be made by the user. The provider can refuse to enter into agreement on providing a requested social service only for three reasons: the provider does not provide the required service, the provider does not have sufficient capacity to provide the required service, the applicant's health condition excludes the provision of the requested service.

Table 4.4: Provision in residential care, facilities and number of beds, 2006

Indicator	Pensioners' houses	Pensioners' lodging houses	Total
Number of establishments	399[a]	142	541
Number of beds	39,621	11,428	51,049
Waiting list	45,631	20,446	66,077

Note: This data only refers to the establishments in the Ministry of Labour and Social Affairs database (mostly public sector).
[a] Including nine common establishments (PH and PLH)
(Source: MoLSA 2007a; 2000)

Since 1994, the number of residential care institutions (pensioners' houses and pensioners' lodging houses) and the number of places provided has constantly increased. But, waiting times for placement can still be between several months and several years (e.g. in Prague). This depends primarily on demand and capacity in the given region and on the interest of applicants in particular facilities. (MoLSA 2005c) It is believed that the large and increasing demand for residential care is caused by the inadequate supply of community services and the limited experience of people who would have alternative options. Finally, residential care facilities still represent a certain level of security for seniors. The feeling of being able to get help whenever needed is the main reason why many still self-sufficient people with no need of nursing care enter waiting lists.

Up to the end of 2006, funding of social services was characterised by different funding regimes for social service providers. There was a different method of financing services provided in regional facilities (from the state budget and budgets of the founders) and in municipal facilities (subsidies per bed from the state budget). (MoLSA 2005c) Since January 2007, use of public resources (subsidies from the state/regional/municipal budget) is declared equal for all social services facilities, and their providers. The primary financing sources for all kinds of social services are the user contributions (using the care allowance), the state budget and the budgets of regional administrative units.

In accordance with the Act on Social Services (§ 101), a subsidy from the state budget can be provided to social services providers who are registered for arranging social services provision. The subsidy is provided for funding ordinary expenses related to the provision of social services in compliance with the medium-term social services development plan. Subsidies from the state budget are provided through regional budgets. Regional authorities are responsible to submit applications for subsidies to the Ministry of Labour and Social Affairs for the next relevant budgetary period. The total amount of a region's subsidy is determined on the basis of the overall annual volume of financial resources stated in the regional medium-term services development plan, the number and amount of care allowances paid, the number of registered social services providers as well as health care residential facilities and their capacities to provide social services.

In accordance with the Act on Social Services (§ 104), specific subsidies by the Ministry of Labour and Social Affairs can be granted to support social services of a nationwide or supra-regional nature, for activities of a developmental nature, training for social services workers, support for social services quality, the preparation of medium-term social services plans as well as extraordinary situations (including, for example, natural disasters). Programmes funded from the structural funds of the European Communities and other programmes of the European Communities may participate in funding the above-mentioned activities in the field of social services provision.

The financial contribution of residents reached more than one third in 2006. While this indicates a substantial increase compared to the mid-1990s, the user contribution slightly declined compared to the year 2000. While different funding regulations applied for public and for non-profit facilities till 2006, new regulations have been implemented in 2007. Since then, the amount of payments to be made by the residents is determined by a Ministry of Labour and Social Affairs Decree. Accordingly, the new cash benefit (see below) should cover most of the payments to be made by users. The maximum limit of reimbursement is CZK 160.00 (€ 5.70) a day for providing accommodation, CZK 140.00 (€ 5.00) a day for all-day boarding and CZK 70.00 (€ 2.50) a day for providing lunch only.

3.2. Community Care

The most widespread form of field social services for elderly people in their home environment are community home care services. These services are provided in the private households or in social services facilities and include: a) assistance with handling self-care acts, b) assistance with personal hygiene or arranging for personal hygiene conditions, c) provision of food or assistance with arranging for food, d) assistance with running a household, e) mediating contacts with the social environment. (Act on Social Services)

Expenditure on community care services increased from CZK 193 million in 1990 to CZK 2,255 million in 2002 and then fell to CZK 1,593 million in 2005. Although the number of clients continues to rise, staff numbers have fallen by more than one third over the last ten years. (see table 4.5) The main reason for this can be seen in the professionalisation of community care services (volunteer community carers are rapidly dwindling in number), while the number of apartments in premises with community care services is rising (service rationalisation). Client participation in cost coverage for community care services has increased tenfold on average, mostly due to a reduction in the number of activities performed for free, an expansion in the range of services on offer and a rise in the rates for individual activities. (Kozlová 2005)

Table 4.5: Financing of community home care services, 1990–2005

	Total expenditure on service in mio CZK/€	Number of service recipients	Number of service employees	Average annual payment by each service recipient (CZK/€)
1990	193.00/6.89	67,043	8,405	112.96/4.03
1995	2,526.00/90.21	86,201	6,372	483.17/17.26
2000	1,540.00/55.00	113,528	5,760	1,316.34/47.01
2005	1,593.00/56.89	111,603	4,821	2,052.27/73.29

(Source: MoLSA 2006a; 2005a; 2000)

The developments in the field of social services have brought positive changes regarding the provision of care in the home of senior citizens in the Czech Republic since 1989. However, the conditions under which this care can currently be given are not considered to be adequate. Basically, there is a lack of consultation services focusing on care for senior citizens, a lack of capacities for interim respite stays and equipment loaning facilities. Community care services which are felt to be lacking most include all-day supervision, night services and other activities to secure the care of the least independent senior citizens.

The providers of community home care services are mostly municipalities, followed by NGOs and the regions. In some specific sectors, such as meals on wheels, laundries or day assistance centres, NGOs, commercial providers or individuals play a comparatively stronger role, while the public sector still dominates. (see table 4.6) There are huge inter-regional differences in the accessibility of community care. The situation is usually better in urban areas than in less populated areas. Some small municipalities are still excluded from the provision of community care services. According to Veselá (2003), community home care services are currently not provided in some areas because of three factors: the locality is too remote (30%), there is no contract between the community and the community home care service provider (26%) or only a few potential clients reside in the area (24%).

Table 4.6: Community home care services (CHCS) by provider, 2006

	Number	Region	Municipality	Churches	Person	Other
CHCS recipients	182,110	3.8%	84.6%	4.6%	0.8%	6.2%
only in houses with care services	20,510	6.6%	81.5%	5.4%	1.8%	4.7%
only meals on wheels	38,455	6.4%	79.6%	6.8%	0.9%	6.1%
CHCS workstations	1,815	2.9%	77.9%	4.1%	6.4%	8.8%
only meals on wheels	926	0.6%	83.3%	1.8%	5.4%	8.9%
Houses with care services	908	0.1%	98.3%	0.4%	-	1.1%
number of flats	29,148	0.1%	98.2%	0.4%	-	1.4%
capacity of flats	35,738	0.1%	98.2%	0.3%	0.1%	1.3%
number of residents	32,426	0.1%	98.0%	0.4%	0.1%	1.5%
Hygiene centres	409	2.7%	83.6%	2.7%	-	11.0%
number of clients	16,663	7.5%	78.6%	3.6%	-	10.3%
Laundries	422	4.3%	87.9%	2.8%	0.2%	4.7%
number of clients	14,463	2.3%	73.2%	1.7%	0.2%	8.7%
Day assistance centres	71	1.4%	77.5%	9.9%	-	11.3%
capacity	690	2.2%	70.7%	12.8%	-	14.2%
number of clients	1,038	1.4%	62.3%	20.4%	-	15.8%

(Source: MoLSA 2007b)

Community home care services (CHCS) are provided to persons with reduced self-sufficiency due to age, chronic disease or disability, and to families with children whose situation requires the assistance of another physical person. Services have been provided to 182,110 recipients in 2007, including 38,455 users of meals on wheels only. The services primarily consist of personal care and assistance and helping persons to maintain their households. The services on offer include food preparation and meals on wheels, shopping services, personal hygiene services and home help services. They are provided to citizens in their homes or in premises with a community care service, in personal hygiene centres, day care centres, canteens for pensioners and laundries. (Kozlová 2005)

Houses with care services (*domovy s pečovatelskou službou*) are increasingly popular facilities. To a great extent, these houses correspond to "sheltered accommodation". Residents live in well equipped flats, have access to several social services and especially have the security of getting help when in need. The main services available comprise the full or part-time presence of a caregiver and supply of meals. In the 1990s – due to the realisation of the "programme for the development of houses with assistance services" – there was a very intensive increase in the number of houses with care services. As many municipalities used the possibility of targeted state grants to build these flats, the number of these flats has more than doubled within a decade. (Mašková 2004)

As outlined before, the funding of long-term care services has been harmonised from 2007. The primary funding source for all types of social services is the user payment now based on the care allowance, the state budget and the budgets of regional administrative units. The amount of the user contributions is regulated by the Ministry of Labour and Social Affairs Decree.

3.3. Payments for Care

Until 2006, two kinds of payments were provided for care. The first one, an "Increase in Pension for Helplessness" (*zvýšení důchodu pro bezmocnost*), was delivered to pensioners whose health or age required care by another person. The aim of this allowance was to help secure the assistance for the recipient on the grounds of helplessness. The second one, a "Contribution for the Care of a Close Person or Another Person" (*příspěvek při péči o blízkou nebo jinou osobu*), aimed to ensure at least basic security in the form of a minimum income, pension and health insurance to informal care-givers who were compelled to give up their gainful employment by providing personal all-day care. Due to the adoption of the Act on Social Services and its promulgation as of 1 January 2007, and the introduction of a newly conceived "Care Allowance" (*příspěvek na péči*), both benefits were abolished.

The care allowance (*příspěvek na péči*) is granted to citizens to secure the assistance required to deal with their difficult social situation. It is provided to persons over one year of age who are dependent on the assistance of another individual for care activities related to their own person and independence. The law distinguishes four levels of dependence. These levels range from mild to complete dependence on the help of another person and correspond to the level of the benefit, ranging between 3,000 CZK (in level I) and 11,000 CZK (in level IV) for those up to the age of 18, and between 2,000 CZK (in level I) and 12,000 CZK (in level IV) for those over the age of 18.

The allowance aims to strengthen people's financial independence as users of social services by providing them with the purchasing power. They can decide on the method of securing assistance themselves and have the opportunity to look for sources of assistance among close persons, other individuals or social service providers. Different forms of assistance can be combined. However, only the carer who provides the greatest amount of care may – on the basis of caring for a person from dependency level II to IV – be credited with care time as compensatory time for retirement pension purposes. According to Labour Office records, the carer may be employed or a student inter alia.

The care allowance is financed from the state budget (through taxes) and is not means-tested. The total number of acknowledged benefit claims ranges from 240,000–250,000 people per month. Almost 70% of recipients are 65 years of age and older, 57% are 75 years or older. Among the younger age groups, those up to 18 years of age account for 7% of recipients, adults between 19 and 65 years of age for 24% of recipients. (MoLSA 2009)

Table 4.7: Care allowance provision according to four levels of dependence, 2009

Level of dependence	Level of the benefit (CZK/€)	
	Persons up to 18 years of age	Persons over 18 years of age
I – mild	3,000/107	2,000/71
II – medium	5,000/179	4,000/143
III – heavy	9,000/321	8,000/286
IV – complete	11,000/393	12,000/429

(Source: Zákon č. 108/2006 Sb.)

4. The Role of the Private Sector

Since 1990, providers of social services do not only include the state, municipalities and towns, but also churches, individuals, civic associations and other NGOs. With voluntary and charitable organisations entering the social services sector and the churches seeing a revival in the social sphere, social services became more privatised, even if still on moderate levels. Many NGOs only act on a local level, while others are active at local, regional and national levels. A very important role is taken by the *Czech Catholic Charity* (*Česká katolická charita*) and *Diakonie of Reformed Churches (Evangelical and Hussite)*, which organise social services for elderly people in all regions. Further NPOs include the *Czech Red Cross, Remedium* or *Senior.* (Holmerová 2006) In particular professionals in the social sphere also took advantage of the opportunity to establish non-state bodies that could immediately be used to start providing modern social services. Overall, however, the development of social services has not been tightly coordinated, and often not very well structured.

Development in this area was mostly hindered because the legal regulations governing the conditions for providing social care services were out of date. Despite numerous legislative interventions, they did not meet the requirements for the provision of social services by non-profit organisations and businesses. State budget funds were channelled to individual entities by different means: primarily as state subsidies for municipal and regional facilities and via grant procedures for non-state entities. These various forms of funding for the same type of services but for different providers have led to the preferential treatment of some entities over others, which made it desirable to establish equal and transparent conditions for all. The new Act on Social Services is the first step towards finding legislative support for efforts to transform the social services system. (Kozlová 2005)

NGOs also act as representatives or lobbyists especially for the interests of those in need of care and informal carers. Some are acting just as lobbyists, others are also providing social services. Some are specialised solely in long-term care, while others work more general on social issues. The *Czech Alzheimer's Society (ČALS - Česká alzheimerovská společnost)* aims to improve the situation of people with dementia, their family care-givers, and lobbies for their rights and interests. In about 30 contact and information points in all regions it provides support oriented towards family care-givers (self-support groups, counselling, respite care). The most important organisations for seniors are *The Union of Retired People of the Czech Republic* (*Svaz důchodců České republiky*) and *Life 90* (*Život 90*). They run various activities for the elderly (meetings, lectures, leisure activities, seniors' telephone etc.), act on behalf of seniors and protect their interests at the local, regional and national level. *Life 90* also offers different types of services (short term stays at respite centres, home alarm systems etc.). The *Czech Helsinki Committee* (*Český Helsinský výbor*) dealing with human rights also focuses on issues concerning seniors, especially those living in institutions. (Holmerová 2006) *SKOK - The Association of Non-Governmental, Non-Profit Organisations Active in the Areas of Social Assistance and Social Health Care* cooperates in preparing laws on social services and organises conferences concerning social and health issues, seminars and training on social services. It endeavours to participate in the formation of social policies through advocacy of the interests and rights of providers and clients of social assistance and social health care services, to support NGOs and their cooperation. (SKOK 2009) With regard to political parties profiled as representing the interests of seniors, there is a very small left oriented *"Party for Life Securities"* (formerly *Pensioners for Life Securities*), which however has never succeeded in an election on the national level.

5. Family Care and Public Support for Informal Care

5.1. Family Care-giving in the Czech Republic

Long-term care is primarily the responsibility of the closest family members and relatives. Where this help is not accessible, public responsibility starts. Act No. 94/1964 Coll. on the Family only regulates the duty of children who are able to maintain themselves to provide their parents with appropriate sustenance if required. Every child meets this maintenance duty with a share corresponding to the ratio of his or her abilities, capacities and financial circumstances in proportion to the abilities, capacities and financial circumstances of the other children.

There is no regular data survey on the number of informal care-givers in the Czech Republic, but several studies on family care and assistance offered to older persons have been made on samples of the population. Research carried out by the Memory Disorder Clinic indicated that 23.5% of Czech families take care of somebody who is not self-sufficient. (Tošnerová 2001) According to Zavázalová et al. (2001), more than 80% of the care provided for senior citizens in the Czech Republic dependent on the help of others, is arranged by the family. The average duration of such care is 4–5 years. Those who most frequently care for relatives and close friends are women (women 64%, men 36%), 80% of whom are employed. Care for a dependent senior citizen is most frequently provided by grown-up offspring (53%), a spouse (21%), relatives (10%) or friends (16%).

Studies have also shown the extensive burdens family care-giving involves. (Barvíková, Bartoňová 2005; Veselá 2002; Tošnerová 2001) About two thirds of all family care-givers feel mentally and physically exhausted. 29% of carers are frequently or very frequently exhausted from 24 hour care. 60% of carers are faced with financial problems, 23% report this as a frequent or very frequent problem. (see table 4.8)

Table 4.8: How people feel in their care-giving situation

Carer's feeling	All "yes" answers in %	Frequently and very frequently in %
Carer is mentally exhausted	70	28
Carer is physically exhausted	69	23
Carer has health problems	68	19
Exhaustion from permanent 24h care	65	29
Lack of finance	60	23

(Source: Veselá 2002)

A relatively high level of intergenerational solidarity in the family is still embodied in the Czech society. But it seems there are no unique motivational mechanisms with universal validity. What features in the decision "to care or not to care" is a mix of love, a matter of course, duty and social and cultural norms. (Možný et al. 2004) In a qualitative explorative study including in-depth interviews with nine main family care-givers (Barvíková, Batoňová

2005) caring for their (grand)parents, these carers treated caring for their dependent parents or grandparents as "commonplace", "duty", "part of life" or "one of life's tasks". Very often, it had been a negative experience with hospitalisation or stays in long-term treatment facilities that influenced the decision of families to take over caring for their close ones. The decision to continue caring is often strengthened by negative experiences or perceptions of staying in long-term care facilities, where the family member suffered physically and mentally. Family carers feel there is a lack of social services (such as respite stay facilities, day care centres or all day supervision) which could help them to manage the situation better. The compensation for difficulties and exhaustion is usually perceived in the strong emotional bond that develops between the caregiver and care receiver, and a certain feeling of assurance that the (grand)parent is well cared for within the resources provided.

However, experiences from practice also prove the existence of financial abuse, unwillingness to care or lack of interest in frail elderly people in families. According to estimates, 3–5% of the elderly face some form of ill-treatment. (Tošnerová 2001) The solution to this problem is often complicated because of its secrecy. Seniors very often conceal such behaviour by their children motivated by the attitude that "it is better to have a bad daughter than no daughter". (Vohralíková, Rabušic 2004) According to nursing home workers, in some cases almost unbearable family situations and the lack of field services are major reasons why seniors withdraw into residential care. (Veselá 2003)

5.2. Public Support for Family Care

Apart from the financial support, the development of new social services enabling frail elderly people to live in their own household and with their community is the main purpose of public support for informal care. Until 2006, all-day carers who met the claim conditions set by the relevant legal regulation were provided with a benefit called "Contribution for the Care of a Close Person or Other Person" (*příspěvek při péči o blízkou nebo jinou osobu*). For the recipients, the state also registered an insurance premium in the health and the pension insurance system. The time in which they provided care is considered compensatory time for pension insurance purposes. However, before the last increase in the contribution in 2005, the amount of the contribution provided was very low and family carers for whom the contribution was the main or only source of income, usually found themselves in a difficult financial situation. A more substantial increase in the contribution has for long been debated, but was considered to be a significant burden on the state budget, for which there was no political will.

From 2007, the earlier benefit has been replaced by the care allowance paid to the person in need of care. If a family member or another person cares for a care allowance recipient, either independently or with the assistance of social services, this person is granted special additional components of social protection. Also, the care allowance is not to be included in the carer's income for the purposes of benefit systems or tax calculations. And carers are in no way restricted in their employment. When caring for a person in dependency levels II to IV, the main carer can become a so-called state policyholder in the public health system. In addition, the period of care-giving counts towards the supplementary period in the pension insurance scheme. (MoLSA 2009)

6. Challenges and Perspectives

The 2006 Act on Social Services is generally perceived as a turning point for social services provision in the Czech Republic, although its implementation produces several challenges and even confusion and fears about its future effects. While it is too soon to really evaluate the impacts, this final section summarises the pros and cons of the new Act as they have been discussed by experts and providers of social services.

The introduction of the care allowance scheme is widely seen as a positive step to enhance care and support for people with disabilities, leading to greater independence and free choice of services. However, social services users and providers expect that the allowance will not be enough to cover the costs of the required services and that it will be necessary to use additional resources. Especially in the case of clients with lower degrees of dependence and lower levels of the care allowance, the amount of the allowance cannot cover the cost of residential care facilities. Therefore, facilities might face problems to balance this situation even if clients' fees are increased to the maximum level allowed by law. On the other hand, this will create an incentive to focus residential care provision on those with more extended care needs.

Other voices object that the Act on Social Services in general responds mainly to the needs and requirements of persons with physical or sensory disabilities. Their interests and rights have been successfully defended by NGOs and lobbying groups since the 1990s, whereas the situation for seniors and people with mental, intellectual or multiple handicaps has been more difficult to improve. It is argued that the motto "people with disability have the right to decide about their life and about the money which they will use to buy social services" is limited where individual decision-making abilities are limited. (Černá 2006) Moreover, service users and providers point out that the new assessment rules relate mainly to acts of mobility and hygiene, which might discriminate other handicaps. (SKOK 2006)

Experts in the field also express doubts about social workers' abilities to examine and objectively consider the dependence degree of the applicants. Even though high demands are placed on social workers' training, they do not have a medical education. Clients can also try to deliberately mystify or hide problems (e.g. someone in the early stages of dementia). Furthermore, the user's need for assistance can radically change within short periods. Other experts point at the risk of allowance abuse by family members, other informal carers or social services providers. It is anticipated that care defined by law or agreed by contract might not be provided and that eventually the increase in clients' independence and self-reliance will not be supported.

With regard to social services provision, the supply of residential care services still prevails over community services. The insufficient range of professional services is perceived as a serious problem and a threat to successful implementation of the new law. Therefore, medium-term social services development planning with the participation of providers and social services users is one of the main principles of the new law. It will proceed on the levels of the ministry, regions and municipalities and should contribute to the equal treatment of social services providers. (SKOK 2006) Since subsidies depend on these plans, in case of omission of any type of social service its provider cannot get a subsidy in this region. Most regions are not experienced in creating such plans and they do not have sufficient skills for strategic planning and decision making. "Existing community development plans are formal, supply and demand are lacking, plans are oriented to existing local providers and their narrow portfolio of activities." (Černá 2007) While the new law has introduced equal treatment in the funding of public and private provision, some still fear that the concentration of power in the regions will lead to preferential treatment of facilities provided by regions and municipalities to the detriment of NGO facilities. As regions and municipalities mostly provide residential care facilities, it would henceforth mean stronger support for residential care compared to other types of social services. On the other hand, the availability of the cash benefit could increase the demand for community services as compared to residential care services which in turn could help the development of a broader public and private mix in service provision.

Finally, a major concern raised with the introduction of the Social Services Act is the financial implications. Preliminary analyses (MoLSA 2009; Průša 2008) confirm that concern. While the government earmarked € 317 million from the state budget for the care allowance in 2007, the total monthly expenditure data for the benefit shows a stable level of between € 50 and € 55 million, which results in about € 650 million (i.e. 0.5% of GDP) when extrapolated to a full year (MoLSA 2009).

With intense debates on potential negative implications of the new scheme the positive effects of recent developments are sometimes overseen. The introduction of the care allowance and the new regulations on social services has been a major step towards developing a more comprehensive long-term care system in the Czech Republic. A number of additional activities promoted by the public sector, practices developed by providers or international projects (such as the "Isolation to Inclusion" project: Isolation to Inclusion 2009) attempt to improve the quality of life of the elderly, to develop support for the independent living of seniors enabling them to stay in their own household, to secure home care for the elderly in the terminal stage of life or to offer training to family members caring for an elderly person. Approaches also have promoted individual specialised care programs (such as drop-in centres of the Czech Alzheimer's Society), the opening of residential care facilities to the public, the development of social services through community planning or crisis intervention and counselling via telephone lines for the elderly. Finally, a major issue is the coordination and integration of health care and social services providing comprehensive responses to the clients' needs.

Bibliography

Barvíková, Jana; Bartoňová, Jitka (2005) Příběhy pečujících rodin (*The stories of caring families*). In: Problematika – generace 50 plus. II. mezinárodní konference, Třeboň 6-7 October 2005, Sborník přednášek, Třeboň, 97–107.

Černá, Milena (2006) Země ústavní péče (*Country of institutional care*). In: E-Bulletin SKOK (online), Vol. 5, December 2006, 1–2. http://www.skok.biz/download/e-bulletin/2006-12.doc (28 July 2009).

Černá, Milena (2007) 5 bodů k otázkám reformy sociálních služeb (*5 points to questions of social services reform*), Discussion document of the civic association SKOK.

Holmerová, Iva (2006) Supporting family carers of elderly people in Europe. The National background report for the Czech Republic. Hamburg: Lit Verlag.

Isolation to Inclusion (2009) Inventory of Innovation. http://www.i2i-project.net/i_by_country.php?c=4&rf=4 (28 July 2009).

Kopecká, Petra (2002) Koncept kvality života seniorů v České republice (*Quality of seniors' life concept in the Czech Republic*). In: Zdravotnictví v České republice, No. 1–2, 71–75.

Kozlová, Lucie (2005) Sociální služby (*Social services*). Praha: TRITON.

Mašková, Miroslava (2004) Evolution of social services for the ageing population. In: Czech welfare state. Changing environment, Changing institutions. Praha: CESES UK FSV, No. 7, 23–39.

MoLSA (2000) Základní ukazatele z oblasti práce a sociálního zabezpečení v České republice ve vývojových řadách a grafech (*Basic indicators of labour and social protection in the Czech Republic – Time series and graphs*). Praha: Ministry of Labour and Social Affairs.

MoLSA (2005a) Základní ukazatele z oblasti práce a sociálního zabezpečení v České republice ve vývojových řadách a grafech (*Basic indicators of labour and social protection in the Czech Republic – Time series and graphs*). Praha: Ministry of Labour and Social Affairs.

MoLSA (2005b) Důvodová zpráva k zákonu o sociálních službách (*Explanatory report on the social services bill*). Praha: Ministry of Labour and Social Affairs.

MoLSA (2005c) Preliminary national report on health care and long-term care in the Czech Republic. Praha: Ministry of Labour and Social Affairs.

MoLSA (2006a) Základní ukazatele z oblasti práce a sociálního zabezpečení v České republice ve vývojových řadách a grafech (*Basic indicators of labour and social protection in the Czech Republic – Time series and graphs*). Praha: Ministry of Labour and Social Affairs.

MoLSA (2006b) National report on strategies for social protection and social inclusion for years 2006-2008. Praha: Ministry of Labour and Social Affairs.

MoLSA (2006c) Pojistně matematická zpráva o sociálním pojištění (*Actuarial report on social insurance*). Praha: Ministry of Labour and Social Affairs.

MoLSA (2007a) Basic indicators of labour and social protection in the Czech Republic – Time series and graphs 2006. Praha: Ministry of Labour and Social Affairs.

MoLSA (2007b) Statistická ročenka z oblasti práce a sociálních věcí (*Statistical year-book on labour and social affairs*). Praha: Ministry of Labour and Social Affairs.

MoLSA (2009) Social services and care allowance in the Czech Republic. Praha: Ministry of Labour and Social Affairs. http://www.mpsv.cz/files/clanky/7033/leaflet_on_social_services.pdf (26 July 2009).

Možný, Ivo; Přidalová, Marie; Bánovcová, Lenka (2004) Mezigenerační solidarita. Výzkumná zpráva z mezinárodního srovnávacího výzkumu – Hodnota dětí a mezigenerační solidarita. *(Research information from international comparative research – Value of children and intergenerational relationship)*. Praha: VÚPSV Praha & Výzkumné centrum Brno.

Průša, Ladislav (2008) New system social services financing: Myths and mistakes. In: ACTA VŠFS, Vol. 2, No. 2, 197–206. http://praha.vupsv.cz/fulltext/Do_1481.pdf (26 July 2009).

SKOK (2006) Vliv nového zákona o sociálních službách na práva uživatelů a poskytovatelu (*The new social services law influence on users' and providers rights*). Praha: SKOK.

SKOK (2009) The Association of Non-Governmental, Non-Profit Organizations Active in the Areas of Social Assistance and Social Health Care. http://www.skok.biz/en/ (28 July 2009).

Tošnerová, Tamara (2001) Pocity a potřeby pečujících o starší rodinné příslušníky (*Feelings and needs of care-givers caring of older relatives*). Praha: Ambulance pro poruchy paměti 3. LF UK.

Veselá, Jitka (2002) Představy rodinných příslušníku o zabezpečení péče nesoběstačným seniorům (*Relatives' views on provision of care for the frail elderly*). Praha: VÚPSV.

Veselá, Jitka (2003) Sociální služby poskytované seniorům v domácnostech (*Social services provided in seniors' households*). Praha: VÚPSV.

Vohralíková, Lenka; Rabušic, Ladislav (2004) Čeští senioři včera, dnes a zítra (*Czech seniors yesterday, today and tomorrow*). Brno: VÚPSV.

Zákon č. 108/2006, Sb., o sociálních službách (*Act No. 109/2006 Coll., on social services*).

Zavázalová, Helena; Vožehová, Sylvie; Zaremba, Vladimír; Zikmundová, Květuše (2001) Vybrané kapitoly ze sociální gerontologie (*Selected chapters from social gerontology*). Praha: Karolinum nakladatelství UK.

5

Long-term Care in Hungary: Between Health and Social Care

László Gulácsi, Katalin Érsek, Kinga Mészáros

1. Introduction

Demographic, social and economic developments will make long-term care a serious challenge for the Hungarian society and the welfare state in the coming decades. The increase in long-term care needs and the measures required to meet them have not been broadly discussed yet and neither have issues of quality and monitoring. Especially in the current situation of budgetary pressure, the funding of policy changes and possible economic implications will have to be given extra attention. The main aim of this chapter is to introduce the current Hungarian long-term care system, provide relevant data and analyse challenges and perspectives for care policies. In studying the current situation in the provision and funding of long-term care, particular attention is paid to the division of responsibilities between the public sector, the private sector and the family, as well as between the health and social care system.

The context of long-term care in Hungary is characterised by a decreasing population (-5.26% since 1989) and demographic ageing. (Eurostat 2009; Iván 2002) Like other European countries, Hungary does not only experience an increase in the absolute number of the elderly population, but also a significant relative growth. The population beyond 65 years of age represented 15.9% of the total population in 2007. According to forecasts, the respective proportion will increase to 33.4% (or almost 3 million elderly people) in 2050. (European

Health for All Database 2008) On the one hand, the country is faced with high mortality rates among men and a strong prevalence of chronic diseases that aggravate old age disability. On the other hand, fertility rates are very low (1.32 in 2007) and differences in terms of life expectancy and healthy life expectancy are increasing among regions of the country. Life expectancy at birth (69.38 years for men, and 77.76 years for women in 2007) is still far below Western European average, but has increased significantly since the 1990s. (Eurostat 2009) As one of the consequences of the differences in life expectancy between men and women, men living in families are likely to be cared for by their spouses, while widowed women often face particularly severe challenges in receiving the necessary care and support.

The increasing needs for care and health services will also bring major implications for the ways in which long-term care is provided in Hungary. Differences in the economic performance have caused considerable migration of the younger generation within the country over the last decades. People have been moving towards the capital Budapest and the Western regions of the country, leaving many elderly people separated from the younger generation in the countryside. Even if family members are able to provide some financial support to their elderly relatives, their capacity to provide care work will probably be more limited in the future. It is very likely that the current demographic and socio-economic developments will create an increasing demand for long-term care services from outside households. To meet these needs, increased public spending on long-term care and major reforms in the existing system will be necessary.

2. From the 1990s to the Current Care System

The development and the current situation of long-term care in Hungary is characterised by split responsibilities of provision and funding arrangements between the health and the social care sector. While there have been attempts to better integrate the two sectors, respective measures remain limited so far.

2.1. The Health Care System

After the political changes of 1990, Hungary and other Central and Eastern European countries returned to the Bismarckian solidarity-based social security system. The responsibility of providing health care was transferred to local and county governments for each level of the health care system – primary care, out-patient care and inpatient care. Only a few institutions of tertiary care, such as university clinics and national medical institutes, remained in the national domain. The Health Insurance Fund (*Országos Egészségbiztosítási Pénztár*, OEP), administered by the National Health Insurance Fund Administration (NHIFA), is responsible for health care services in the whole country. Running costs are generally covered by social health insurance contributions from the Health Insurance Fund. The Health Insurance Fund has sub-budgets for different types of services (primary care, out-patient care, acute and chronic in-patient care, etc.), which are capped with a national budget ceiling. Government grants and subsidies from facility owners, mainly local governments, can be provided additionally to cover capital costs. With the recent reform of health care in Hungary, a purchaser-provider split was introduced to the system. Most general practitioners are responsible for a certain catchment area (territorial supply obligation) and have a gatekeeper role towards secondary and tertiary care provided by specialists. GPs' revenues combine capitation fees based on a special point system for different age groups, a fixed fee covering overhead costs, a supplementary fee to eliminate income differences due to location and additional reimbursement for patients not registered with their practice. Acute inpatient care is financed through the *Homogén Betegségcsoportok* (HBCS) system, which was implemented from 1993 and follows a similar approach as the Diagnosis Related Groups system (DRG). (Egervári 2007)

The Hungarian health care system has an ambivalent structure. While the responsibility of delivering health care is decentralized giving local authorities a strong influence as owners of health care institutions, financing health care is highly centralized. Although the NHIFA has local offices (branches) in each Hungarian county, they do not have competences to make independent decisions. (Boncz et al. 2004) The NHIFA faced increasing deficits over the last years, which reached over 30% of total revenues between 2003 and 2005. These budgetary issues have since become a major driver of health reforms and reform debates in Hungary, aiming mostly at cost-containment and a reduction of hospital beds. (Boncz, Sebestyen 2006; Gaál 2004; Boncz 2003)

2.2. The Social Care Sector in Hungary

The Hungarian Social Act (Law Act 1993/III) was the first major step in defining responsibilities in the field of social care in the 1990s. The 20 county self-governments are responsible for the provision of residential care, while local self-governments (3,168 in 2005) have to ensure the provision of community care in private homes. A licence system was introduced, allowing for the operation of residences and for access to public funding via a so-called normative, which is a pre-defined level of reimbursement per service unit. These changes in regulation led to the opening of several new residences and a substantial increase in non-profit run institutions. At the same time, split responsibilities between health and social care became an increasingly important issue in the debate about the future provision of long-term care. The NHIFA started a programme for mixed health and social services in 1999, which included the provision of services in the private home of the elderly person and domestic hospice care. With a modification of the Social Act in 1999, the concept of operation licences has been further clarified. An additional classification of providers into public, non-public and church-related institutions determines access to and level of public funding.

2.3. Care Responsibilities between the Health and Social Sector

Split responsibilities, the fragmentation of competences and a lack of coordination between the relevant players in the health care sector and the social care sector are seen as major barriers in the current Hungarian long-term care system. In health issues, the Ministry of Health and the NHIFA have the key responsibilities in organising and funding services. In the social care sector, apart from the Ministry of Social Affairs and Labour, self-governments on the county and the municipality level play the major role in sustaining institutions and services. Even though the two sectors work largely isolated, there are parallel responsibilities in the provision of services for frail elderly and disabled people. The actual care provision is largely determined by what the two sectors make available, rather than by defined competences.

The Law Act Nr. LXXIX of 2001, a modification of the 1993 Social Act, and the establishment of the Social Welfare Committee (an inter-ministerial strategic planning committee) were first attempts to strengthen coordination between health and social care. The underlying objective was to develop comprehensive standards and to systematically collect statistical and financial data for strategic planning in the sector. In 2003, the establishment of a Care Insurance Fund within the NHIFA was proposed as a response to better integrate the two sectors. The proposal was revisited in 2006, but not supported by the Ministry of Finance. The National Development Programme 2004–2006 and the National Strategy Reports for 2006–2008 contain strategic concerns in the field of long-term care as well. However, the concepts and recommendations presented were not implemented, again mainly due to a lack of funding in the field. After that, the creation of Multipurpose Sub-region Associations in 2007 was a remarkable initiative to better integrate social and health services. (see section 6) Besides the cooperation of the two sectors, other major current issues in the Hungarian long-term care system include the further clarification and reorganisation of the residential care sector, substantial investments in community care and the creation of a sustainable system of funding. (Interview Csillik)

3. Public Provision and Funding of Care

About 6% of the Hungarian population over 60 years of age use services provided by the public long-term care system. However, it is assumed that between 25% and 30% of the same age group are in need of some form of care or support. (Bácskay 2004) Basic community care and specialised institutional care services will be discussed in further detail below. Community care services are provided in both the health and the social sector. The health care sector covers nursing care, while the social sector comprises home help, meals on wheels, a bell-alarm system, administrative help and clubs for the elderly. The same division also exists for specialised institutional services, where the health sector includes nursing wards and general chronic care wards in hospitals. These services are not specifically aimed at elderly people, but at providing rehabilitation, nursing care and hospice care for chronically ill people. In the social sector, specialised institutional care includes residential care centres for long-term or short-term housing, as well as day care centres.

3.1. Residential Care Provision

Residential Care in the Social Sector
Residential care in the social sector is organised in two types of institutions, in short-term care institutions and old people's homes. Short-term care institutions *(átmeneti elhelyezést nyújtó intézmény)* provide accommodation and care for a limited period of time. Their primary aim is to enable frail elderly to get back to their private homes and be able to live on their own. They help the elderly person to perform every day activities, such as bathing, dressing, eating, getting in and out of bed or chair without permanent home help. The second task of short-term care institutions is respite care, with which they temporarily relieve informal care-givers from their care-giving duties and allow them to take time off. According to the Social Act, such institutions should be available in every settlement with more than 10,000 inhabitants. In reality, however, respective infrastructure is provided in only 40% of these settlements. (HCSO 2006) In 2006, 3,062 patients were looked after in 156 institutions with a total capacity of 3,120 beds. This figure amounts to 80.1 beds per 100,000 inhabitants and to an occupancy rate of 98%. (HCSO 2007) About two thirds of all beds are provided by the public sector, while most beds in the private sector are provided by non-profit organisations. (see table 5.1)

As the second type of institutional care in the social sector, old people's homes *(idősek otthona)* provide long-term accommodation and a wide range of care services. According to the Social Act, these residential care institutions should serve elderly people who are not self-sufficient, but whose health status does not require continuous hospitalisation. Residence includes hotel services and a care component (medical attendance, nursing care, personal care). In 2005, there were 793 old people's homes with 48,818 beds. They provided services to an average of almost 47,000 residents, which is about 2% of all elderly citizens. Bed density in old people's homes is 485 beds per 100,000 inhabitants. (HCSO 2007; 2006) Similar to short-term care institutions, public authorities run most of these permanent residencies (63%), mainly on the level of local governments or counties. Non-profit providers also hold a considerable share (37%), while private enterprises only operate few institutions. (see table 5.1)

Table 5.1: Beds by provider in short- and long-term residential institutions, 2006

Provider	Beds in short-term residential institutions	As % of total	Beds in old people's homes	As % of total
Local government	2,077	66.57	16,035	32.85
County, capital government	17	0.54	14,231	29.15
Central state budget institutions	0	0.00	50	0.10
Multipurpose sub-region association	0	0.00	249	0.51
Public sector total	2,094	67.12	30,565	62.61
Church	62	1.99	7,377	15.11
Public services company	628	20.13	6,474	13.26
Association	169	5.42	691	1.42
Foundation	127	4.07	3,654	7.48
Non-profit sector total	986	31.60	18,196	37.27
Private sector total (public enterprises)	40	1.28	57	0.12
Total	3,120	100.00	48,818	100.00

(Source: HCSO 2007)

The total number of facilities in the residential care sector has almost doubled between 1994 and 2004. The main reason for this lies in the strategy of non-profit organisations, which have established new homes with a more familiar atmosphere and a smaller number of beds. (Bácskay 2004) Occupancy rates are close to 100% and waiting lists illustrate the significant lack of capacity. Even though data on waiting lists is limited, existing information indicates that the number of potential residents on waiting lists has increased from around 30% to 60% between 1994 and 2004. In addition to the lack of capacity, there are also regional discrepancies. Residential care settings are not available in one third of all Hungarian settlements. Furthermore, adequate services for elderly

111

in need of more intense care and for the specific needs of people with dementia and mental health problems are still of very limited availability. (Interview
Csillik)

Residential Care in the Health Sector

Two types of hospital wards focus on the provision of long-term nursing care
in the health care sector – chronic wards *(krónikus ágyak)* and nursing wards
(ápolási ágyak). Both are a regular part of hospitals, financed by the NHIFA
and designed as transitional care units. While permanent medical supervision
is provided in the chronic ward, patients who do no longer require specific
medical treatment stay in the nursing ward where assistance and care are provided by trained nurses. Due to the lack of places in residential care settings
in the social sector, these wards often work as an intermediate solution while
searching for alternative care settings. If there are no beds available in social
care institutions, patients are sometimes also sent home despite serious chronic
health conditions due to the increasing pressure on hospital budgets. As a consequence of the lack of home nursing and home help, many elderly soon get
back to the hospital as acute care patients. It is estimated that approximately
one third of all patients in the inpatient sector are aged 65 years and over.

Care for frail elderly people in hospitals who do not need medical care,
however, has increasingly been targeted for its cost-containment potential and
growing economic pressure in the health sector has led to a major programme of
acute care bed reduction in the recent past. (Österle, Gulácsi 2007) Altogether,
acute bed capacity was cut by almost 16,000 beds while the number of chronic
care beds went up by about 7,000 beds. In the course of this programme, between 2006 and 2008 the total number of beds (acute and chronic) decreased
from 80,252 to 71,440 beds. Twelve former hospitals have been transformed
into chronic care settings.

3.2. Community Care Provision

Community Care in the Social Sector

With the 1993 Social Act, responsibility for community care was transferred to
local governments. According to the Act, all local authorities have to provide
domestic care *(házi segítségnyújtás)* as social basic care for people who need

help to maintain their independent conduct of life. The range of potential services covers housework, shopping, health support and help with administrative routines. Access to these services is based on an assessment of social needs arising from the health condition. The assessment is done by a general practitioner and has to be renewed every two years. Without certification from a GP, services can be provided for a maximum of 60 days due to social needs.

The number of social service recipients has been rather stable over the past years. In 2005, 106,702 patients received social catering while 45,130 received domestic care. However, the required services were offered by less than two thirds of the local authorities in 2003 and services were rarely available over night or during weekends. In general, community care services are more developed in larger cities but scarce in rural areas. However, several projects have been started to improve the situation of elderly in the countryside as well. In smaller villages, the homestead and village caretaker system *(falu-és tanyagondnok)* attempts to improve access to basic social care. It provides support and care in villages with less than 600 inhabitants and in peripheral settlements with less than 400 inhabitants. A major role of these caretakers is that of an organiser, helping people in their contact with the authorities and other organisations. Self-governments of settlements with more than 3,000 inhabitants have to provide day-care centres *(idősek klubja)* for their population. Citizens can spend their days in these clubs, satisfy their hygienic needs and receive catering and other community help services there. The preventive approach of these centres is of particular importance, as they allow for early contact with the professional support system. In 2003, the service was provided for about 40,000 people by 1,300 clubs. (HCSO 2006) Another widely available service is social catering *(szociális étkeztetés)* which provides warm food at least once a day for those who are not able to cook for themselves. This service is mostly provided through organisations like schools and nursery school caterings. In 2004, about 71% of the settlements and 93% of the population in need were covered. (HCSO 2005) The bell-alarm system or indicator-based home help system is a 24-hour service for those who can maintain an independent life, but might need help in a crisis situation *(jelzőrendszeres házi segítségnyújtás)*. This service has to be provided in every municipality with more than 10,000 inhabitants and comprised 6,000 carers *(gondozó)* in 2004. It requires a functioning social and health support system, but also technological innovation as phone access is still limited in some of the poorest settlements. (Bácskay 2004)

Community Care in the Health Sector

Home nursing and home hospice care are the two main types of community care services in the health sector. Home nursing *(házi szakápolás)* is health care provided by a professional nurse and replaces nursing in the hospital, where the health status still requires highly trained care. This focus on special nursing tasks is the main difference to home care services provided in the social sector, where a more diverse bundle of services is offered. Following a medical assessment by a doctor, access to home nursing is free. However, as home nursing is funded by the NHIFA, there are certain limitations to its provision. The provider of the nursing services needs to be contracted with NHIFA and acts within a given spending limit. In each case, the service is limited to 56 visits per year. Each visit can take between one and three hours. Additional visits can only be provided with an authorisation from the NHIFA. Since 2004, NHIFA also funds home hospice care, which includes nursing as well as physical and mental support for patients and their relatives. (Hegedűs 2005) The need must be attested by a general practitioner and funding is restricted to 50 days, although it can be extended by 50 additional days if necessary. As hospice care also comprises nursing care, there is no additional funding for home nursing within the health sector.

Towards Integrated Community Care

The fragmentation between the health care sector and the social care sector has been addressed by a number of projects in recent years. A major example is the project ISZER *(Integrált Szociális és Egészségügyi Rendszer –* Integrated Social and Health System), which was started to develop personalised services and care programmes for people in need of care over 65 years of age. It aimed at the promotion of independent living, empowering the elderly population and reducing the amount of institutionalized long-term care. Earlier experiences showed that a lack of domestic help often leads to prolonged institutionalisation after acute care in hospitals. In order to improve coordination of services, institutions such as hospitals, day hospitals, specialised chronic care institutions and residential homes were involved in the programme. However, the project was suspended due to a lack of funding and political support. Another approach to improve the integration of services is a novel geriatric model programme in Budapest. It attempts to strengthen transfer between theory and practice and to improve continuous training for doctors, nurses and public health specialists in the field of health and social care for the elderly. (Széman 2004) Unfortunately, no major further attempts towards a more integrated provision of care have been established since then.

3.3. Payments for Care
Similar to other countries in Central and South Eastern Europe, informal care-giving is the major source for helping frail elderly people in Hungary. Given the lack of community care services, the nursing fee (*ápolási díj*) often represents the only public support for informal care. The benefit was introduced with the Social Act 1993 and is administered and funded by the local authorities. It is paid for the care of chronically ill persons beyond 18 years of age, the general benefit level being equal to the minimum pension (HUF 25,800 in 2006, about € 100). Depending on the income level of the person in need of care, it can be lowered to 80% or extended to 130%. Given the low level of the benefit, it does not suffice to establish a regular employment contract. However, when the nursing fee is received for providing care, the period is recognised in the old age pension insurance scheme. Figures on the number of nursing fee recipients show large variations, ranging between more than 70,000 persons in 2004 and about 40,000 in 2005. This discrepancy can be explained by the big differences in take-up (which in turn are at least partly caused by the discretionary power of local authorities in making decisions on the benefit) and by a lack of reporting the developments. (HCSO Database 2008)

While cash for care programmes have been introduced or extended in many European countries in the past two decades, this is not to be expected in Hungary soon. Neither an extension of the nursing fee programme, nor the introduction of a cash-oriented scheme currently plays a role in the Hungarian discussion on the future of long-term care.

3.4. Funding of Long-term Care

Parallel to the differences in organisation, service provision in the health and the social care sector follows different principles of funding. In the social sector, funding is based on annually determined budgets which are then transferred to providers according to specific reference units of care, e.g. residential care beds. From the social service provider perspective, services are covered by a combination of subsidies from the public budget (only partly related to individual needs), contributions from self-governments and co-payments by recipients. The individual contribution of the users ranges – depending on the specific service – up to a maximum of 20% or 30% of the monthly income for domestic services and 80% of the monthly income in the residential care sector.

In residential care, the basic subsidy per resident and year was HUF 700,000 (€ 2,833) and HUF 800,000 (€ 3,241) in the case of dementia care in 2007. Additional funding is available when extended services become necessary, either as an additional monthly subsidy or via a tendering procedure. These public subsidies cover about 60% of the total operational costs of residences. An additional 25% of costs are covered by residents or their family members. What remains (on average 15%) has to be covered by the provider's own resources. (Interview Csillik)

Until 2005, funding of community care services was based on subsidies related to the number of inhabitants of the given self-government. Since then, financing is related to the number of service users. In 2007, the subsidy was HUF 111,500 (€ 451) per patient for domestic help, HUF 40,000 (€ 162) for indication based domestic help and HUF 81,200 (€ 329) for social catering. According to estimations, these normatives only cover about 38% of the operational costs for domestic care provision and 72% of operational costs for catering services. (Cziráki 2007) The contributions of users are limited to between 20% and 30% of their regular income, depending on the type of service. As in residential care, this leaves a substantial amount of costs to be covered from other sources.

Unlike in the social sector, the provision of long-term care services in the health sector is strictly limited. Care provision in chronic and nursing wards is based on daily subsidies, which amounted to HUF 5,200 (€ 21) in 2007. Depending on the type of chronic care, additional funding follows a multiplier system. In 2007, the multiplier was 1.2 for chronic care or rehabilitation, and 1.5 for intensive rehabilitation and hospice care. (see table 5.2) Co-payments by users have to be made for specific additional care or extended comfort services. From 2003 to 2007, the basic daily subsidy in the health sector was increased by almost 50%. In the same period, subsidies remained rather stable in the social sector. Home nursing funded by the health sector was provided to 66,348 recipients in 2005, with an average of 17 visits each. Over the years, there has been a substantial increase in the number of recipients, while the average number of visits has remained relatively stable. (NHIFA Database 2008)

Table 5.2: Financing health sector provisions through subsidies (2003–2007)

	2003	2004	2005	2006	2007
Chronic daily allowance	3,500	3,900	4,050	4,900	5,200
HUF (€)/day	(14)	(15)	(16)	(19)	(21)
	Multiplying factors				
Nursing in nursing department	0.9	1.2	1.2	1	1
Chronic care	1.2	1.5	1.5	1.2	1.2
Rehabilitation	1.5	1.6	1.6	1.2	1.2
Intensive rehabilitation	-	2.1	2.1	1.5	1.5
Hospice	1	1.5	1.5	1.5	1.5

(Source: Interview Csillik)

4. Civil Society and Private Sector Activities

With the changes in the economic and political situation after the transition, civil society in Hungary became increasingly active in different societal sectors. Furthermore, a growing number of non-profit organisations became active in the provision of social services. These non-profit providers particularly mushroomed in areas where public provision was limited or non-existent. They attempted to emphasise client-orientation and flexibility in responding to the needs of the population. (Jenei, Kuti 2003; Kuti 1999)

However, the relationship between the state and civil society organisations has often been contradictory. (Jenei, Kuti 2003; Széman 2003) On the one hand, administrative hurdles and limited public funding have long hindered the extension of non-profit initiatives. On the other hand, rhetoric support for the development of civil society is strong and specific measures have been taken to financially support it. One important example is the 1%-scheme. Since 1996, individuals can donate 1% of their personal income tax payment to a non-profit organisation of their choice. Many organizations, especially those working in education and social care, benefit from this scheme. (Széman 2004)

In the field of long-term care, the 1993 Social Act opened care provision to non-profit organisations. From that point on, a licence was necessary to operate a service and to have access to public funding. Church-related institutions were even given additional financial incentives. (State Audit Office of Hungary 2003) It is estimated that about 8% of 49,000 non-profit organisations registered in 2004 (HCSO 2004) work in the field of social care, among which about 20% are active in the more specific field of long-term care for elderly people. (Interview Csillik) In the residential care sector, non-profit organisations account for 32% of all institutions and 37% of beds. The major providers are either church-related institutions or so-called public service companies. In the community care sector, non-profit organisations have been particularly active in developing provisions in less serviced areas and in initiating new programs, e.g. to improve the integration of health and social services. (Széman 2004)

Compared to non-profit organisations, the private market sector plays an almost negligible role in the Hungarian long-term care system. Though international provider chains and regional initiatives have made attempts to enter the market, their activities remain very limited or they even withdrew from the market again. One reason for the limited success of for-profit initiatives is that only a very small proportion of the population can afford to pay for long-term care from their own resources. Another limiting factor lies in the public funding scheme, which limits access to the respective normative paid for long-term care services for private for-profit providers. (Cziráki 2007)

5. Family Care

Families have traditionally taken on the responsibility to provide care for their elderly and/or to financially support them. With the 1993 Social Act, responsibility for the provision of social care was given to local authorities. While this has led to an overall extension of long-term care services, the actual provision still remains limited, unavailable in some parts of the country and character-ized by large regional variations. Due to the limited availability of services and the fragmentation between health and social care, care needs are still pre-dominantly covered by help and support provided within families. When taking on care-giving duties, families are often confronted with enormous physical, social and economic burdens. The large proportion of elderly with very low pensions below the poverty line is especially vulnerable.

There is a huge lack of systematic information on the situation of fam-ily carers in Hungary. Existing evidence (for an overview see Széman 2004) shows that those over 50 years of age are heavily involved in family care-giv-ing. Apart from family members living in the same household, daughters and daughters-in-law are the main providers of family care. Similar to the develop-ments across Europe, traditional forms of family care are increasingly under pressure. Apart from changes in living arrangements, higher (female) employ-ment participation and an increase in retirement age (which previously was just 55 years of age) shape the situation in Hungary. (Széman 2004) The lack of studies on family care in Hungary also is an indicator of the still limited public recognition of care work provided within family networks. The major govern-ment response to family care is the nursing fee scheme (see above) which is connected with pension insurance coverage. While the nursing fee provides some basic support, it remains much lower than the minimum income earned in gainful employment.

6. The Future of Long-term Care in Hungary

During the last twenty years, the Hungarian long-term care system has been characterised by an extension of publicly funded provisions and an increase of non-profit sector activities. The Social Act 1993 is to be seen as the major source and starting point of these developments but the current level of formal care provision is still far below that of most Western European countries. Peo-ple in need of long-term care and their family members often find themselves in highly precarious situations. But due to different regional policies and huge dif-ferences in economic performance, the situation varies largely across the coun-try. Additionally, the individual situations differ depending on whether health or social care provisions are available. Two of the major factors that block further reforms concern the severe budgetary limitations on national, regional and local levels, but also the fact that long-term care is not on the agenda of the major decision makers in the policy process.

There have been repeated proposals to extend public responsibility in long-term care, to harmonise developments in the health and in the social care sector and to establish long-term care as a separate pillar in the welfare system. (Interview Csillik; Interview Dózsa; State Audit Office of Hungary 2008) However, proposals made by expert groups in the public administration or put forward by experts and professionals working in the field rarely expanded into a broader public debate. The problematic separation of the health and social care sector was the starting point of a proposal made in 2007. According to this plan, long-term care should become part of the social insurance system. However, it remained unclear whether long-term care should be covered in the context of the existing structures of health insurance or whether a separate scheme should be established. Besides promoting a more integrated system, this and other plans also emphasise the role of long-term care services in the community and the improvement of the relationship between the public sector and non-profit providers. However, all these plans would require substantial investment and it seems there is little political will for extension under the current financial situation.

As in other European countries, long-term care is becoming a major challenge for the Hungarian society. While this and the problems of the current situation are recognised in various policy papers and reports, no consequences have been drawn so far and no adequate responses have been developed. Apart from extending financial and professional resources, more systematic research on the sector is necessary. More comprehensive data collection and research would help both the public debate on long-term care and the development of standards and practice guidelines to ensure a cost-effective and high quality care system.

Bibliography

Bácskay, Andrea (2004) Az idősek szociális gondozása (*Social care for the elderly*). Budapest: Hungarian Central Statistical Office.

Boncz, Imre (2003) The Hungarian health insurance system. In: Hospital, Vol. 5, No. 5, 24–25.

Boncz, Imre; Nagy, Julia; Sebestyen, Andor; Korosi, László (2004) Financing of health care services in Hungary. In: The European Journal of Health Economics, Vol. 5, No. 3, 252–258.

Boncz, Imre; Sebestyen, Andor (2006) Financial deficits in the health services of the UK and Hungary. In: Lancet, Vol. 368, No. 9539, 917–918.

Cziráki, Andrea (2007) Szociális szolgáltatási rendszer megújítása (*Renewal of the social services system*). In: Szociális Menedzser, Vol. 1, 2–9.

Egervári, Ágnes (2007) Homogén Gondozási Csoportok, a "HGCS" (*Care Related Groups "CRG"*). In: Szociális Menedzser, Vol. 1, 16–19.

European Health for All Database (2008) Copenhagen: WHO Regional Office for Europe. Available from: http://www.euro.who.int/HFADB (15 October 2009).

Eurostat (2009) Eurostat Database. Available from: http://epp.eurostat.ec.europa.eu (1 December 2009).

Gaál, Péter (2004) Health care systems in transition: Hungary. Copenhagen: WHO Regional Office for Europe on behalf of the European Observatory on Health Systems and Policies.

Hegedűs, Katalin (2005) Hospice Magyarországon 1991–2005 (*Hospice care in Hungary 1991–2005*). In: A hospice ellátás területi és minőségi fejlesztése. Budapest: Hungarian Hospice-Palliative Association.

HCSO Database (2008) Online database for the Hungarian Central Statistical Office. Available from: www.ksh.hu (15 October 2009).

HCSO Hungarian Central Statistical Office (2004) Időskorúak Magyarországon (*Elderly in Hungary*). Budapest.

HCSO Hungarian Central Statistical Office (2005) Statistical yearbook for welfare statistics 2004. Budapest.

HCSO Hungarian Central Statistical Office (2006) Statistical yearbook for welfare statistics 2005. Budapest.

HCSO Hungarian Central Statistical Office (2007) Hungarian health statistic yearbook 2006. Budapest.

Iván, László (2002) A magyar népesség idősödésének kérdései és kihívásai (*Issues and challenges in connection with the ageing of the Hungarian population*). In: Kulin, Ferenc (ed) Kölcsey Füzetek. A Kölcsey Intézet Kiadványa.

Jenei, György; Kuti, Éva (2003) Duality in the third sector: The Hungarian case. In: Asian Journal of Public Adminstration, Vol. 25, No. 1, 133–157.

Kuti, Éva (1999) Different Eastern European countries at different crossroads. In: Voluntas - International Journal of Voluntary and Nonprofit Organizations, Vol. 10, No. 1, 51–60.

Law Act (1993) Évi III. törvény a szociális igazgatásról és szociális ellátásokról *(Act III., Law on Social Administration and Social Benefits)*. Available from: http://net.jogtar.hu/jr/gen/hjegy_doc.cgi?docid=99300003.TV (15 October 2009)

Law Act (2001) Évi LXXXI. törvény a szociális igazgatásról és szociális ellátásokról szóló 1993 évi III. törvény módosításáról. *(Amending Act On the Law on Social Administration and Social Benefits)*. Available from: http://net.jogtar.hu/jr/gen/hjegy_doc.cgi?docid=99300003.TV (15 October 2009)

NHIFA Database (2008) Online database of the national health Insurance Fund. Available from: http://www.oep.hu (15 October 2009).

Österle, August; Gulácsi, László (2007) Das Gesundheitssystem in Ungarn: Entwicklungen, Herausforderungen und Reformen *(The health care system in Hungary: Developments, challenges and reforms)*. In: Soziale Sicherheit, Vol. 60, No. 9, 418–429.

State Audit Office of Hungary (2003) Jelentés a helyi önkormányzatok tartós szociális ellátási feladatainak ellenőrzéséről az idősek otthonainál *(Auditing the discharge of local government obligations related to ongoing social provisions in retirement homes)*. Report No. 0317. Budapest: State Audit Office of Hungary.

State Audit Office of Hungary (2008) Jelentés az önkormányzati kórházak és bentlakásos szociális intézmények ápolásra, gondozásra fordított pénzeszközei felhasználásának ellenőrzéséről *(Audit of the utilization of funds appropriated for nursing by hospitals and residential social institutions of local governments)*. Report Nr. 0820. Budapest: State Audit Office of Hungary.

Széman, Zsuzsa (2003) The welfare mix in Hungary as a new phenomenon. In: Social Policy and Society, Vol. 2, No. 2, 101–108.

Széman, Zsuzsa (2004) Services for supporting family carers of elderly people in Europe. Characteristics, coverage and usage. National background report for Hungary. Hamburg: EUROFAMCARE.

Interviews

Csillik, Gabriella (Expert, Ministry for Social Affairs and Labour), Personal communications, 2007, 2008.

Dózsa, Csaba (Health Economist Expert), Personal communications, 2007, 2008.

6
Long-term Care Policy in Romania: A Hesitant Response to a Pressing Need

Livia Popescu

1. Economic and Demographic Context

1.1. Economic Performance

The Romanian economy performed very poorly in the first decade of the post-communist era. It experienced severe declines from 1990 until 1992 and 1997 until 1999. Growth resumed modestly in 2000 and has since then continued at a faster pace. Despite high growth rates in 2004 to 2007, the country is still lagging behind all EU member states, except Bulgaria. In 2007, the estimated GDP per inhabitant in PPS (€ 10,100) represented only 42.5% of the EU27 average and its further increase in 2008 will have a modest effect on this disparity. (Eurostat 2009; National Institute of Statistics 2008a). Inflation has been devastating for many years. In 1993 it even reached peaks as high as 256%. For the first time in the post-communist era, the consumer price index had a single digit value (9%) in 2005 and fell to 4.8% in 2007. According to 2007 data, GDP was created predominantly in the service sector (49.7%) and industry (23.1%), while agriculture and construction contribute with 6.6% and 9.1% respectively. In recent years, services and construction showed the highest growth rates. (National Institute of Statistics 2008a)

1.2. Demographic Characteristics

During the first ten years of transition, changes in the economy led to a surge in poverty and a serious decline in the living standard for the majority of the population. Economic hardship impacted negatively on several demographic indicators. Both birth rate and life expectancy at birth fell during the 1990s. The negative trend of the first indicator is entrenched, while the decline in average life expectancy did not persist beyond the year 1998. The general fertility rate diminished by nearly half and the birth rate fell from 16 newborns per 1,000 (1989) to 10 per 1,000 (2007) over the last 18 years. (National Institute of Statistics 2008a) After an apparent decline from 1993 to 1997, average life expectancy resumed its positive trend. Subsequently, the average calculated for 2005 to 2007 was higher than for 1988 to 1991 for both men and women. The difference reached 2.61 years for the male population and 3.49 years for females. However, compared to most EU member states, average life expectancy is relatively low. At present, it is over 75 years only for female population while it remains below 70 years for men. Average life expectancy is consistently higher in towns than in villages, for both men and women. (National Institute of Statistics 2008a)

Due primarily to the fall in the birth rate, the Romanian population is ageing steadily. In 2007, the number of people over 65 years of age represented 14.86% of the total population. The increase was particularly high for the oldest age groups. It reached 45% for persons aged 75 and over, while the number of „young" elderly (60 to 74 years old) was rather constant. (National Institute of Statistics 2008a; 2008b) The ageing process is more amplified in rural areas

Table 6.1: Proportion of elderly population, 1990–2007

Proportion of elderly as % of total population	1990		1995		2000		2007	
	M	F	M	F	M	F	M	F
65+	8.8	11.9	10.2	13.7	11.3	15.2	12.4	17.2
65-69	3.8	4.6	4.4	5.1	4.4	5.3	4.2	5.1
70-74	1.7	2.5	3.0	4.1	3.5	4.4	3.7	4.8
75-79	1.9	2.7	1.2	1.9	2.1	3.2	2.6	3.8
80+	1.4	2.1	1.6	2.6	1.3	2.3	2.0	3.4

(Source: National Institute of Statistics 2008a; 2006)

and particularly significant among the female population. In 2007, the proportion of elderly persons was higher in the countryside than in towns both in absolute and relative terms. Demographic forecasts indicate that ageing will continue at a high pace. The share of the elderly group (65 and over) is likely to represent between 14.9% and 15.2% of the total population in 2015. If the current scenarios are correct, the percentage will double until 2050. (Maccheroni 2007; Ghețău 2004)

1.3. Economic Vulnerability of the Elderly Population

The average employment rate among persons over 65 years of age is 14.2%. Participation in income generating activities is substantially higher among the rural aged population (24.3%) than among urban elderly (2.1%). (Institutul National de Statistică 2007) Overall devaluation of wages and social benefits resulted in a serious decrease in living standards, particularly in the first decade of the transition period. The average pension fell in relation to both its 1990 level and to the average wage. In 2008, the average pension calculated for the state social insurance program surpassed its 1990 real value for the first time. The same year, its ratio to the average net wage reached 45.8%. (Casa Națională de Pensii si Alte Drepturi de Asigurări Sociale Website 2009)

The post-socialist pension system fostered strong inequalities. Some of them are the logical result of insurance-based schemes while others are produced by the piecemeal, inconsistent legislative process. An important difference exists between non-agricultural (State Social Insurance Fund) and agricultural occupations (Farmers' Fund). Despite recent corrective measures, the average pension of retired farmers, who represent 17.3% of all pensioners, is 2.3 times lower than the amount paid in the state social insurance program. Variables such as age and gender generate additional variances. Pensions that are paid to women are lower than the amounts received by men for all the categories of pensioners. The biggest gender gap exists for the full retirement pension, where women's average pension is merely 65.1% of the one calculated for men. (Institutul National de Statistică 2009) The oldest pensioners receive the lowest amounts, due to both variation in the qualifying conditions and irregular indexation. The recalculation process that was initiated in 2005 led to a minor decrease of this generation gap.

Data from the 2007 national Household Budget Survey indicates that the level of income per capita was relatively high in households headed by retired persons. It reaches 89.9% of average income and places pensioners second, after households run by employees. Households headed by retired persons spend about 45% out of their total consumption expenditure on food, slightly more than the share spent by the total population. As expected, the share of medicines and medical products is more important in the case of pensioners' households than in the total population. Nearly 23% of their non-food expenditure is spent on these items. (Institutul National de Statistică 2008a)

Even though 95% of the elderly population receive a pension, 40% of the households headed by persons over 65 cannot afford to keep their home adequately warm and 38% of them have insufficient means to eat meat or fish every second day. In 2007, the poverty rate for the retired population was estimated to be 15.7%. The percentages of poor are higher among persons over the age of 65 (19%) and among female pensioners (17.6%). Introduction of the minimum social pension in April 2009 raised in some measure the standards of living of nearly 1,000,000 elderly. (Ministry of Labour, Family and Social Protection Website 2009; Institutul National de Statistică 2008b; 2008c)

1.4. Persons in Need of Long-term Care

Statistics on the population in need of long-term care are lacking and available estimates vary significantly due to differing modes of calculation. The numbers for 2000 range between a minimum of 122,406 (the estimated number of persons certified as handicapped) and a maximum of 576,140 (total persons with self-reported long-term physical incapacity). (National Institute of Statistics 2001) Based on 2005 demographic data, the Draft Law on the protection of elderly rights (2006) estimates a minimum of 125,250 dependent elderly. This represents 3% of the population over 60 years. Moreover, 38.4% of the elderly over 65 declared a long standing illness or disability in the 2007 European Quality of Life Survey. (Eurofund Website 2009)

Since 2004, the National Authority for Handicapped Persons has reported regularly on the number of certified handicapped persons. The number of elderly persons in need of care (certified handicapped persons aged 65+) was 135,431 in 2006 and 198,088 in 2008 compared to 98,959 in 1990, 111,546 in

1995 and 122,406 in 2000. (Ministry of Labour, Family and Social Protection 2009; 2008; National Institute of Statistics 2008a; 2006; own calculations for 1990, 1995 and 2000) This group requires constant and intensive care. However, it is reasonable to believe that numerous dependent old people do not even register for a medical assessment. Consequently, the number of certified handicapped elderly should be regarded as the lowest estimate of the population in need of long-term care.

The increase in the share of handicapped elderly parallels the ageing of Romanian society that occurred in the last 17 years. In 2007, 5.3% of total old persons were certified as handicapped and subsequently became entitled to long-term care provisions. (Ministry of Labour, Family and Social Protection 2009; National Institute of Statistics 2008a)

2. The Current Long-term Care System

2.1. Post-1989 Long-term Care Policy

Personal social services were lowly developed during communist times. The regime focused on the big components of the social protection system such as pensions and health care. These were work-status based and responded to collective needs. Official ideology either ignored particular individual needs or considered them as being part of the family's responsibility. (Ferge 1991) Until 1989 Romania had nothing but residential care services for the elderly, which offered only a small number of places. Placing aged members in residential care was considered an extreme measure and was often not acknowledged to outsiders by the respective family. (Popescu 2004)

Since Romania faced serious child protection issues during the first decade of transition, care for elderly was not acknowledged as a problem until the late 1990s. It slowly reached the public policy agenda and was eventually regulated in 2000. Law 17/2000 was the first to deal specifically with social assistance for elderly persons. It illustrates the shift from the prevalent medical approach to the social one. Elderly persons, who are defined as "persons having reached the retirement age", are entitled to social assistance as a "right". The same act classifies the degrees of dependence based on a national evaluation grid of the elderly person's needs. In 2003, another legal provision set the structure, principles and responsibilities for social services, including those for the elderly. The distinction was made between primary social services and specialised social services. The former are mostly community or proximity service provisions. An additional component, namely the home nursing service, was introduced by the First Law on Social Health Insurance in 1997. However, the National Unique Social Health Insurance Fund (*Fondul Naţional Unic de Asigurări Sociale de Sănătate*) did not contract this kind of service before 2003.

Despite these developments, long-term care is not defined explicitly in Romanian legislation. The current system consists of two components which are based on distinct approaches. Long-term care is either viewed as a dependency situation or as a disability/handicap condition. There is no separate scheme for long-term care. Services such as residential homes and community care are provided within the elderly social assistance system. Residential care is also organised as part of special assistance provisions for disabled persons. Elderly with medical certification of a handicap are eligible for these residences, called "assistance and nursing homes". The degree of handicap is defined according to a set of criteria that takes into account the "intensity of medical problems and the appropriate need for care, support and permanent supervision of the person". Four categories are subsequently distinguished: serious, accentuated, medium and light handicap. (Order no. 762/1.992) Serious handicap indicates the need for permanent care, support and supervision by another person. Mental illness is among the medical conditions that may cause a handicap and so are Alzheimer's and Parkinson's diseases.

Until the late 1990s, care for elderly was provided either in residential care or within families. Since 2005, several governmental acts have aimed to increase the quality of life of old people and reduce the risk of their social exclusion. The revision of the legislation, which was prompted by Romania's accession to the EU goes along with the key European and UN documents. The Governmental Strategy 2005–2008 places the development of services for the elderly within the reform of the social assistance system. It argues for an integrated coherent system of social and medical service provision while emphasising the role of domiciliary care. Subsequently, a 2006 national programme targets the reduction of costly residential care through the development of community/home care. (Decision no. 1665) Domiciliary nursing can be provided within the health insurance system if the county funds contract it with local providers.

The long-term care system is a mixed private-public responsibility. Administration, funding and service provision are all shared within the partnership framework that is stipulated in the legislation. Within this context, the private sector is understood as consisting solely of non-governmental (not-for-profit) organisations. The decentralisation principle governs current policy documents and statements. However, its implementation process has not been completed for the time being. Within the public sector, responsibility is also split. Social services for the elderly in general are the responsibility of both the county and the local/municipality councils. The Ministry of Labour, Family and Social Protection establishes the priorities at the national level and constitutes the decision-making agency for national policies and programmes. Centrally as well as at the county level, it plays the key methodological role by evaluating and monitoring social services. Accreditation and quality standards for elderly care were regulated in 2003. The legislation established the obligation of social services providers to be accredited by a distinct body and subsequently to comply with the minimum standards in their functioning. (Decision no. 1665)

Long-term hospitalisation for social reasons, including old-age related problems captures the attention of the authorities periodically. Since 2004, Law 99 concerning the administration of public sanitary units at the local level regulates the organisation of units of "medico-social assistance". County and local councils have the option to convert some health care units into medico-social ones. These services provide residential care for chronic patients who require permanent or temporary supervision, assistance, care and treatment. They are funded jointly by the local councils, health funds and payments from residents. (Draft Law on the protection of elderly rights 2006)

2.2. Funding Mechanisms of the Long-term Care Provisions

The prevalent funding of long-term care in Romania is public. The main sources are: central/state budget, county and local budgets and health insurance county funds. In principle, the central budget finances programmes of national interest while the local and county councils are responsible for the funding of direct service provision. Local authorities have the possibility to obtain funding from the central state budget for construction works or improvements to the facilities for social services. The process has a competitive character and is organised by the Ministry of Labour, Family and Social Protection. Due to this mixed funding, county budgets for social services are not typically covered by official statistics. Some categories of revenues and expenditure are included in the state budget while others are part of the local budgets. The costs of medical services and products are covered by the contributions paid by employers and employees/self-employed to the National Unique Social Health Insurance Fund and the county funds respectively.

Given the fragmented funding of long-term care, it is difficult to estimate the total expenditure for these services. The figures in table 6.2 reflect the central part of the costs paid from the state budget for all social assistance services.

Table 6.2: Public expenditure for social assistance services in RON/€[a], 2008

State budget[b]	Local budgets[c]	Subsidies for NGOs	Total
27,631,138/	98,423,956/	13,101,740/	139,156,834/
7,467,875	26,601,069	3,541,011	37,609,955

[a] Exchange rate 2008: € 1.00 = RON 3.7
[b] Expenditure included in the ministerial budget as "financing of social assistance institutions of public interest" and „programmes of national interest"
[c] Expenditure for "hostels for elderly persons"
(Source: Ministry of Labour, Family and Social Protection 2009)

Public money finances both benefits and service delivery in the public sector. Direct service provision in the third sector is subsidised as well. The subsidy per capita is in strict relation to the type of service (domiciliary, community or residential care) and based on competition for projects. In 2009, the amount of the monthly subsidy varied between RON 120 (€ 29) and RON 250 (€ 60). (Law Clarification 2009) It is estimated that the state central budget allocated about € 13.5 million (0.1% of the state budget expenditure) to the entire non-governmental sector in 2006. About 82% of this amount came from the Ministry of Labour, Family and Social Protection. (Fundatia pentru Dezvoltarea Societătii Civile, Centrul de Asistență pentru Organizațiile Neguvernamentale 2007) Although there is no official reporting on the finances of the non-governmental sector, it is very likely that the share of public money in its total expenditure is currently very small. Local councils can also allocate subsidies for this sector.

In the case of home nursing, per capita services are reimbursed to the providers by the health funds, regardless of the public/private (non-governmental) division. Cost-sharing for long-term care services and particularly for residential ones depends on the user's income and cannot exceed 60% of it. The regulatory framework of these payments is provided by the law while the actual amount is decided locally or at the county level. Allowances and complementary personal budgets for handicapped persons are financed by taxes through the state budget.

3. Long-term Care in the Welfare System – An Unfulfilled Promise

3.1. Residential Care – Eligibility, Coverage and Quality Standards

The legislation adopted in 2003 and 2006 (Law 47/2006 on the national social assistance system) enforces and defines the different levels of responsibility (state, county and local councils) in social services. Residential care was reframed in compliance with the newly stated principles of service provision. The main reform consisted in the decentralisation of funding and decision-making in residential care. At present, the responsibility is delegated completely to the local and county level. Public-private partnership is another essential principle as it allows the county and local authorities to buy services from the private/ non-profit sector. However, the share of the non-governmental sector in residential care is relatively small.

The outcomes of decentralisation in the organisation and funding were not altogether positive because it preceded the decentralisation of tax collection. Many local authorities are lacking financial resources and therefore many regional inequalities became conspicuous. Support from the state budget is sometimes decided on political "sympathy" or "lobbying" and not necessarily in relation to the problems or needs of the respective communities.

Service Provision and Eligibility

There are two categories of public residential facilities: "care and assistance centres" and "hostels for elderly". The County Public Directorate for Social Assistance comprises all the specialised public social services at the county level. It is the main provider of residential care for persons with more complex needs, including elderly who are certified with a degree of handicap. Subsequently, the Directorate is responsible for the first type of facilities. The latter are managed by the local authorities (local councils) and offer services to less dependent users.

The eligibility criteria used for public services and for publicly funded non-governmental organisations are stipulated in the legislation. (Decision no. 1665) They refer to both the medical condition and the economic situation of the person. In order to be considered for a place, a person should meet at least one or more of the following conditions:

- a demonstrated need for special permanent medical care that cannot be granted at the person's home,
- incapacity to fulfil daily domestic activities,
- lack of any legal family support or incapacity of the respective family members to fulfil their legal obligation,
- lack of housing and/or personal income.

By law, priority is given to the most emergent and serious cases. A person should be considered for a place in public residential care if one or more criteria are met and if there are open places. The decision on acceptance belongs to the County Public Directorate for places in its subordinated facilities, to the local authority (mayor) for the residential care provided locally and to the county directorates of the Ministry of Labour, Family and Social Protection for the non-governmental facilities that receive subsidies from the state budget. The statistical report issued by the Ministry of Labour, Family and Social Protection covers solely the "hostels for elderly persons" (*cămine pentru persoane vârstnice*). In 2008, the number of these facilities was ten times higher than in 1990 while the number of places multiplied by six.

Table 6.3: Number of places in hostels for elderly, 2008

Residential care provider	Number of beds	As % of total	Persons on waiting lists	Waiting persons as % of existing places
Public sector	6,076	79.8	1,310	21.5
Non-profit sector	1,538	20.2	1,605	104.0
Total	7,614	100.0	2,418	31.7

(Source: Ministry of Labour, Family and Social Protection 2009)

The county and local administrations provide more than three quarters of the places while the non-governmental sector stays behind the public sector with about one fifth of the whole residential capacity. 7,005 additional places exist in "centres for care and assistance" (*centre de îngrijire si asistentă*) for disabled adults. About 3% of the total certified handicapped elderly is institutionalized in such centres.

In spite of the recent increase, the present capacity of residential facilities is far from meeting the need as demonstrated by the number of persons on waiting lists both for public and non-governmental services. The demand exceeds the cumulative capacities of both sectors by about 30%. (see table 6.3) At the same time, it is very much possible that many persons applied for a place in both sectors. Medico-social units are typically placed in rural areas and many of them encounter financial difficulties. Even so, their capacity increased 2.7 times between 2003 (858 beds) and 2006 (2,365 beds). (National Institute of Statistics 2007) The Program of the incumbent government aims at transforming them into residential long-term care facilities. (Government of Romania 2008)

Public Financing, Cost-Decision and Cost-Sharing

County and local budgets have the responsibility for funding public residential care. The state budget also contributes to "re-equilibrate" or compensate the county budgets if they lack the necessary resources. Decentralisation of the decision-making process was furthered by Law 281/2006 that amended the 2000 Law on Social Assistance of Elderly Persons. The average monthly cost of residential care, previously decided by a national authority, is now entirely dependent upon the decisions taken by the county or local councils.

Non-governmental organisations which provide services in more than one county are entitled to subsidies from the central budget. For those active in just one county, subsidies are to be paid by the local budget. The amounts are decided upon evaluation of the organisations/services and they typically only cover a small proportion of the total cost of the care.

In 2008, the total expenditure for residential care in both sectors amounted to € 32,227,246. Public facilities, which are under the responsibility of local councils, spent the biggest proportion of the sum (83.3%).

Table 6.4: Expenditure for residential care facilities[a] in RON/€, 2008

Residential care provider	Expenditure	As % of total
Public sector[b]	98,423,956/26,601,069	83.3
Non-profit sector	20,816,855/ 5,626,177	16.7
Total	119,240,811/32,227,246	100.0

[a] Homes for elderly
[b] Financed by local councils
(Source: Ministry of Labour, Family and Social Protection 2009)

In the public sector, clients are required to pay up to 60% of their net income to cover the cost of maintenance in residential care. If this maximum share does not cover the total cost, the difference must be paid by the person's legal caretakers. The same rule applies to residents with low or no disposable income. The obligation to pay is firstly extended to the spouse of the person and secondly to his or her children. If neither the resident, nor the spouse, nor the children (legal caretakers) have the necessary financial resources, the cost will be subsidised by the county or local council, depending on the subordination of the respective facility. Informal payments or gifts are occasionally offered to care personnel by residents or their family members in order to get "improvements" to the care services. However, the extent of the phenomenon cannot be documented.

3.2. Emerging Community Care

Responsibility, Funding and Eligibility

Community care was legislated for the first time in 2000. Law 17/2000 mentions the main types of community services and asserts that local authorities have the major responsibility in organising and financing them. As a general rule, local administrations share the funding of community care services with the central public administration. Programmes of national interest and complementary resources for underdeveloped areas are to be supported by the central government. In addition, the state budget subsidises non-governmental services in compliance with the same criteria as for residential care. Home nursing is contracted out by county health insurance funds.

Cost sharing is also required in community care. The amount paid by the user depends on the type of service and is decided by the local councils. Users whose net income is less than a specific threshold (five times higher than the eligibility threshold for social aid) are exempted from payment. In 2009, the eligibility level for the social aid benefit or the guaranteed minimum income was RON 125 (€ 30) for a person living alone per month. The same year a minimum level of pension was set at RON 350 (€ 84). Therefore, many low income pensioners are exempt from paying for services. In fact, few community services require any payment at all.

Similar to residential care, community care is organised in a double track system as well: socio-medical dependency and handicap. For those in dependency, eligibility is decided by a socio-medical board which is appointed by the local authorities. In the case of medical certification of the handicap, the decision is taken by a special medical board that is appointed by the county health authorities. Priority criteria are not strictly regulated, but in principle it is the emergency of the person's condition that dictates the result. For any service where public money is involved, the decision is ultimately taken by the responsible authority (county public directorate for social assistance or the mayor). Religious organisations may use membership or religious affiliation among their criteria of admission, but they rarely state it explicitly.

Service Provision

The non-governmental sector pioneered community care in Romania and made its case to the authorities. At present, these services include day centres, home care, meals on wheels and domiciliary nursing. In spite of their variety, coverage is very limited. Even in the capital city, it does not exceed 10% of the population in need, a figure which was reported by a non-governmental provider. (Dobre, Roth 2005)

People with socio-medical dependency are entitled to a caretaker who is authorised to perform this job and is employed by the municipality/council. If the county medical board certifies a serious handicap, the elderly person has the right to a personal assistant on conditions stipulated by the legislation on handicapped persons. The personal assistant is employed by the local authority as well. The authorisation of caretakers for the elderly started in just a couple of counties in 2003. Initially, the complicated procedure discouraged both authorities and potential candidates. Therefore, the number remained low until the procedure was simplified recently. The educational requirement for caretakers and personal assistants is identical: completion of the minimum compulsory level of education (ten years). Law 448/2006 concerning the protection and promotion of the rights of handicapped persons allows exceptions from this rule if relatives perform this job. An additional distinction is made between "personal assistant" (PA) and "professional personal assistant" (PPA). The local council continues to be the employer for the first category of personal assistants whereas the county council has to pay for the second one. Besides authorisation, the PPA is required to follow yearly training offered by the employer as opposed to training every second year for the PA. The PA is employed just to care and protect persons with a serious handicap. PPA is meant to "care and protect" handicapped persons who lack housing or sufficient income (income below the average salary), according to an individualised plan of service delivery. Expenses for meals, hygiene items, housing etc. for a person with a "serious or accentuated handicap" must be paid to the PPA by the county directorate. (Draft Law on the protection of elderly rights 2006) Three years after its adoption, the legal provision regarding the PPA is still inoperative. (Lazar 2009)

Habitually, both caretakers and personal assistants look after more than one client. Family members can be employed both as caretakers for dependent elderly persons or as a personal assistant for a handicapped person. In the first case, care work can partially or totally reduce the time of paid work outside the house. In 2006, the government launched a two year programme of national interest, which aims to develop domiciliary services. The objective was to train and authorise 10,000 caretakers for dependent elderly persons. They are expected to provide services to an estimated number of 40,000 dependent old people in their homes. The programme is financed from the central budget. (Decision no. 1665)

There are important differences between counties in the number of providers and available services. In some counties all types of services are provided while in some others none are. The number of clients also varies due to differences in the development of community care services and their capacity to meet the demand. Detailed information on community care services has only been available since 2007. The provisional data for the first three quarters of the year show that the non-profit sector is the major provider of domiciliary care, supporting 65.7% of the average number of users per month. In addition, it owns one third of the places in day care centres. (see table 6.5)

Table 6.5: Provision of community care, January–September 2007

Community care provider	Domiciliary care		Day care centres	
	users/month	% of total	no. of places	% of total
Public sector[a]	5,729	34.3	2,021	64.8
Non-profit sector	10,977	65.7	1,098	35.2
Total	16,706	100.0	3,119	100.0

[a] Financed by county and local councils
(Source: Interview Docsanescu)

Home nursing was legislated in the late 1990s, but the county health insurance funds only started to reimburse it in 2004. In 2006, the National Unique Social Health Insurance Fund expenditure for such activities rose by 70.6% relative to the previous year. From 2006 to 2008 home nursing services doubled each year both in numbers and costs. However, domiciliary nursing merely represents 0.1% (0.05% in 2006) of the total expenditure for medical services and items. (Casa Națională de Asigurări de Sănătate 2008) The non-profit sector started domiciliary nursing and remained the main provider in this area.

The example of Cluj county illustrates the general trends in community care provision. The day care centres tend to be created by the public sector rather than by the non-profit sector. Home nursing is largely supplied by five NGOs (e.g. *Caritas, Centrul de Ingrijire pentru Vârstnici*). Two organisations offer humanitarian help to the elderly, wheelchairs and meals. The "meals on wheels" service is basically non-existent. Just one organisation (*Pro Vobis*), which predominantly works with volunteers, provides occasional domestic help in the city of Cluj.

3.3. Cash Benefit Scheme

There is no general cash benefit or personal budget for dependent elderly people in the Romanian welfare system. Handicapped persons are nevertheless entitled to an allowance when their degree of handicap is a serious or accentuated one. The benefit is also provided to elderly if they fall into these categories. The "Monthly Indemnity for a Handicapped Adult" (*Indemnizație lunară pentru adultul cu handicap*) is cashed by the handicapped person for his or her free use. The benefit is financed by taxes, from the central budget, and without any regional variation. Persons certified as having a severe and accentuated handicap are solely eligible for the benefit if they are not in residential care or cared for by a professional personal assistant. Until December 2006, the benefit was means-tested and provided only to handicapped persons without personal income. In the case of those with an income, the amount was reduced to 50% (severe handicap) or 30% (accentuated handicap). Law 448/2006 repealed the means-testing and set up a personal complementary budget (*Buget personal complementar pentru persoană cu handicap*). The latter is meant to substitute for services that were previously provided free of charge (e.g. subscription to radio and TV, telephone connection etc.). In addition, eligibility was extended to persons with a medium degree of handicap. (see table 6.6)

Regular statistical reports document data about the total number of benefit recipients, regardless of age. Table 6.7 shows a steady increase in the number of benefit recipients between 2000 and 2008, which is caused primarily by the increase in the total number of persons who are certified as handicapped.

Table 6.6: Summary of eligibility conditions for the monthly indemnity for non-institutionalized handicapped persons and the complementary personal budget, 2009

Handicap level	Needs	Age	Income	Indemnity[a]	Complementary budget[a]
severe handicap	Very high intensity of medical problems, permanent care, support and supervision	18+	No condition	202.00 (€ 47)	91.00 (€ 21)
accentuated handicap	High intensity of medical problems, semi-permanent care, support and supervision	18+	No condition	166.00 (€ 39)	68.00 (€ 16)
medium handicap	Medium intensity of medical problems	18+	No condition	None	33.50 (€ 8)

[a] Amount in RON (€), exchange rate November 2009: € 1.00 = RON 4.26
(Source: Draft Law on the protection of elderly rights 2006)

Table 6.7: Average monthly number of allowance recipients (persons with severe and accentuated handicap), 2000–2008

	2000	2004	2006	2007	2008
Number of recipients[a]	143,797	181,144	285,373	427,175	493,282

[a] Excluding handicapped persons with visual impairment
(Source: Ministry of Labour, Family and Social Protection 2009; National Institute of Statistics 2007)

People with severe and accentuated handicaps represent 90% of the total handicapped population. Their degree of handicap entitles them to the indemnity, but given that the benefit was means-tested at that time, only about 65% of them received it until 2006. Since the cancellation of the means-testing in January 2007, the coverage of the benefit rose to 89.4% of the total non-institutionalised adult population. Complementary personal budgets are paid to 590,248 persons. Persons aged 65+ represent 1/3 of the adults who are certified as being handicapped (all degrees of handicap included) and they probably have a similar share among the benefit recipients. (Ministry of Labour, Family and Social Protection 2009)

4. Pioneering Long-term Care:
The Non-Governmental Services

4.1. Legal Framework and Funding Arrangements

It was not until 2000 that the Romanian parliament replaced the 1924 Law governing NGOs with a new and more comprehensive legal framework. The Governmental Ordinance 26/2000, which was adopted by the Parliament in 2005 as Law 246, aimed to facilitate access of non-governmental entities to private and public resources, as well as to encourage partnerships between NGOs and public authorities. Associations and foundations are defined as legal persons, or entities, of private law, without patrimonial aims. Compared to the 1924 Law, which was re-enacted in 1990, the new act provides more favourable conditions for the creation and registration of an NGO. The association or foundation becomes a legal entity when, following the court decision, it is included in the Registry of Associations and Foundations that is held at the local court. The new legal provisions introduced the concept of "public utility" in relation to associations and foundations. Such a status is granted to NGOs that meet certain criteria, including that the organisation's activity is of general or community interest. Once granted, the "public utility" status is assigned for an unlimited period of time. Following recognition as a public utility, the NGO has a set of rights and obligations that include preferential access to financial support from state or local authorities (Draft Law on the protection of elderly rights 2006; Jenkins et al. 2001)

The income sources of NGOs may include membership fees, interest and dividends from savings and investments, donations, sponsorships, subsidies from state or local budget, dividends from their own for-profit ventures or direct economic activities. The economic activities must have an accessory character and the "profits" obtained from the for-profit subsidiaries must be used to achieve the main goals of the organisation. Public money from the central state budget is available to non-governmental entities through subsidies, non-reimbursable funding and programmes of national interest. From these sources, the entire non-governmental sector received an amount estimated at RON 47,730,373 (approximately € 13.5 million) or 0.1% of the state budget expenditure in 2006. Most of this funding (64% of the total) was channelled through the programmes of national interest, while the direct subsidies per user only represented 9%. The Ministry of Labour, Social Solidarity and Family (presently Ministry of Labour, Family and Social Protection), which is responsible for social services, had the biggest share (83%) of the budgetary allocation to non-governmental organisations. (Fundația pentru Dezvoltarea Societății Civile, Centrul de Asistență pentru Organizații Neguvernamentale 2007)

The current legal framework stimulates local public authorities to create partnerships with the non-governmental sector or to contract services from it. Among the organisations surveyed in 2006, 40% received funds from local authorities through public-private partnerships. Additionally, it is a common practice to create such partnerships in order to access European funding. The practice of social contracting is still tentative due to legislative, administrative and cultural blockages. (Fundația pentru Dezvoltarea Societății Civile 2007b)

The Fiscal Code (Law 571/2003) allows income earners to direct a proportion of their yearly income tax to a "non-profit entity". Originally limited to 1%, the sponsoring ceiling doubled one year after implementation of the regulation. The citizens' participation increased gradually as did the amounts donated. In the first year of implementation (2005), less than 150,000 tax payers participated. The number multiplied by four in the next year and exceeded 1.3 million in 2008. The sums directed to non-profit organisations increased ninefold since the first year of implementation and now reached almost RON 110 million. (Asociatia pentru Relatii Comunitare Website 2009)

Given the difficult economic situation of the country in the first decade of transition, international financial aid contributed importantly to the improvements in residential facilities as well as in services and staff training both in the public and private/non-governmental sectors. The largest share of non-profit services funding still comes from international institutional donors (international NGOs, foreign governmental agencies, etc.). Since 2006, the prospective integration of Romania into the EU caused a reduction in international funding. As a result, the competition for both public and private domestic funding increased appreciably.

The majority of NGOs provide direct services which is also the case in the area of long-term care. The non-profit sector is not only an important actor in social services delivery but has also prompted innovative practices and improvements in quality standards over the years. At the end of 2006, a year after the introduction of compulsory accreditation, there were more accredited private/non-governmental entities than public ones. (Fundaţia pentru Dezvoltarea Societăţii Civile 2007a) The non-profit sector plays an essential role in long-term care provision. In 2007, NGOs carried out the majority of home care activities. Additionally, they hosted one fifth of the persons in residential care and assisted 11% of the persons in day care centres. (Interview Docsanescu)

4.2. Caritas Confederation: A Best Practice in Home Care and Domiciliary Nursing

The *Caritas Confederation* established its network of domiciliary care services in Romania in 1997. At present they encompass home nursing, personal/domestic care and support activities for the elderly and their families in 159 localities in Romania. Between 2006 and 2008, the number of assisted persons doubled and reached nearly 16,000. (Confederaţia Caritas România 2008)

Table 6.8: Home care services provided by Caritas, 2008

	Domiciliary nursing	Personal and domestic care	Community services
Number of activities	1,733,737	778,093	311,545

(Source: Confederaţia Caritas România 2008)

The organisation manages to deliver services in both urban and rural areas. According to a 2005 survey, about 41% of their home nursing users are from rural areas, which is an exceptional performance for a community care provider in Romania. Most users (79%) are elderly with a temporary or permanent need for medical care and 44% are above 75 years old. A survey carried out in 2005 showed that the overwhelming majority of users and family members expressed a high degree of satisfaction with the care activities delivered by *Caritas* centres. (Roth et al. 2006)

Caritas initiated innovative services in Romania and contributed significantly to the development of community and home care. Without any doubt, the organisation prompted the development of public-private partnerships in social service provision and the professionalization of long-term care activities.

Given its religious affiliation, the *Caritas Confederation* was active in counties with an important proportion of Roman-Catholic population. The organisation is present predominantly in counties from Transylvania. Subsequently, its impact is regional rather than national. About two thirds of service users are of the Hungarian minority and about 60% are Roman-Catholic, but there is no reported ethnic or religious discrimination in the service delivery. (Roth et al. 2006)

5. Family and Other Informal Care

The Family Code does not state any legal caring obligation of children towards their parents. Nevertheless, family members are expected to care for each other in case of illness or dependency. However, Law 17/2000 refers explicitly to the obligation of the family (spouse and children) to support the dependent person at least financially, namely by a contribution to the cost of residential care.

The European Quality of Life Survey (EQLS 2003) shows that 18% of the respondents who live in a household with at least one person over the age of 65 perform daily care for elderly or disabled relatives. Many of the respondents combine daily housework with caring for children and elderly family members each day. (Mărgineanu et al. 2006) Similar to other low-income countries in the EU, the engagement in family care is above the European average. Such a pattern is not surprising in a country where 95% of the aged handicapped persons live in their homes while community care services are underdeveloped. The average time spent in care duties each day is higher among women than men. People with lower income are also more involved in caring activities. (Mărgineanu et al. 2006) Findings of the 2007 Eurobarometer confirm that Romanians support traditional family care when an elderly parent needs regular help. More than 65% of the respondents consider that living with the parent or providing him/her regularly care are the best options in this situation. (European Commission 2007)

Even though informal employment of caretakers is not uncommon, there is no systematic data about this phenomenon. In urban areas, demand considerably exceeds the supply. Recruitment tends to be informal as well, but not necessarily using neighbourhood networking. A report by the European Commission pointed out that many female migrant workers from Central and Eastern Europe work abroad formally or informally as domestic helpers, caretakers for children and elderly. (Dobre, Roth 2005) Data provided by a 2007 survey on secondary school pupils indicates that 55,000 of them have mothers working abroad. More than half of these women perform housekeeping and caring activities. (Toth et al. 2007)

6. Prospective Changes and Trends

The public scene is currently dominated by the debate about the reform of the pension system. The present government argues that financial problems are created by the "unproductive" elderly, rather than drafting long-term care policies. Legislation enacted in 2004 to 2006 has not yet been fully implemented. At the same time, a few proposals to change the present system are expected to reach the agenda of the parliamentary debate. They indicate some of the possible developments of the long-term care system.

A governmental document from 2005 acknowledged the need to create a more coherent system of residential care for elderly persons, to unify the regulations concerning services and to integrate medical and social services. The "Programme of National Interest on the Development of Domiciliary Care", which was adopted by the government in 2006, aims to prevent and reduce costly residential care. Accordingly, the 2006 draft, the "Law on the Protection of Rights of Elderly Persons" defines long-term care coherently and has an integrated approach to service provision. The needs of old age are considered in terms of dependency and not handicap. In addition, residential services are regarded as a second option, to be adopted only if home care is inappropriate to the particular case. The Ministry of Labour, Family and Social Protection, the initiator of this law, supported at the time the introduction of a dependency allowance to be paid to elderly persons in need of care. It is designed as a means-tested benefit and funded by the state budget. The eligibility threshold per family member is established at the average pension level. Elderly persons will be eligible regardless of the form of care (domiciliary or residential, formal or informal), but the level of the benefit takes the type of care into account. In the case of informal care, the amount will be limited to 50% of the standard one. The level of the benefit will be adjusted to the degrees of dependency certified by a medical board. In its final statement, the draft law recommends the introduction of an insurance-based scheme for long-term care within five years after the adoption of the current act. (Draft Law on the protection of elderly rights 2006) It is expected that the existing legal provisions on externalisation of social services will be implemented soon and will contribute to upgrading both the efficiency and quality of services. The direct provision of services by the public sector is likely to diminish when public funds will be used for contracting them out to the private sector more extensively.

In the 18 years following the fall of communism, the oldest section of the Romanian population increased both in relative and in absolute terms. In 2008, elderly persons (65+) reached 3,200,000 and represented 15% of the total population. (Ghețău 2009) Nearly 5% of them have a definite need of long-term care, which is medically certified as a handicap. Another proportion of the elderly, still to be estimated, experiences different degrees of dependency in their daily life. In spite of demographers' warnings on ageing and its continuous amplification, the political response to this new social problem was both tardy and hesitant. It was not until 2000 that care for elderly persons was legislated from a non-medical perspective. Even until now, the long-term care system has preserved two tracks of eligibility. One is based on medical certification of the handicap while the second also takes into consideration the social dimension of dependency.

Romania's long-term care system is essentially service based. No personal allowance is provided unless a person is handicapped. Responsibility is delegated completely to the local and county level, but the contribution of the central budget is still prevalent in the public sector. In spite of recent increases in capacity, neither residential nor community services come close to the actual demand of care. The non-profit sector plays an important role in long-term care, particularly in domiciliary care and nursing. It can access public funding and enter partnerships with local authorities in service delivery. Nonetheless, many non-governmental organisations rely on international rather than domestic money. At the same time, public authorities tend to compete with non-governmental entities in the direct provision of services. Consequently, the advances in contracting out are minimal and there are no reasons to expect a change of attitude in the near future. Both traditional values and the weakness of services prevented any substantial "de-familiarisation" of long-term care in Romania so far. (Saraceno 2004) In terms of quality in care services, Romania's rating of 4.4 is the second lowest in the EU27. (Anderson et al. 2009). Yet, politicians do not consider long-term care a priority. The national programmes for community care did not materialise as planned while the projected law on the protection of elderly rights has not reached the parliamentary agenda for the past four years. Long-term care policy needs to bridge the gap between institutionalised promises and institutional practices.

Bibliography

Anderson, Robert; Mikuliç, Branislav; Vermeylen, Greet; Lyly-Yrjanainen, Maija; Zigante, Valentina (2009) Second European quality of life survey – overview. Luxembourg: Office for Official Publications of the European Communities.

Asociatia pentru Relatii Comunitare Website (2009) Informatii despre prevederea 2% (*Information on 2% income tax dedication*). http://www.doilasuta.ro (21 February 2010).

Casa Naţională de Asigurări de Sănătate (2008) Raportul Anual pe anul 2007 (*2007 Annual report*). http://www.cnas.ro/pdf/rptcnas/RAP_CNAS_2008.pdf (16 November 2009).

Casa Naţională de Pensii si Alte Drepturi de Asigurări Sociale Website (2009) (*National House of Pensions and Other Social Insurance Rights*).
http://www.cnpas.org/portal/media-type/html/ (15 December 2009).

Confederaţia Caritas România (2008) Raport annual 2008 (*Caritas annual report 2008*).
http://www.caritas.org.ro/depozit/raport_CCR_2008_RO.pdf (22 February 2010).

Decision no. 1665 (2008) On the update of benefits provided in Art. 58 (4) of Law no. 448/2006 on the protection and promotion of disabled persons.
http://www.mmuncii.ro/pub/imagemanager/images/file/Legislatie/HOTARARI-DE-GUVERN/HG1665-2008.pdf (10 February 2010).

Dobre, Suzana; Roth, Maria (2005) Emerging care services for elderly in Romania. In: Studia Universitatis Babes-Bolyai – Sociology, Iss. 2, 3–17.

Draft Law on the protection of elderly rights (2006)
http://sas.mmssf.ro/compendiumLegislativ.php?id=296 (20 December 2009).

Eurofund Website (2009) European quality of life survey 2007 – mapping the results. http://www.eurofound.europa.eu/areas/qualityoflife/eqls/eqls2007/2eqls_05_03.htm (21 December 2009).

European Commission (2007) Health and long-term care in the European Union, Special Eurobarometer. Luxemburg: European Commission.

Eurostat (2009) Eurostat Database. Available from: http://epp.eurostat.ec.europa.eu (16 December 2009).

Ferge, Zsuzsa (1991) Recent trends in social policy in Hungary. In: Adam, Jan (ed) Economic reforms and welfare systems in the USSR, Poland and Hungary. London: Macmillan.

Fundatia pentru Dezvoltarea Societătii Civile; Centrul de Asistență pentru Organizații Neguvernamentale (2007) Analiza mecanismelor de finanțare directă de la bugetul de stat pentru organizavii neguvernamentale în Romania (*Analysis of direct funding mechanisms of non-governmental organisations by the state budget*). Bucureşti.

Fundatia pentru Dezvoltarea Societătii Civile (2007a) Locul si rolul organizatiilor neguvernamentale pe piata de servicii sociale din Romania (*The place and role of non-governmental organisations in the social services market*). Bucureşti: FDSC.

Fundatia pentru Dezvoltarea Societătii Civile (2007b) Reforma contractării sociale în Romania (*The reform of social contracting in Romania*). Bucureşti: FDSC.

Ghețău, Vasile (2004) Anul 2050: va ajunge populatia României la mai puțin de 16 milioane de locuitori? O viziune prospectiva asupra populatiei României în secolul 21 (*Year 2050: Will the Romanian population decrease to less than 16 million? A prospective vision on the population of Romania in the 21st century*). Bucureşti: Academia Română.

Ghețău, Vasile (2009) Dezechilbre şi procese demografice (*Demographic unbalances and processes*). In: Preda, Marian (ed) Riscuri şi inechităţi sociale în România (*Social risks and inequalities in Romania*). Iasi: Polirom

Government of Romania (2008) Government program 2009-2012. Chapter on family, child protection and equal opportunities. http://www.gov.ro/capitolul-9-familia-protectia-copilului-si-egalitatea-de-sanse_l1a2082.html (11 February 2010).

Institutul Național de Statistică (2007) Forța de muncă în România. Ocupare şi şomaj în anul 2006 (*Labour force in Romania. Employment and unemployment in 2006*). Bucuresti: INS.

Institutul Național de Statistică (2008a) Coordonate ale nivelului de trai in România (*Coordinates of the living standard in Romania*). Bucureşti: INS.

Institutul Național de Statistică (2008b) Condiţiile de viaţă ale populaţiei din România (*Living condions of the population in Romania*). Bucureşti: INS.

Institutul Național de Statistică (2008c), Dimensiuni ale incluziunii sociale în România (*Dimensions of social inclusion in Romania*). Bucureşti: INS

Institutul Naţional de Statistică (2009) Numărul de pensionari si pensia medie lunara (*The number of pensioners and average monthly pension*). Bucureşti: INS

Jenkins, Robert; Popescu, Livia; Edwards, Richard (2001) The post-communist welfare state and the role of the non-profit sector in Hungary and Romania. Paper presented at ARNOVA 30th Annual Conference, 29 November 2001 – 1 December 2001.

Law Clarification (2009) on the application according to the Law No. 34/1998. http://www.mmuncii.ro/ro/581-view.html (13 February 2010).

Lazar, Florin (2009), Persoanele cu handicap (*Persons with handicap*). In: Preda, Marian (ed), Riscuri şi inechităţi sociale în România (*Social risks and inequalities in Romania*). Iasi: Polirom

Maccheroni, Carlo (2007) Implications of demographic change in the enlarged EU on patterns of saving and related consumer's behaviour. In: European Papers on New Welfare, Paper No. 8/2007. Trieste: The Risk Institute.

Margineanu, Ioan; Precupeţu, Iuliana; Tzanov, Vassil; Preoteasa, Ana Maria; Voicu, Bogdan (2006) First European quality of life survey. Quality of life in Bulgaria and Romania. Luxembourg: Office for Official Publications of the European Communities.

Ministry of Labour, Family and Social Protection (2008) Quarterly statistical bulletin on labour and social protection, 1/61. http://www.mmuncii.ro/pub/imagemanager/images/file/Statistica/Buletin%20statistic/2008/Asistenta1(61).pdf (20 November 2009).

Ministry of Labour, Family and Social Protection (2009) Quarterly statistical bulletin on labour and social protection, 1/65. http://www.mmuncii.ro/pub/imagemanager/images/file/Statistica/Buletin statistic/2009/asistenta sociala1_65.pdf (20 November 2009).

National Institute of Statistics (2001) Romanian demographic yearbook. Bucharest: NIS.

National Institute of Statistics (2006) Romanian demographic yearbook. Bucharest: NIS.

National Institute of Statistics (2007) Romanian statistical yearbook. Bucharest: NIS.

National Institute of Statistics (2008a) Romanian statistical yearbook. Bucharest: NIS.

National Institute of Statistics (2008b) Romanian statistical yearbook, Time series 1990–2006. Bucharest: NIS.

Order No. 762/1.992 (2007) Medical and psychosocial criteria for the disability classification. http://www.mmuncii.ro/pub/imagemanager/images/file/Legislatie/ORDINE/O762-1992-2007.pdf (10 February 2010).

Popescu, Livia (2004) Politicile sociale est-europene intre paternalism de stat si responsabilitate individuala (*East-European social policies between State paternalism and individual responsibility*). Cluj: Presa Universitară Clujeană.

Roth-Szamoskozi, Maria; Berszan, Lidia; Diaconescu, Maria; Haragus, Paul Teodor; Mezei, Elemer; Oanes, Cristina; Rebeleanu, Adina; Rusu, Dan Octavian; Szabo, Bela; Haragus, Mihaela; Steinebach, Cristoph; Kösler, Edgar (2006) Die Evaluierung der Hauskrankenpflegedienste der Caritas: Entwicklung, Zielsetzungen und Methoden (*Evaluation of home nursing services by the Caritas: Development, aims and methods*). In Studia Universitatis Babes-Bolyai. Sociologia, 95–110.

Saraceno, Chiara (2004) De-familiarisation or re-familiarisation? Trends in income-tested family benefits. In: Knijn, Trudie; Komter, Aafke (eds) Solidarity between the sexes and the generations. Transformations in Europe. Cheltenham: Edward Elgar Publishing.

Toth, Georgiana; Tufiş, Paula; Păun, Georgiana; Şerban, Monica; Mihai, Ioana-Alexandra (2007) Efectele migratiei. Copiii ramasi acasa (*Effects of migration. Children left alone at home*). Bucureşti: Fundaţia Soros România.

Interviews

Docsanescu, Dorina (Department of Social Inclusion and Social Assistance, Ministry of Labour, Family and Social Protection), Personal Interview, 17 March 2008.

7
Ageing and the Welfare Mix Policy in Serbia

Marija Kolin

1. The Wider Context of Population Ageing

During the recent past, social protection of the elderly has been under the cumulative negative effects of a general social crisis, widespread economic collapse and political instability. As a result of the drastic economic decline that took place in Serbia over the last decade, the majority of the population has been exposed to mass poverty. The position of the elderly has been seriously jeopardised, especially for those who live alone in rural areas, without pensions or other social protection measures. The socio-economic situation in the country improved after political changes and macroeconomic reforms in 2000, but the wider circumstances continue to be unfavourable for the most vulnerable population of the elderly.

In the context of long lasting social deprivation, the basic empirical findings taken from the Second Report on the Implementation of the Poverty Reduction Strategy in Serbia 2007 show that the population group most at risk of poverty are the elderly over 65. They make up almost a quarter of the total number of the poor. Altogether, more than 10% of the elderly live below the absolute poverty line. (Government of Serbia 2007a) According to recent statistical data, the average pension income is RSD 21,000 or around € 200 per month (exchange rate: € 1.00 = RSD 95.00). (Statistical Office of the Republic of Serbia 2009) The most vulnerable elderly in Serbia are the "oldest old" (80 years and over), elderly households in isolated rural areas, older women, single-person households (without surviving kin) and refugees, especially those in refugee camps. Findings from a study show that every fourth elderly needs some kind of assistance in daily life at home or with outdoor activities. (Kolin 1997) In addition, the recent Help Age International survey documents that older people in Serbia often feel socially excluded and exposed to negative stereotypes and other side effects of the transition. The same source confirms that the most difficult problems facing the elderly are the poor quality of life of them and their families, their marginalised position in the family and the absence of services within the local community. (HelpAge International 2002b)

Apart from that, the recent social and economic transformation processes have been accompanied by a profound demographic transformation and changes in the population age structure. Serbia experienced an increase in the proportion of older people, resulting in 1.28 million elderly persons or 17.7% of the total population (7.4 million) in 2006. Above all, relevant demographic estimates conclude that the population's ageing process will intensify further over the next few decades. (Penev 2005) According to a medium-term projection, the number of persons above 80 will double over the next 50 years. The "older-old" population will then represent one quarter of the population. (Amity Report 2007) This demographic shift puts further pressure on social provision in areas such as pensions, social protection and healthcare for the elderly. Moreover, these changes will increase the demand for long-term care and personal assistance. Demographic changes have already resulted in a higher need for social services in local communities. However, existing capacities are still highly insufficient and availability is regionally uneven. Taking all programmes for the elderly into consideration, just about 10% of those aged 65 and over receive some type of care services or benefits. (Government of Serbia 2007a) Various causes have contributed to the poor development of social welfare for the elderly, but financial shortfalls and an uneven distribution are the main reasons for limited achievements.

Due to the significant erosion in public schemes over the last decade and the profound demographic transformations, families have to take enormous burdens in care-giving for the elderly today. (Amity Report 2007; Kolin 2005b; Milic 2004b) This development will have an additional influence on growing demands for social protection measures over the next few decades. At the same time, family impoverishment due to unemployment and the economic crisis puts additional difficulties on the care for the elderly family members. It can be expected that as the still strong primary networks and their protective capacities now undergo the consequences of modernization processes and changes in the family structure, these informal networks will be less capable to obtain care and security for the elderly in the future.

2. Stakeholders in Long-term Care and Major Gaps

2.1. Historical View

Understanding the functioning of the social protection system for the elderly in Serbia is hard, if the political and socio-economic problems of the last decade are not considered. The inherited welfare system was rather generous, with a moderately developed network of residential institutions and established service provision at the local level, including adequate sources of financing and subsidies for underdeveloped municipalities. However, turbulent political circumstances and the severe economic deterioration over the past decade caused a general decline in social protection for the elderly. During the time of dramatic political circumstances, ethnic conflicts, wars, international sanctions, isolation and finally the NATO bombing in 1999, all social resources were exhausted and the position of the elderly severely deteriorated. The most difficult issue was the situation in old people's homes. The number of elderly people seeking accommodation increased whilst they were faced with shortages in accommodation, poor facilities and social services, inadequate quality of health care and very basic problems related to heating, equipping premises, purchasing clothing and supply of medical equipment. (Kolin 1998)

However, important changes have taken place in the provision of long-term care over the last decade. With the legal opportunity to privatize social provision, a new network of services emerged. A number of voluntary and non-profit organisations, as well as self-organised groups with different missions and activities were established in the 1990s. The majority focused on a wide range of social problems dealing with the assistance of vulnerable groups, supplying healthcare institutions with the necessary medical equipment, organising treatment for sick and elderly populations or offering assistance to the disabled. In addressing deprivation, non-profit sector organisations are involved in providing services in local communities, home care help, soup kitchens or other kinds of support directed at the inherited networks of long-term care institutions for the elderly. (Kolin 2005a)

After the change of government in October 2000, and despite the political situation and social turbulence that still hinders the process of modernisation, the reform process focused on the social and economic system. However, policies for the elderly in need of care remained rather marginalised. The main efforts of the new government have been directed towards finding criteria for more efficient social protection and the provision of a safety net for the poorest citizens and the most vulnerable social groups. Above all, the Poverty Reduction Strategy Programme (PRSP), which was introduced as a joint effort by UNDP, the World Bank, the IMF, the Norwegian Government and the Catholic Relief Service, started to promote the provision of social assistance to the poor and vulnerable groups during the period of transition. The PRSP aims to contribute to reducing human poverty and social exclusion by promoting and supporting the development of community level services. Furthermore, the reform of the pension insurance system and the regular delivery of pension incomes has been one of the priorities over the past few years. These changes have improved the position of the poorest strata in society, but despite reform efforts and substantial donor funding, the social safety net against poverty and the provision of social services at the community level still do not adequately cover the needs of the frail elderly population.

2.2. Main Characteristics of the Current Situation

The currently applied concept of social policy towards the elderly is not essentially different from the classic socialistic welfare system developed before 1989. At the formal level, the social welfare system is based on the Law on Social Protection and Social Security of Citizens which was adopted in 1991 and amended several times since then. It is characterised by a centralised approach on planning residential capacities and by insufficient resources at the local level that do not respond to the real needs of the beneficiaries. (Law on Social Welfare and Provision of Social Security of the Citizens) Long-term care in Serbia is not organised as a separate system and responsibilities in social protection for the elderly are shared between different actors. The main stakeholders are the Ministry of Labour and Social Policy (MLSP) and the Ministry of Health (MH) at the central level, while local governments and social welfare institutions – primarily Centres for Social Work (CSW) and homes for the elderly – are the main stakeholders at the local level.

The central Serbian government is still the key player in defining and introducing regulatory frameworks and passing strategy programmes. The majority of revenues for funding long-term care schemes are from the state budget. The Ministry of Finance and Regional Development is responsible for legislation regarding the collection of contributions for compulsory social insurance and social assistance revenues. Although the responsibility for establishing social rights and related processes, as well as the necessary resources, are with the central government, local governments play an important role in providing social protection. (Law on Local Self-Government) According to the Decision for Social Protection that determines the level of social welfare provision by local communities, municipalities must provide money transfers for urgent needs (medical supplies, food, heating), home assistance, day care centres, shelters for homeless people, funeral reimbursements for the poor and soup kitchens. In addition, local governments have to support clubs that provide psycho-social support for the elderly at the local level.

The network of long-term care institutions and care related cash benefits is predominantly established and supported by the MLSP, while other sectors, especially health protection and pension insurance, may provide additional long-term care support. (Law on Pension and Disability Insurance; Law on Social Welfare and Provision of Social Security of the Citizens) The most important governmental institution that regulates, coordinates and provides services are the Centres for Social Work. These Centres with multidisciplinary professional social work teams are well developed in each municipality. However, in order to receive support, an elderly person has to apply for protection in the respective CSW and cope with a complex procedure. This often poses a great challenge, especially for those living in rural areas or those who are already immobile and without family support. (Amity Report 2007) In the last decade, these centres have increasingly been complemented by international and national non-governmental and humanitarian organisations and a newly established network of privately owned homes for the elderly.

Considering health facilities for long-term care for the elderly, there is only one hospital department with 177 beds specialised in health treatment for the elderly in Belgrade. In addition, there is a directive that between 10% and 15% of all hospital beds must be available for older patients and end-of-life care, but only for a maximum of 30 days. However, because of the shortage in community services, it is still quite common that elderly become hospitalised and accommodated there for long-term care, even more so as elderly citizens are legally entitled to free health treatment. However, the organisational and management structure of health facilities is currently subject to a profound restructuring and reform process, not least because of the large deficits that health funds have experienced over the years while investment in infrastructure has been neglected. It is expected that this will increasingly hinder the hospitalisation of long-term care patients.

According to present regulations, long-term care beneficiaries are adult persons who are accommodated in public social welfare institutions – shelters, old-people's homes and pensioners' homes, adult disabled people's homes, or combined institutions during the relevant year. These institutions provide temporary or permanent accommodation (including meals, social care and health protection) for adults and aged people without means of subsistence and family care, as well as for physically and mentally handicapped who are incapable of independent living. (Law on Social Welfare and Provision of Social Security of the Citizens)

2.3. Estimated Needs and Financial Gaps

So far, there is no appropriate statistical data that offers reliable evidence about the long-term care needs of the elderly in Serbia. Hence, approaches on needs estimation must start from the age structure of the population and data collected in specific research projects on the needs of the elderly. According to estimates of a Gerontological Society expert, about half of those aged 80 years and over (which is currently about 70,000 people) are in need of care. (Interview Dinic) In addition to this most vulnerable group in need of long-term care, potential beneficiaries of support are found among the entire elderly population. Another recent survey estimates that between one quarter and one third of the elderly could be considered as potential beneficiaries – that is between 300,000 and 400,000 elderly from a total population of 1.28 million aged 65 years and over. (Kolin 2005b)

One of the important features connected with these estimates is the health situation of the elderly in Serbia. According to expert estimates, four out of five elderly persons suffer from some kind of health problem, most frequently from multimorbidity. (Interview Dinic; Republican Institute for Social Protection 2006) At the same time, utilisation of health care services is very low, especially with regard to home visits by physicians, nurses or social workers. According to official statistics, life expectancy at birth (70 for male and 75 for female) in Serbia is much lower than in the EU (75 for male and 82 for female on average) – a fact that can at least partly be explained by the poor level of health protection, including deficiencies in preventive care and health education. (Statistical Office of the Republic of Serbia 2009; Matejic, Bjegovic 2005)

Various factors have contributed to the poor development of social services for the elderly, but the lack of financial means is generally considered the major reason. Public social expenditure as a proportion of GDP is 14.5% in Serbia. The largest share, however, is spent on pensions (10.6%). As a consequence of recent pension reforms, the relative share of pension expenditure has declined even though the number of recipients has increased. (Government of Serbia 2007a) Major difficulties in the provision of long-term care arise from the fact that financial resources for social protection and community care are extremely limited in Serbian municipalities. On average, just about 2% of municipal budgets are spent on social protection at the local community level, which should cover day-care service centres, home care and assistance, support for pensioners' clubs and capacities for organising community programmes. (Ministry of Labour and Social Policy 2005) While recent decentralisation efforts in social welfare aim at a greater variety of services to respond to local needs more adequately, such programmes are constantly faced with insufficient financial resources and a lack of professional capacities that would assure wider coverage in the local community.

3. The Key Welfare Programmes

3.1. Residential Care

The major welfare programmes on long-term care are provided through residential facilities set up across the country for those who are incapable of independent living and do not have access to family care. The network of 45 public residential institutions for the elderly (organised as gerontological centres, residential homes or departments) are predominantly inherited from the socialist period and provided by the central government. As recorded by the clearing house, the Gerontological Society of Serbia, these institutions accommodated 9,299 beneficiaries in 2008, with the largest one being in Belgrade (631 places). Admission to these institutions is under responsibility of local CSWs as they review applications and make decisions about acceptance. Priority criteria for admission are determined by one's (in-)ability to perform daily activities and upon the potentials of family members to look after the needy elderly. The existing capacities are far below the current needs and waiting lists are extensive throughout the whole country.

Together with 17 officially recognised private residential institutions for the elderly, homes for the elderly accommodate 9,782 beneficiaries altogether. The welfare mix strategy has its legal recognition in the Serbian welfare system and started to develop during the 1990s. Private residential capacities for the elderly are developing slowly due to the rigid legislative constraints. However, the network of private residential care institutions has been growing in the recent past. (Dinic 2006) The majority of these new homes for the elderly are close to the capital Belgrade and regional centres such as Novi Sad. Besides the private residential care institutions that passed through the regular procedure by MLSP, there are other private residential institutions not officially registered by the authorities. As some of these homes are registered in other sectors than social protection (e.g. in tourism), they are not monitored and supervised by the authorities or professionals. According to estimates, there are more than 50 such institutions providing care for the elderly. (Dinic 2006)

Funding of places in residential care settings is based on a combination of central governmental support and user contributions. Residents are required to contribute to the costs according to the level of their pension income. In addi-

Table 7.1: Number of elderly accommodated in residential homes in Serbia, 1990–2008

	1990	1995	2000	2005/06	2008
Number of public facilities	37	37	39	42	45
Number of private facilities	-	-	7	7	17
Total number of beneficiaries[e]	8,321	8,916	9,113	9,339	9,782
in public facilities (%)	100	100	97	97	95
in private facilities (%)	0	0	3	3	5

[e] estimated

(Source: Dinic 2006)

tion, dependency level, family status and ownership of an apartment are taken into account when calculating the fee. In public homes, the maximum user contribution amounts to RSD 30,000 (€ 300), but costs for a bed might amount up to € 1,200 in the private sector. The contribution by MLSP, on average, is between 10% and 20% of the costs. If users or relatives are unable to contribute from their own income or their assets, costs are entirely covered by MLSP. This exception is the case for about 20% of users accommodated in public residential institutions.

Apart from the aforementioned lack of an appropriate approach to the regulation of private institutions, missing capacities and the quality of services are the major concerns in the development of the residential care sector in Serbia. (Ministry of Labour and Social Policy 2005; HelpAge International 2002a) According to the Gerontological Society of Serbia, less than 1% of the 1.28 million elderly people are currently accommodated in one of the long-term care institutions. Capacities are insufficient, characterised by an uneven territorial distribution and persons placed in these residential institutions do not have official representatives to advocate their rights. A significant number of municipalities do not even have any residential capacities for those who need this kind of protection. (Republican Institute for Social Protection 2006; Ministry of Labour and Social Policy 2005) However, strengthening the development of residential capacities has become one of the strategic objectives of current Serbian welfare policies for the elderly. According to the National Investment Plan 2007 (Government of Serbia 2007b), new residential homes with small accommodation capacities (20–50 beneficiaries) will be built for the elderly in five municipalities (*Užice, Priboj, Čačak, Sremska Mitrovica* and *Bosilegrad*).

According to the major reform document – the Social Welfare Development Strategy – the existing public long-term care network is insufficient, overcrowded, poorly maintained, often isolated from the inner city and run by professionals who have inadequate skills and capacities to deal with the multidimensional needs of the elderly. (Ministry of Labour and Social Policy 2005) The same document underlines that in the current system of social welfare, the dominant model of professional work is based on the classic "medical approach" that focuses on identifying individual's deficiencies and pathological conditions and behaviour. This medical model is essentially paternalistic as it makes beneficiaries passive, stigmatises them and does not account for their strengths and potentials. Although formal professional qualification is high, employees in social welfare institutions often lack the specific knowledge and skills required in this sector. Inappropriate professional competence and a lack of motivation due to the inadequate infrastructure often lead to situations where the needs and problems of the elderly remain insufficiently satisfied. New standards have recently been set up in the reform process on welfare policy for the elderly, but it will definitely require long-term efforts to improve skill building.

3.2. Community Care

Community care (*kucna pomoc i nega*) is provided on a mixed welfare basis, including public, non-profit and for-profit actors. The current public schemes in community care still derive from the times of socialism, when home care was introduced to support elderly through the welfare and health sector. Community care is first of all provided as a health treatment by the network of health centres. During the 1990s, these types of services were withdrawn due to deterioration in the established level of social protection. Starting from 2002, services provided by the Ministry of Health were restarted and organised through health centres in municipalities throughout Serbia. However, it is reported that coverage of these services provided by the health care centres is still not adequate. New private arrangements and agencies have been established in order to fill this gap in health services for the elderly. One of the best known is *ARWEN,* which was established in Belgrade. However, private service provision is expensive, even for the many elderly with an average income. (Dinic 2006) In addition to the health centres, other specialised health institutions provide care and support for elderly in their home. The Institute for Gerontology, Home Treatment and Care is active in Belgrade and provides health treatment and help at home without means testing. Eligibility depends on the health status of the potential user. The respective authorities claim that around 1,500 beneficiaries are covered by a range of the different services provided by the multidisciplinary medical staff per day. (Interview Zigic)

Apart from these health-centred services, social care services are provided by local governments, MLSP and Social Innovation Fund (SIF) partnership projects. Additionally, there are programmes and activities organised by numerous voluntary organisations, self-help groups, religious organisations and other civil groups. (see table 8.3) The Law on Social Protection and Social Security of Citizens gives local self-governments and municipalities the responsibility for social protection programmes, including home and day care centres, while MLSP is responsible for the respective framework regulation. Funding of these social care services is based on public resources and user contributions, which depend on income and family status. The respective regulations, however, vary across municipalities. Despite the local responsibility for providing community care, these services are not developed in line with citizens' needs. Deficiencies in financial resources and related shortages, poor professional capacities and a lack of expertise for organising community programmes negatively affect many elderly.

Recent evidence documents that only 39 municipalities (out of 167 in Serbia) provide home care services for the elderly. (Amity Report 2007) The majority of these programmes are implemented in larger cities and regional centres (with large variations), while particular services are almost non-existent in most rural communities and in the south eastern part of Serbia. (see table 8.1) It is estimated that 2,500 elderly persons receive care at home while additionally 17,000 elderly persons are covered by the clubs for the elderly organised by local communities. Clubs for the elderly have been developed in 42 municipalities and are financially supported by local authorities (mainly by providing the adequate premises). These programmes are organised by CSWs and provided by MLSP and local governments in Serbia.

Table 7.2: Community care providers and estimated number of beneficiaries, 2007/08

Provider	Programme	Number of beneficiaries
Local government/CSW in 39 municipalities	Care at Home	2,500
Local government/CSW in 42 municipalities	Support for Clubs	17,000
Institute for Gerontology, Home Treatment and Care	Health Care	1,500
SIF partnership projects in 58 municipalities	Help at Home	3,500
NGOs and religious groups	Care at Home	17,000
Red Cross	Care at Home	10,000

(Source: European Commission 2008; Amity Report 2007; Dinic 2006)

In developing social welfare services, local governments are often supported by international donors' programmes. In recent years, the SIF established by MLSP and supported by EU/EAR, UNDP, the World Bank and the Norwegian government prioritises community social services for the elderly through governmental and non-governmental partnerships at the local level. (SIF Social Innovation Fund 2009) So far, SIF has financed 88 projects in different municipalities that enhance the quality of social welfare for the most vulnerable population in Serbia. As the number of elderly people increases and resources are limited (dealing with those who are "oldest-old", living alone in isolated rural areas without kinship or extended family), SIF supports 58 municipalities with 3,500 elderly beneficiaries through appropriate programmes. (Amity Report 2007) These programmes include day care centres, volunteer activities, services delivered at home and different kinds of psycho-social support. The ambition is to provide innovative services as a supplement to existing public services. Further improvements of partnership projects would require a new legal framework that encourages local service development and capacity building, to strengthen non-profit sector activities and the competences of their volunteers.

As an alternative to institutional care, foster care for an elderly has recently been promoted as a community based programme by relevant stakeholders. As a substitute to long-term care in residential institutions, these services are provided with the aim of maximising the independence of the elderly. The caregivers help the elderly by providing a private room in their home, meals, laundry, assistance with personal activities of daily living and nursery (as needed). They are paid per month, depending on the care needs of the person living in their household. Foster care is still a pilot programme supported by SIF and carried out with 76 beneficiaries in 18 municipalities. However, according to a relevant professional view, this new type of care can be important to meet the exploding needs for long-term care. (Dinic 2008) In addition, new day care centres for the elderly which are also supported by SIF provide care for 50 beneficiaries, but the sustainability of these programmes is questionable.

According to estimates, 40,000–50,000 elderly in Serbia have been provided with at least some of the services for care at home. (Dinic 2006) Considering estimates that 300,000–400,000 elderly people are in need of some kind of support in their home, community care currently just reaches a small segment of those in need. The lack of capacity in residential and community care provision means that other providers, primarily the family, have a large burden in caring for elderly family members. (see section 5)

3.3. Payments for Care

People who are incapable of fulfilling basic needs themselves (if they cannot dress, feed or walk without the help of another person) are eligible for a cash compensation for help (*novcana naknada za pomoc i negu drugog lica*). This benefit scheme was inherited from socialist times and still is the most important welfare programme for the elderly and disabled in Serbia. (Law on Pension and Disability Insurance; Law on Social Welfare and Provision of Social Security of the Citizens) The benefit level is determined by health status and family structure and amounts to an average of € 55 per person per month. Taken as a whole, € 16.8 million per year are spent on this benefit which is currently received by 63,000 users, mostly elderly. The benefit is provided through MLSP and the pension insurance system in the entire country. With this broad coverage, the cash benefit is of major importance for the sustainability of family care. (Interview Kozarcanin)

4. Private Sector and Civil Society Activities

The development and growth of the private sector and civil society activities has been one of the most significant changes in Serbian social policy during the past decade. Apart from a sizeable growth of private non-profit and for-profit actors, the involvement of these actors in experimental projects and public-private partnerships is of increasing importance. Following the democratic transition in Serbia, the third sector mobilised its organisational capacity to become more responsive to increasing poverty and vulnerability during the transition process. In a situation of limited local funds, the role of the international community and civic organisations has been decisive in the provision of community care in Serbia. Due to the increasing number of elderly people and the limited resources of governmental institutions to meet the corresponding needs, various third sector actors started to provide welfare services to the elderly, especially those who are "oldest-old" and live alone in isolated rural areas without kinship or extended family. The majority of these organisations offer home care, nursing, domestic help or other support for vulnerable, elderly people in order to improve their quality of life. It is estimated that at least 10% of between 300 and 400 NGOs specialising in social protection provide community social services for the elderly. More specifically, in addressing deprivation of the elderly on the local level, civil society organisations are active in providing care and support at home, visiting and transport services, training for care workers, psychological support and relaxation. (Kolin 2005a)

During the 1990s, many organisations with a background in one of the major churches have renewed their social programmes again after decades. Providing direct help and social services to the elderly has historically been one of their most important activities. Since the 1990s, they have restarted or intensified these activities, including nursing and medical treatment, food provision and home assistance. It is in particular chronically sick persons with weak family support who are supported by these religious groups. The biggest network in Serbia is *Caritas Yugoslavia* which is supported by the international welfare organisations of the Catholic Church. Also increasingly involved in providing services for the elderly and sick people is *Philanthropy*, the humanitarian organisation of the Serbian Orthodox Church (to which 78% of the population belong). Another major non-profit player is the *Serbian Red Cross* that started programmes implementing personal care, psycho-social support and other support schemes for the elderly at home. *Red Cross* programmes for the elderly currently cover 83 municipalities with 10,000 beneficiaries. (see table 8.2)

A recently published monograph (Dinic 2006) documents that 68 third sector actors are active in providing some kind of help, advocacy, psycho-social support, education or services for the elderly. It is estimated that these organisations reach about 27,000 elderly people. Currently, the role of the non-profit sector in long-term care protection is mostly supplemental. Many services are only for the short term and often not integrated into wider social planning. As government support for third sector programmes is still weak, sustainability strongly depends on international donor programmes. The development of public-private partnerships on the local level can be a major way forward. However, a lack of experience challenges both governments and third sector actors.

It is worth mentioning that there are also many private specialized personal assistance agencies providing home care services. In particular middle class families are turning to this solution as they want to keep their elderly family members out of nursing homes. In that context, services also flourish in grey markets providing help to the elderly often without proper regulation, monitoring and evaluation.

5. The Role of Informal Family Networks

Given the lack of public and private provision of care from outside households, families, friends and neighbours provide the largest share of care for the frail elderly population. Family values still highly disapprove of neglecting parents and older relatives. (Amity Report 2007; Kolin 2005b; Milic 2004a; Kozar-canin 2003) This tradition of caring for the elderly within the family is also reflected in people's expectations, as 82% of the elderly people expect support from the family according to the Amity Report. Almost one third expects support from friends or neighbours, while expected support from various formal sector actors is only up to 3%. (see table 8.2)

Table 7.3: Expected sources of support for the elderly in need

	Not expecting support	Expecting Support
Political parties	98%	1%
Local government	96%	2%
Non-governmental organization	93%	3%
Association of Citizens	89%	3%
Centre of Social Work	91%	3%
Religious Groups	91%	3%
Neighbours	48%	27%
Friends	46%	30%
Family	8%	82%

(Source: Amity Report 2007)

According to the Family Law (2005) and The Law on Social Welfare and Provision of Social Security of the Citizens, there is a legal responsibility of children and parents to care for and financially support their elderly or handicapped family members. (Family Act; Law on Social Welfare and Provision of Social Security of the Citizens) Social protection should only be provided when the family's inability to take on that responsibility is proven. Besides legal obligations, the traditional pattern of solidarity and mutuality in care-giving for the elderly is still strong in Serbia. Research data on family relations shows that two thirds of families in Serbia are actively or passively providing help for elderly, either for an elderly living alone or in the same household. They are involved in caring on a daily basis by keeping in touch, supplying various forms of support and assistance or by spending leisure time with them. (Milic 2004b)

Recent research points out that 80% of the elderly are supported by family members through home help in everyday activities, care-giving, resolving health problems or financial support. (Amity Report 2007) However, the burden of care-giving within families is quite unequal. The large majority of primary informal care-giving is unpaid and most care work is done be female family members, especially wives or daughters. Very often, family carers are retired or unemployed, or stay at home to take over the role of care-giver. Many care-givers live in extremely unfavourable social conditions (unemployment and poverty-stricken families) without any public support for their informal care provision. In these situations, mutual solidarity and sharing resources within family networks has become a major survival strategy. (Kolin 2005b; Milic 2004a; Bogićević et al. 2003; Kozarcanin 2003)

More distant relatives and neighbours are an important additional source of care work, but they mostly act as secondary helpers and only assume primary responsibility when spouses or adult children are not available. Secondary help and assistance is mostly based on the principle of mutual support. Although statistics are unavailable, there are indications that a variety of arrangements are applied when primary responsibility for care is taken over by the informal sector. There are, for example, arrangements where care-giving and housing are combined, either on a more informal basis of care-giving for accommodation or on the basis of formal contracts, where life-time support is given for housing or other basic provisions. (Ubavic 2005)

Furthermore, many day-care services are provided by individuals who work unregistered, based on mutual agreements between users and providers. However, even this kind of care is only affordable for families with higher incomes. (European Commission 2008) As younger generations move to the cities, rural and remote areas become dominantly populated with elderly. As formal care primarily targets urban residents, elderly living in rural areas are deprived of both formal and non-formal care.

There is no systematic research on potential abuse of the elderly, either in institutional care settings or in the context of private homes. However, there is some evidence of physical and mental abuse of elderly in the health system as reported by the European Commission Report 2008 (European Commission 2008). Several reported homicides of older persons in 2007, deaths caused by suicide and deaths due to unintentional accidents point at the issue that is not publicly disclosed. This especially underlines the vulnerability of this population and the need for new prevention programmes.

6. Current Challenges and Trends

Various factors have contributed to the poor development of appropriate social protection measures for the elderly in Serbia, causing a situation where less than 10% of the elderly benefit from social protection programmes. The lack of diversified forms of support in the living environment and shortages in residential capacities are noticeable among the existing services for the elderly. Even though total spending for social benefit schemes is 14.5% of GDP, this is mostly taken up by pensions and money transfers. Findings from several studies point out that the elderly are inadequately informed about the availability of social services and programmes provided for them, while those who are poorest are the least informed. (European Commission 2008) The majority of the elderly in need only receive cash compensations and less than 1% is accommodated in one of the existing residential care settings.

According to statistical projections, demographic ageing will have lasting effects on the Serbian age structure. The number of persons over the age of 80 will double in the next 50 years and the "older-old" population will represent one quarter of the total population by then. Considering substantial changes in family patterns and growing needs for long-term care, a comprehensive reform of social protection and social insurance for the elderly will be one of the most important issues for policymakers, especially at the local level.

Although the inherited welfare system in Serbia has been rather generous, particularly with regard to health protection and social welfare for the family, negative impacts of the economic and social crisis have led to the erosion of social protection and health care for the elderly. In these unfavourable social circumstances, public protection for the elderly has seriously deteriorated. (Republican Institute for Social Protection 2006; Ministry of Labour and Social Policy 2005; HelpAge International 2002a) The still traditional and conservative pattern of social protection for the elderly gives priority to "residential" care and institutional services. As the residential capacities for elderly in need of long-term care are insufficient or regionally and functionally inaccessible, current debates focus on transforming existing institutions and developing new services to improve the quality of life for those who already reside in institutions. According to the National Strategy on Ageing adopted in 2006, which is the most significant document for future programmes for the elderly, improvement in long-term care is one of the most important policy issues in Serbia. This is especially true in regions where residential capacities are missing and in big cities (Belgrade and Novi Sad) that do not meet the existing needs.

The new approach promotes social cohesion and community care services. In developing this new approach, the key component would be a welfare strategy in which the public, private and voluntary sectors cooperate in creating social policy programmes. The National Strategy for Ageing (2006) and the Strategy for Development of Social Policy (2005), the most important documents on social protection for the elderly adopted in the recent past, largely focus on the growing gap between increasing needs and limited public resources for care. Considering the rising need for nursing homes, these documents underline the role of the government not only in providing more capacities, but also in creating opportunities for private and voluntary organisations to grow.

In order to improve the operation of social welfare institutions, several projects were implemented within the framework of the National Investment Plan 2007. According to this document, smaller accommodation capacities, nursing centres for pensioners, residential communities and other alternative approaches to care for the elderly should be fostered in the future. In the context of social services, the stated strategy recognises that the biggest challenge is the development of alternative social welfare, supporting day care centres, home-based social care and other solutions according to the deinstitutionalisation trend in the social policy reconstruction process. (Ministry of Labour and Social Policy 2005; Bošnjak 2003; Law on Local Self-Government)

Recently, long-term care for the elderly has become an increasingly urgent issue for many municipalities in Serbia. It was already argued that due to the high level of centralisation and the limited funds in municipal budgets, community based services have not developed in accordance with the needs of the elderly. The centralised approach to planning and financing residential capacities, alongside insufficient resources at the local level, has created a bungling network of institutions which do not respond to the real needs of the beneficiaries and do not provide adequate services. With regard to the main strategy documents (Republican Institute for Social Protection 2006; Ministry of Labour and Social Policy 2005) it could be concluded that current reform debates aim at strengthening decentralisation in social welfare. With this, municipalities would have to contribute to the development of a greater variety of more feasible local services for beneficiaries in their own living environment.

Furthermore, the accepted Social Welfare System Development Action Programme (2006) foresees the extension and enhancement of protection measures and their quality for the most vulnerable groups, while the problems of the elderly are always the focus of attention. The development of services at the local community level and the active involvement of non-profit organisations are underlined by the document. The initiated health care reform also includes the introduction of primary and secondary health care and visits for home treatment as a favourable service option that is now lacking to a significant degree.

In accordance with the modern European concept of social protection for the elderly, future programmes are planned to strengthen the role of local communities in protection, care and different types of support for the elderly in their living environment such as home help, day care facilities and other social services in the community. Due to the great number of needy elderly, still insufficient residential capacities and weak achievements in community care, foster family placement has been recognised as one of the solutions that could bridge this gap. For now, only 76 elderly people have been accommodated in a foster family's apartment through 18 CSW and supported by SIF. Foster family care is supported by relevant governmental strategies such as the Social Welfare Development Strategy and the National Strategy for the Elderly and will, according to professionals (Dinic 2008), become a significant social protection measure for long-term care in the future.

The development of community-based services and the promotion of a mixed welfare concept to strengthen social cohesion at the local level still remains the main concern of the relevant stakeholders, primarily the MLSP, the municipal network of centres for social work, health institutions and the specific social protection network of residential care for the elderly. In this situation of shortages of the adequate social policy programmes, most elderly people needing long-term care live at home or in the home of their family members. In the described unfavourable situation, which is characterised by a uniform, low quality, an overcrowded network of long-term care institutions and insufficient community care services at the local level, informal networks often provide all the necessary care. According to relevant research, two thirds of families in Serbia are involved in caring for the elderly on a daily basis. (Milic 2004b) The family is a major provider of help and support for elderly and it is usually wives and daughters who provide personal social services and housework on the base of family mutuality and solidarity.

As described, the whole system of long-term care for the elderly is characterised by a lack of funding and a lack of knowledge because of missing systematic research. Future efforts in this domain should enable policy makers to better understand the related issues and to handle policy in a more adequate way. The current absence of a proper needs assessment is one of the main problems also raised by the Social Welfare Development Strategy adopted by government. Such a needs assessment would be a significant precondition for the future development of welfare services in a way that corresponds to the actual requirements and needs. Further reforms and developments of welfare services, both on the national and local level, should be based on reliable research and a comprehensive database.

According to the deinstitutionalisation process, current reform debates clearly focus on improving alternative social welfare programmes that would support day care centres, home-based social care and other solutions in community-based services. In general, new trends and perspectives focus on fostering public-private relationships, improving trust in civil society service providers and, above all, on creating better tailored community care services. (Republican Institute for Social Protection 2006; Ministry of Labour and Social Policy 2005) Taken as a whole, social protection of the elderly has to overcome existing problems, improve the quality of services and realise that the main aim of long-term care is to provide and strengthen the elderly in living independently as much as possible.

Bibliography

Amity Report (2007) Vaninstitucionalna zastita starih ljudi u Srbiji (*Community care of the elderly in Serbia*). UNDP supported unpublished Report. Beograd.

Bogićević, Biljana; Krstic, Gorana; Mijatovic, Bosko (2003) Siromaštvo i reforma finansijske podrške siromašnima (*Poverty and reform of financial support to the poor*), Ministarstvo za socijalna pitanja i Centar za liberalno-demokratske studije. Beograd: Goragraf.

Bošnjak, Vesna (2003) Deinstitucionalizacija u socijalnoj zaštiti (*Deinstitutionalisation in social welfare*), Socijalna Misao, Reforme u socijalnoj zaštiti (*Reforms in social welfare*). Beograd: Čigoja štampa.

Dinić, Dragana (ed) (2006) Mreža gerontoloških kapaciteta u Srbiji-Vodič za dijasporu (*The network of gerontological capacities in Serbia – Guidance for the Diaspora*). Beograd: Gerontological Society of Serbia.

Dinić, Dragana (ed) (2008) Detekcija i hraniteljstvo starijih ljudi (*Detection and foster family placement for the elderly*). Beograd: Gerontological Association of Serbia.

European Commission (2008): Social protection and social inclusion in the Republic of Serbia. Beograd: Economics Institute.

Family Act: http://www.minrzs.gov.rs/docen/propisi/zakoni/Family_law.doc (30 December 2009).

Government of Serbia (2007a) Second report on the implementation of the poverty reduction strategy in Serbia. http://www.prsp.gov.rs/download/Second_Progress_ Report on_the_Implementation_of_the_Poverty_Reduction_Strategy_ in_Serbia_2_8_2007.pdf (30 June 2009).

Government of Serbia (2007b) National investment plan 2007. http://www.prsp.sr.gov.yu/engleski/dokumenta.jsp (30 June 2009).

HelpAge International (2002a) A Generation in Transition: Older people's situation and civil society's response in Eastern and Central Europe. London.

HelpAge International (2002b) State of the world's older people by region, Eastern and Central Europe. London.

Kolin, Marija (1997) Demographic and social problems on ageing. Paper presented to international conference – Demographic and social aspects on ageing, 9–20 June 1997, Valleta, Malta. International Institute for the Elderly: United Nations.

Kolin, Marija (1998) Social policy for the elderly. Background section on Yugoslavia, unpublished paper prepared for Open Society Institute. Budapest: LGI.

Kolin, Marija (2005a) Neprofitne organizacije – novi socijalni partneri (*Non-profit organisations. New social partners*). Beograd: Argument.

Kolin, Marija (2005b) Položaj starih u Srbiji i programi promena (*Current position of the elderly and social changes*). In: Institute of Social Sciences (ed) Staračka domaćinstva i izbegličke porodice (*The old households and refugees*). Beograd: Institute of Social Sciences.

Kozarčanin, Lidija (2003) Starost između države i porodice (*The elderly between government and family*). Beograd: Sluzbeni glasnik.

Law on Local Self-Government: http://www.osce.org/documents/fry/2002/03/125_ en.pdf (30 December 2009).

Law on Social Welfare and Provision of Social Security of the Citizens: http://www.minrzs.gov.rs/cir/index.php?option=com_docman&task=doc_ download&gid=289&Itemid=224 (30 December 2009).

Law on Pension and Disability Insurance: http://www.minrzs.gov.rs/cir/index.php? option=com_docman&task=doc_download&gid=285&Itemid=226 (30 December 2009).

Matejic, Bojana; Bjegovic, Vesna (2005) Needs assessment among elderly population in Serbia. http://www.ijic.org/portal/publish/articles/000035/article.htm (June 2009).

Milic, Andjelka (2004a) Transformacija porodice i domacinstva – zastoj i strategija prezivljavanja (*Family and household transformation and survival strategy*). In: Milic, Andjelka (ed) Drustvena transformacija i strategije drustvenih grupa (*Social transformation and strategies of social groups*). Beograd: Institute of Sociological Research, Faculty of Philosophy.

Milic, Andjelka (2004b) Stari i strategije porodicnog zbrinjavanja i nege (*Old people and family care*). In: Milic, Andjelka (ed) Drustvena transformacija i strategije drustvenih grupa (*Social transformation and strategies of social groups*). Beograd: Institute of Sociological Research, Faculty of Philosophy.

Ministry of Labour and Social Policy (2005): Social welfare development strategy. Beograd.

Penev, Goran (2005) Staračka domaćinstva i izbeglice (*The old household and refugees*). In: Institute of Social Sciences (ed) Staracka domacinstva i izbeglicke porodice (*The old households and refugees*). Beograd: Institute of Social Sciences.

Republican Institute for Social Protection (2006) Nacionalna strategija o starenju (*National Strategy on Ageing*): http://www.zavodsz.gov.rs/PDF/Nacionalna%20 strategija%20o%20starenju.pdf (30 June 2009).

SIF Social Innovation Fund (2009) Ministry of Labour and Social Policy. http://www.sif.minrzs.gov.rs/ (30 December 2009).

Statistical Office of the Republic of Serbia (2009) Statistical pocketbook of Serbia 2009. http://webrzs.stat.gov.rs/axd/dokumenti/razno/statkalendar2009.pdf (30 June 2009).

Ubavic, Milenko (2005) Pravni osnov za integraciju imovine starackih domacinstava i izbeglih i raseljenih lica radi ostvarivanja zivotne i ekonomske simbioze (*Legal basis for integration of the property of old households and refugees and displaced persons in order to ensure existential and economic symbiosis*). In: Institute of Social Sciences (ed) Staracka domacinstva i izbeglicke porodice (*The old households and refugees*). Beograd: Institute of Social Sciences.

Interviews

Dinic, Dragana (Gerontological Society of Serbia), Personal Interviews, October 2006, February 2008, June 2009.

Kozarcanin, Lidija (Social Policy Institute), Personal Interview, October 2006.

Zigic, Ljiljana (Director, Institute for Gerontology, Home Treatment and Care), Personal Interview, November 2006.

Sagdati, Sanije (Belgrade Gerontological Centre), Personal Interview, November 2006.

Trkulja, Maca (Director, Centre for Social Work Zemun), Personal Interview, November 2006.

8
Long-term Care in the Slovak Republic

Helena Kuvíková, Jana Štrangfeldová, Lenka Topinková, Katarína Vidličková

1. Introduction

Slovakia has seen significant socio-demographic changes over the last decades, which will continue to challenge and profoundly shape social policies. The growth of the post-productive population and decreases in the pre-productive and productive population will have major consequences for the country, not least for the organisation of its health and long-term care system. With regard to long-term care, increasing needs will arise from two major sources. Firstly, the increase in the elderly population will lead to an increase in care needs. Secondly, while families currently play the main role in providing care for the frail elderly population, there is increasing pressure on their role as informal carers. As a consequence, a re-evaluation of current social policies and substantial investments in the long-term care infrastructure will be required to address these socio-demographic challenges. (Bednárik, Bodnárová 2005)

This article attempts to evaluate the current state of long-term care in Slovakia by analysing the existing approaches to support people in need of care. It outlines the current system of financial assistance for elderly, the services provided in residential and community care, as well as services organised and funded in the health care sector or in the social care sector. Additional sections deal with the growing importance of private long-term care providers and with the dominant role of family care-giving. In the final section, the article discusses potential directions for future long-term care policies in Slovakia in the light of current challenges and policy proposals.

2. Long-term Care in the Slovak Welfare System

Long-term care does not exist as a separate social protection scheme in Slovakia. Instead, different welfare sectors provide assistance and support schemes for long-term dependent people. The main regulatory actors, also closely involved in funding and quality monitoring, include: ministries (in particular the Ministry of Health, the Ministry of Labour, Social Affairs and Family and the Ministry of Finance), eight regional self-governments, municipal self-governments, health insurance companies and social insurance companies. The group of service providers includes public, private and non-profit organisations and a large number of informal carers, mostly family members, but also friends and neighbours.

The Slovak social security system is comprised of three pillars: the social insurance system, state social support and social assistance. Long-term care is not organised as a separate pillar in the social protection system, but as a combination of the first pillar (health insurance following social insurance principles) and the third pillar (social care following social assistance principles). The pillar of social assistance was called social care until the year 1996. With the Law Act No. 195/1998 Coll. on Social Assistance, new principles have been introduced. Social assistance is provided to citizens or families when social insurance and state social support do not secure their basic needs. Social care was replaced by social assistance to accentuate the primary responsibility of the citizens and their families in solving insufficient social situations they might find themselves in. This shift is also described as a change from passive and paternalistic social care to more motivating and activating social assistance. In contrast to social insurance and state social support, where rights and eligibility criteria are exactly defined, social assistance is based on an individualised approach. The new regulatory framework also presents a shift from defining social care for specific social groups towards defining tools of social assistance. Furthermore, it emphasises a welfare mix, involving regions and municipalities as well as private actors, charities and third sector organisations.

Since January 2003, competences in the area of social services have gradually been shifted to self-governing bodies (municipal and regional self-governments). As a consequence, social services for long-term care (outside the health sector) are now almost fully decentralised. The ministries (Ministry of Health and Ministry of Labour, Social Affairs and Family) are responsible for supervision and for issues related to education and the training of professionals in the area of health and social services. They also make financial contributions to the funds of social service providers. Financial assistance for people in need of long-term care also remains the responsibility of the state and is administered by the Offices for Labour, Social Affairs and Family. The regional self-governments manage the provider registers of health and social services, decide on registration applications, negotiate contracts with private providers and contribute to the funding of social services. (Woleková, Petijová 2007)

With Law Act No. 448/2008 Coll. on social services, a new regulatory framework became valid in 2009. The overall aim is to foster social inclusion and to better meet the needs of people in adverse social situations. It provides new approaches to the cooperation between state authorities and providers in the private sector and defines the basic terms and relations in the delivery of social services. It also introduces new types of social services, defining them as services of public interest. While it emphasises the non-profit orientation of the activity, it also allows businesses and individuals on a self-employed basis to register as social service providers. The new legislation did not, however, establish long-term care as a separate welfare sector. Long-term care therefore remains a responsibility shared between health, disability and social care policies and is divided between different governmental levels. Services provided for dependent elderly people are funded from different sources, including federal, regional and local budgets, social insurance contributions, private means and donations. Not least, this fragmentation complicates any attempt to identify and measure long-term care expenditure. According to an earlier Slovak study, long-term care expenditure accounts for about 0.62% of GDP, including health and social care and covering all age groups. This share even amounts to 0.9% if a wider definition, including all social sector expenses for severely handicapped and elderly people, is applied. (Woleková et al. 2004) According to OECD reports, public long-term care expenditure in Slovakia accounts for 0.3% of GDP. Following Eurostat measurements, this share is slightly higher, amounting to 0.4% of GDP.

3. The Provision and Funding of Long-term Care

Apart from the family as the main provider of long-term care, services and support in long-term care are built on three pillars: the provision of places in residential care settings, the provision of social services in the private environment of the dependent person and financial assistance, paid either to the person in need of care or to the person providing care. It is estimated that about one quarter of all citizens with a long-term illness or disability are provided with residential health and social services (about 22,000 persons). More than 76,000 citizens are provided with help and support in their private environment. They either use services provided at home or receive financial assistance which can be granted for personal assistance or given directly to informal carers.

3.1. Residential Care

Residential care in Slovakia is provided in health care institutions and in social care institutions. But the total number of residential places does not cover the demand. Long waiting lists for places in long-term care institutions indicate the current discrepancy between demand and supply, which is also caused by the lack of services in the community care sector. The new social services legislation acknowledges the importance of community care development. It stipulates that needs should primarily be provided in the private environment of the elderly person. Only if these services cannot satisfy the specific needs or are unavailable, access to residential care should be provided. The residential care sector has recently focussed on new community oriented institutions, adding more complex packages of nursing services to institutions that have previously mainly focused on residence only.

In the health care sector, residential long-term care is provided in different kinds of facilities. These include geriatric wards in hospitals, long-term care wards, geriatric centres or clinics, hospices, sanatoria and a few nursing homes that belong to the health sector. In 2005, the total number of these facilities was 111. The two most important types of facilities (geriatric wards and long-term care wards or sanatoria) together provided about 2,800 beds. These figures, however, can only serve as a rough indicator for the number of long-term care beds in the health sector, as these beds serve very different objectives. They can be intended for geriatric health care, palliative care, rehabilitation or intermediate stays before being transferred to a social service institution or back to the private environment.

In the social sector, services have been provided by 579 institutions in 2008, 436 of them institutions for adults. These institutional facilities for adults provide 28,676 beds. (Závodná 2008) In 2008, 28,676 places have been available in the two major types of facilities for adults: 15,427 places in the 224 pensioners' homes and 13,249 places in the 212 pensioners' sheltered housing homes. A second major group of institutions are nursing service facilities and nursing service stations. Nursing service facilities provide nursing care services for clients that require full-time services in an institutional facility. 1,776 places were available in 92 facilities in 2008. Additionally, 118 places are held by five nursing service stations that provide services to clients staying in their private environment. (Závodná 2008)

Funding of social service facilities is characterised by a mix of state budget subsidies (accounting for about a quarter of total funding), contributions by self-governmental regions (accounting for about half of total funding), receipts

Table 8.1: Institutional facilities in the social sector by region, 2008

Institutions providing social services	Number of institutions	Places Total	Adults	Children
Total	579	35,501	28,676	6,825
Bratislava region	49	3,786	3,021	765
Trnava region	71	4,310	3,791	519
Nitra region	77	5,092	4,301	791
Trenčín region	71	4,111	3,453	658
Žilina region	73	4,656	3,903	753
Banská Bystrica region	99	4,658	3,666	992
Prešov region	82	4,488	3,536	952
Košice region	57	4,400	3,005	1,395

(Source: Závodná 2008)

from the municipalities and social security funds and contributions made by the residents (amounting to about 20% of total funding). (Závodná 2008)

According to the law, access to the facilities should follow the need for long-term care and not the economic background of the potential resident. There is no preferential treatment of people with low incomes, as social assistance principles in funding should offer them equal opportunities to enter residential care settings. However, given the highly restricted budgetary situation of the institutions, it is sometimes reported that people who can make more substantial financial contributions are favoured.

3.2. Community Care

In the past, social care was mostly provided by large scale specialised institutions across the country. Therefore, the concept of community care does not have a strong tradition in Slovakia. It is only with recent changes in the legislation on social services, that the concepts of community care and community planning of social services have received broader attention. Community care is developed on the grounds of national priorities for the development of social services and recognises local requirements. The new legislation has also broadened the potential range of services that can be offered in the community care sector. In 2007, 22,760 citizens have been provided with long-term care services in their private households. Additionally, transportation services have been provided to 2,173 people. (Ministry of Labour, Social Affairs and Family 2009) Furthermore, assistance is given to more citizens in the form of financial support for informal long-term care or for personal assistance. (see below)

Care provided by Agencies of Home Nursing Care (*ADOS – Agentúra domácej ošetrovateľskej starostlivosti*) form the core of community care in Slovakia. These agencies, which have been operating since 1997, are usually health care organisations focusing on nursing care in private homes. Their services are meant for patients in need of specialised long-term care without required hospitalisation or for patients who have just been released from hospitals. Patients are usually chronically ill and partially or completely immobile. The nursing care and rehabilitation provided by ADOS has to be prescribed by the attending physician and approved by the health insurance. The costs are then covered by health insurance, but there are strict rules regarding the duration of each visit. Some of the agencies also provide additional social care services. However, as health insurance funds do not pay for social care, costs have to be covered by patients themselves. The majority of Agencies of Home Nursing Care is located in the East of the country, more than one third in the two Eastern regions of Prešov and Košice. This indicates that in the Western part of the country, in particular the Bratislava and Trenčín region, respective services are provided by other community care organisations.

3.3. Payments for Care

There are three different forms of financial support for people in need of care or their informal carers: care allowances, financial support from social assistance and personal assistance. (Bednárik 2004) The intention of the care allowance is to provide informal carers with a basic income. It is paid to them directly. The benefit is income-tested and can only be granted if care is provided to a person over 6 years of age for at least 20 hours per week. In 2009, the care allowance amounted to € 206 per month for one dependent person or € 275 if care is provided for two or more dependent persons. Due to means-testing, the average benefit paid to informal carers is substantially lower. Given the low actual level of the benefit, it does not create an incentive to leave formal employment, but can provide some support for the financial situation of poor households. It turns out that many of the recipients were unemployed before. By the end of 2007, the benefit was paid to 51,000 carers, a quarter of them beyond 60 years of age. Total public expenditure on the care allowance has decreased in recent years and amounted to about € 85 million in 2008 (compared to about € 92 million in 2006). (Ministry of Labour, Social Affairs and Family 2009)

Further financial support can be granted through benefits for specific circumstances, such as assistance for home adaptation, for transportation or for buying and repairing aids. The respective benefit is paid directly to the dependent person. The third type of financial support for long-term care is the personal assistance allowance. This direct payment scheme was strongly advocated by the representatives of disability groups. After a pilot phase in 1997–98, the scheme was implemented in 1999. The aim of this scheme is to help dependent people to gain autonomy, providing them with support for the work of personal assistants. While family carers were not the primary target of this scheme, it developed to be an important measure of supporting informal care. Different from the care allowance described above, the personal assistance allowance focuses on dependent persons below 65 years of age and is related to their work activity. Only in recent years, coverage has been extended beyond 65 years of age if the person has received it before. The number of recipients has been increasing steadily since the introduction of the scheme in 1999. In 2008, it was paid to about 6,000 recipients, with less than 2% being beyond 65 years of age. Total expenditure was about € 18 million in the same year. (Ministry of Labour, Social Affairs and Family 2009)

4. The Role of the Private Sector

Long-term care services – outside family and other informal networks – are provided by the state, regions and municipalities, non-profit and for-profit organisations. The role of the private sector, in particular the non-profit or third sector, became particularly important in the process of transformation. It profoundly shaped the development of services in many areas, including the field of social care. Non-profit sector development also influences public policies. It strengthens civil society and offers alternative services in health and social care. The existence and growth of the non-profit sector is determined at least partly by the fact that public institutions are unable or unwilling to adequately tackle problems in the fields of health and social care. The extension of public services is limited by budgetary pressure but also by ideological preferences. As a consequence, public support in the form of legislative and financial regulations and financial support from the private sector have created space and demand for new organisations in the non-profit sector. (Kuvíková 2006; Kuvíková, Hullová 2004)

In the past, the majority of long-term care services were provided as residential care, mainly in large institutions financed by the state. The transformation process started a redefinition of the underlying principles. In the recent past, changes have been driven by the objective of providing care in the private home of the dependent person or in a day care centre. The aim is to enable dependent persons to choose individual services, to provide activating services and to include them in the process of assistance. Parallel to these developments, the role of non-profit organisations in long-term care provision became more important. Services in the community, including a wide range of counselling, home care and day care centres, are increasingly provided by nonprofits, particularly in urban areas. According to the Ministry of Labour, Social Affairs and Family (2009), 4,131 employees worked in the provision of long-term care in non-profit organisations in 2008. Another 1,785 worked in the field as volunteers. Profit-making companies are not excluded from providing health or social services in long-term care, but are not provided with public funds. Given that only a small proportion of the population is able to pay for these services out-of-pocket, their market share in this sector is very small. (Koldinská, Tomeš 2004)

Non-profit organisations willing to enter the field of social care have to register as a social service provider. They can exist in five different legal forms: as civic associations, as foundations, as non-investment funds, as public benefit organisations or as church organisations. More than half of the non-profit organisations in the field of health and social services are organised as public benefit organisations. Registration for this kind of NGO has to be approved by a regional council office. The law permits public benefit organisations to carry out additional commercial activities the condition that the additional business activity does not threaten the quality, extent and accessibility of the services and that this enterprise will help to achieve a more effective use of its property. Any profit gained from such an activity must be used solely to provide public welfare services. (Law Act No. 213/1997) The second major provider group is formed by health and social service providers that are organised as civic associations. They are legal entities organised by citizens or other legal entities in order to represent their common interests. Their registration is approved by the Home Office. The third largest group of provider organisations are church related organisations.

In 2008, 416 nongovernmental organisations have been active in the provision of social services. (see table 8.2) While the number of organisations has increased since 2007 (396 NGOs in 2007), the number of people provided with their services has decreased from about 54,000 to about 43,000. (Ministry of Labour, Social Affairs and Family 2009)

Table 8.2: Number of non-government providers of social services, 2007–2008

	2007	2008
Total number of non-government providers of social services	396	416
Nursing care	101	94
Public catering	44	40
Transport services	23	25
Care provided in institutions of social services	269	294
Other social services	35	46
Total number of people provided by their services	54,103	42,896
Nursing care	4,731	4,361
Public catering	8,420	7,986
Transport services	3,983	3,746
Care provided in institutions of social services	9,256	11,003
Other social services	27,882	32,603

(Source: Ministry of Labour, Social Affairs and Family 2009)

The total income of non-profit social service providers is made up of transfers from the state and municipality budgets, from contributions paid by the clients and from donations. Public contributions accounted for about 55% of their total income in 2008, mostly from the budget of the municipalities. (Ministry of Labour, Social Affairs and Family 2009) State budget contributions are limited to capital transfers and some common transfers. About one third of the total budget comes from payments made by service users. The remaining budget share (accounting for about 8% in 2008) is composed of sponsorships, donations and public collections. Part of the donations come from dedicated tax shares, as citizens can assign 2% of their income tax payments to certain NGOs.

5. The Role of the Family

The attitude of the Slovak society towards the issue of taking care of family members is ambivalent. According to opinion and value surveys, the family takes the first place in a scale of values. On the other hand, as a result of 40 years of socialist regime, people are used to the state taking care of ill and frail elderly people. An aspect that has long shaped values in the Slovak society is a particular inheritance procedure in some regions. Accordingly, the youngest child is supposed to take care of his or her parents until they die. They might inherit their house or some assets in return, but might also just have the duty. Similar arrangements can also be found in inheritance contracts, when one child commits her- or himself to take care of the parents, who give her/him the largest part of the inheritance in exchange. The other children abandon the right to ask for more assets for this reason. There are no in-depth studies on these customs and contracts, but they are – at least in some regions – deeply rooted in society.

While there is little systematic evidence about the dimension of family care in Slovakia, families definitely play a major role in providing help and support to dependent relatives. They are recognised in the legislation in two different ways. First, they are considered as co-funders of social services. For residential care and community care services, the income of the recipient and of close family members is taken into account. It is only when their income is below a specific threshold, which is related to the minimum subsistence level, that no contributions have to be made by family members. Secondly, family members are recognised and supported as informal carers. In the case of the care allowance the means-tested benefit is paid directly to informal carers, whereas the personal assistance allowance is paid to the dependent person, but again with the intention to support informal care arrangements. (see section 3.3) Thirdly, there is a bundle of additional measures addressing informal carers. Most importantly, if a carer receiving the care allowance is not in any formal employment, social insurance contributions are covered by the state. Other support services for informal carers include counselling, respite care or measures that attempt to facilitate the care and work balance. Most of these activities, however, are very limited in availability, often only provided in the context of pilot programs.

A recent study focused on family carers and, more specifically, on recipients of the care allowance and the personal assistance allowance aged 18–64. (Repková 2008) It shows that 60% of informal carers provide help and support for dependent individuals beyond 65 years of age. The patterns of family caregiving are quite similar to those in other countries. The large majority of 82% of all informal carers are women. While women often act as family carers when they are in their employment age, male carers mostly start providing care after they retired. (Repková 2006) Almost half of the carers are between 51 and 65 years of age but only a small proportion is in regular employment alongside the provision of informal care. According to the study, 45% of family carers in the employment age started care-giving when they were unemployed. In these cases, where unemployment leads to very low household income, the care allowance provides an important financial support. (Repková 2008)

6. Conclusion

The latest legal changes on social services in Slovakia bring about a new philosophy in the relations between the relevant actors, the delivery of social services and the general range of services. They emphasise principles such as activation, quality and supervision and refer to new types of services, including interpretation services, mediation of personal assistance, social rehabilitation activities, aids or relief services.

Activating the client refers to the provision of social services which consider individual development plans, making social services tailor-made for each individual client. This approach now has to be followed by all social service providers. It aims at improving the quality of the services and at recognising the individual goals, needs and abilities of service recipients. The provider is obliged to keep written individual records about social service delivery and to evaluate its progress, as far as possible, with the recipient's participation. If the recipient faces serious restrictions in major activities, the individual development plan has to contain social rehabilitation activities to lower the rate of dependency.

After quality management has become a major issue in the health care sector, the latest legislative changes also brought it to the area of social services. Quality concerns include procedural, personal and operational features. Social service providers are obliged to ensure quality by fulfilling requirements on staff qualification and infrastructure development, e.g. in buildings that are used by people with handicaps. Closely related to the quality objective is the introduction of independent supervision (a social service inspectorate) to guarantee the recognition of human rights and to ensure social service quality. Finally, a major aim of the reforms is to increase the objectivity in assessing dependency and the related provision of services and financial support. These objectives clearly indicate a new philosophy in the provision of social services. However, the current economic recession and the already precarious financial situation on the level of regions and municipalities might create substantial limitations in developing the required infrastructure and in providing the necessary means to achieve the objectives. Before the new legislation was enacted, the Ministry of Labour, Social Affairs and Family expected substantial additional costs to arise from the new policies, in particular on the level of regions and municipalities.

Finally, there are some general issues that will have a major impact on the way long-term care is addressed in Slovakia in the future. While there have been major legislative changes in the recent past, long-term care is not established as a separate welfare sector and neither even established as a concept systematically used in policy-making and debates. It is partly covered by provisions from the health or disability sector, and to a larger extent by the social sector. This fragmentation hinders communication and cooperation between the sectors. It also leads to difficulties in systematically collecting data on long-term care, as data collection in the health and the social care sector are not harmonised. And data collection in the social care sector does not systematically distinguish long-term care services from other social services. This, in turn, limits the opportunity for subsequently monitoring and evaluating the situation of people in need of long-term care and the developments in the long-term care sector in general. Furthermore, and related to the above mentioned concerns, there is a general lack of information on the individual level and a lack of awareness on the level of public debates. The capacity and quality of services do not meet the real needs of the dependent population. Ageing populations, changing lifestyles and family structures, and growing expectations for a better service quality will further increase the pressure to respond to these needs by developing services that are affordable, better integrated and cost-effective.

Bibliography

Bednárik, Rastislav (2004) Stav sociálnej ochrany na Slovensku (*Status of social protection in Slovakia*). Bratislava: Centre for Study of Labour and Family.

Bednárik, Rastislav; Bodnárová, Bernardína (2005) Starnutie populácie – Výzva na zmeny v službách pre starších ľudí (*Ageing of population – Call for changes in services for older people*). Bratislava: Centre for Study of Labour and Family.

Koldinská, Kristína; Tomeš, Igor (2004) Social services in accession countries. In: Social Work & Society, Vol. 2, No. 1, 110–117.

Kuvíková, Helena (2006) Možnosti rozvoja mimovládnych organizácií v krajinách Vyšehradskej skupiny (*Possibilities in development of non-governmental organisations in the W-4 countries*). Banská Bystrica: EF UMB.

Kuvíková, Helena; Hullová, Danica (2004) The nonprofit sector in the Slovak Republic. In: Zimmer, Annette; Priller, Eckhard (eds) Future of civil society. Wiesbaden: VS Verlag für Sozialwissenschaften.

Law Act No. 213/1997 on Non-Profit Organisations

Law Act No. 195/1998 Coll. on Social Assistance

Law Act No. 448/2008 Coll. on Social Services

Ministry of Labour, Social Affairs and Family (2009) Report on the social situation of the population of the Slovak Republic for 2008. Bratislava.

Repková, Kvetoslava (2006) Family care in Slovakia through gender optics. Bratislava: Institute for Labour and Family Research.

Repková, Kvetoslava (2008) Situácia rodinných opatrovateľov/liek vo svetle sociálnych štatistík (*The situation of family carers in the light of social statistics*). Bratislava: Institute for Labour and Family Research.

Woleková, Helena; Gonda, Peter; Howe, Anna (2004) Porovnanie dlhodobej starostlivosti v krajinách OECD a na Slovensku (*Comparison of long-term care in OECD countries and Slovakia*). Bratislava: MZ SR.

Woleková, Helena; Petijová, Martina (2007) Sociálne služby na Slovensku (*Social services in Slovakia*). Bratislava: SOCIA.

Závodná, Soňa (2008) Zariadenia sociálnych služieb v Slovenskej republike v roku 2008 (*Social service facilities in the Slovak Republic in 2008*). Bratislava: ŠÚ SR.

Interviews

Bušová, Božena (Director of the Home Care Agency "Harris"), Personal Interview, May 2007.

Nahálka, Peter (Department of Social Affairs and Health Care at the Office of Self-Governing Region Banská Bystrica), Personal Interview, November 2006.

Potaš, Marián (Agency of Employment, Social Affairs and Family), Personal Interview, November 2006.

Tatár, Peter (Vice Mayor, Bratislava Regional Self-Government), Personal Interview, May 2007.

Woleková, Helena (CEO of the SOCIA-Social Reform Foundation, former Minister of Labour and Social Affairs), Personal Interview, May 2007.

9
Needs and Beads:
The Emerging Long-term Care System
of Slovenia

Vito Flaker, Barbara Kresal, Mateja Nagode

1. Gradual Social Transition

Slovenia is a small country (just over 2,000,000 inhabitants, 20,273 km²) of great diversity, situated at the crossroads of different cultures, climates and flows (political, traffic). Historically, it was part of the Austro-Hungarian Empire (parts of it also of the Venetian Republic) until the 1st World War. In 1918, it became part of the Kingdom of Yugoslavia and a federal unit of the socialist state with a great degree of autonomy after the 2nd World War. Slovenia gained independence in 1991, changing its political, economic and social system. It shares the destiny of many other countries that previously had a socialist political and economic system. It had to confront the same adverse consequences recorded elsewhere (decline in standard of living, increased poverty, changes in values – individualism, fast-profit hedonism, deconstruction of the "social state", increase in unemployment, housing shortage etc.), although the price of transition in Slovenia does not seem to have been as high as elsewhere. In comparison with other countries in transition, it is the most successful in many economic and social indicators.

After the initial shock and fall of the economy (–8.9% GDP), a high rate of economic growth was established in the following years (5.4% in 1999, 3.1% in 2001, 4.4% in 2004, and 6.8% in 2007). (Statistical Office of the Republic of Slovenia 2008) The employment rate in Slovenia also increased continually, amounting to 66% in 2005 and to 68.8% in 2008. (Urad Republike Slovenije za makroekonomske analize in razvoj 2009) Under the circumstances of economic restructuring, the social security system functioned relatively efficiently. Expenditure on social security has varied between 22% and 24% of GDP since 1996. In 2006, the country has spent 22.1% of its GDP on social protection, compared to an EU average 25.8%. (Eurostat 2009) The highest share of expenditure is related to old-age benefits (37.9%) while sickness and health care expenditure represents around a third (32.1%). The rest comprises unemployment (3.0%), family and children (8.6%), disability (8.5%), survivors (7.5%), housing (0.1%) and others (2.6%). Long-term care expenditure amounted to 1.15% of GDP in 2006 and is also increasing. (Urad Republike Slovenije za makroekonomske analize in razvoj 2009; Jacović 2008)

According to national statistics, Slovenia faced its highest unemployment rate at 14.5% between 1993 and 1998, before it decreased to 11% in 2004 and to 8.9% in May 2009. However, unemployment has increased in the recent past due to the financial and economic crisis. The unemployment rate measured according to the ILO and EU standards was between 7.4% in 1998 and 6.0% in 2006, has decreased to less than 5% in 2007 and 2008, and increased again to 6.0% in 2009. (Eurostat 2009) One of the main problems on the labour market today is a very low employment rate among older workers. In 2007, only 33.5% of the population aged between 55 and 64 were in active employment. This share has been increasing slightly over the last years, partly due to the old-age insurance reform. Other problems concern the fairly high unemployment among young people (37.6% among youth aged 15–24 in 2007), a high percentage of long-term unemployed and a high unemployment rate for people with lower education. (Ministry of Labour, Family and Social Affairs 2006c) Social transfers have contributed significantly to the lowering of poverty risks. The at-risk of poverty rate was 11.5% in Slovenia in 2007. Excluding social transfers, the rate would have been two times higher than that. Unemployed persons, households without employed family members, elderly women, single parents and big families show the highest risk of poverty. (Urad Republike Slovenije za makro-ekonomske analize in razvoj 2009; Javornik 2007).

Demographic trends in Slovenia point towards an increasing number and share of older people. Slovenia had 249,046 people over the age of 65 in 1995, their share in the total population amounting to 12.5%. In 2008, this age group accounted for almost one fifth of the total population and its share is projected to have reached 35% by 2060. Life expectancy in Slovenia is among the highest in new EU Member States and it is increasing continually. A boy born in Slovenia in 2005/06 can expect to reach almost 75 years while the average life expectancy for girls is 82 years. Over the last three decades, male life expectancy increased by 8.3 years and female life expectancy by 7.7 years. (Vertot 2007) While the budgetary burden of age-related expenditure is still maintainable today, projections show that it could increase quickly due to population ageing. Social security will therefore have to be adapted to the future demographic structure of the Slovenian population. The pension system has already undergone a long-term reform but international bodies (EU, IMF) claim that it will need more balancing in the public expenditure. However, there is no consensus regarding this issue in Slovenia. (Government PR and Media Office 2006)

2. Long-term Care Within the Social Security System

As a consequence of the Austro-Hungarian heritage, the Slovenian social security system follows the Bismarckian model. It is based on compulsory public social insurance for different social risks. The first scheme of compulsory social insurance covering the risk of work injuries was introduced in 1887 and compulsory sickness insurance followed the year after. Pension insurance for white-collar workers goes back to 1907 and the first unemployment benefits were established in 1918. However, it took until 1937 before the general compulsory system of pension insurance was introduced and a special unemployment insurance scheme was established. (Kresal 1998)

During the 1990s, the independent Republic of Slovenia adopted its own legislation in the field of social security. It encompasses all benefit schemes covered by the ILO Convention No. 102 on social security, as well as a social assistance scheme that provides a minimum means of subsistence. The social security system in Slovenia actually consists of five parts: health insurance

(Health Care and Health Insurance Act), old-age and disability insurance (Pension and Disability Insurance Act), unemployment insurance, (Employment and Insurance Against Unemployment Act), parental insurance and family benefits (Parental Care and Family Benefits Act) and social assistance (Social Care Act). Health, disability and old-age insurance are social insurance schemes which are financed through the contributions of employers and employees (as well as other insured persons). Besides the compulsory social insurance schemes there are different voluntary, supplementary social insurance schemes. In health care, nearly all insured people (approx. 98%) have voluntary supplementary health insurance as well. By contrast, supplementary voluntary insurance for old-age pensions are not that widespread in Slovenia. Family protection is a mix of concepts of social insurance and social assistance, as parental insurance is financed by contributions while other benefits are tax-funded. In addition, there is a system of social care and assistance based on the principle of subsidiarity which is funded from the state or municipal budget. However, the users are obliged to participate in payments for care services depending on the type of the social services and the ability of the user to pay for the services needed.

Insurance for long-term care is supposed to be introduced as a new field of social security in the near future. In 2006, the first proposal for legislation regulating long-term care was prepared, but it has not yet been enacted yet and its future prospects are unclear. (Cvetko et al. 2007) In the Government's Working Programme for the year 2009, the enactment of long-term care legislation is scheduled for May 2010. (Normativni program dela Vlade RS za leto 2009) Long-term care in Slovenia is currently provided in different ways. Some services are provided in the form of institutional health care, including non-acute hospitalisation treatment, comprising mainly intermediate care and prolonged hospitalisation provided by nursing departments, health visiting service and home health care. The other part of the services is provided within the scope of the social care system. These services include day care and residential care, home help services, family assistance, sheltered housing and different social care programmes for people with disabilities, including personal assistance. For individuals in need, a social assistance cash-benefit is provided which can be used for informal help or to pay for the required services. Cash benefits for long-term care can be granted to recipients of old-age and disability pensions, beneficiaries of social assistance, persons who are unable to work due to serious disabilities, war-disabled persons and war veterans. (Ministry of Labour, Family and Social Affairs 2006c)

Table 9.1: Total expenditure on long-term care by funding source and sector, 2003/2006

	In mio € (current prices)		Structure in %		GDP share in %		Real index	Real annual growth in %
	2003	2006	2003	2006	2003	2006	2006/2003	2003–2006
Total	267	333	100.0	100.0	1.08	1.09	114.6	4.7
Public	202	257	75.7	77.2	0.82	0.84	116.9	5.3
Private	65	76	24.3	22.8	0.26	0.25	107.4	2.4
Health care	164	208	61.4	62.5	0.66	0.68	116.6	5.2
Social care	103	125	38.6	37.5	0.42	0.41	111.5	3.7

Note: ltc = HC.3 + HC.R.6.1 according to the methodology of the SHA and JQ 2007 (Source: SORS – Preliminary estimates for the Joint Questionnaire (JQ) of Eurostat, OECD and WHO for Slovenia, December 2007)

Table 9.2: Expenditure on long-term care by number of users and percentage of resources in health and social care, 2004

Type of expenditure	Number of users	Expenditure in %
Health care	48,705	47.45
Residential care	15,727	39.95
Community care	32,978	7.50
Social care	21,719	24.41
Residential care	16,686	21.30
Community care	5,033	3.10
Cash benefits	30,015	27.89
Total		
Residential care	16,686	61.07
Community care	38,011	11.05
Cash benefits	30,015	27.89

(Source: Calculated on the basis of figures presented in the Draft of the Long-Term Care and Long-Term Insurance Act; Ministrstvo za delo, družino in socialne zadeve 2006)

Data on long-term care expenditure shows a steady growth in expenditure in absolute terms, but the share in GDP remains relatively steady. There is, however, a greater increase in public expenditure and health costs, while the shares of private spending and the social care sector have slightly lowered. The bulk (almost half) of the long-term care expenditure is spent on health care. However, the majority of health care is provided residentially in social care homes. Social care homes, namely, provide both social (including accommodation) and health care and can sometimes be difficult to distinguish in practice.

A much higher share of users receive community care services than residential care - but expenditure is structured the opposite way. Residential care is almost six times more expensive than community care. Cash payments also represent a considerable share of total expenditure and a significant part of this sum is received by people in residential care. Residential care is clearly the dominant part of the present long-term care provision in Slovenia, with cash payments contributing both to living in the community as well as to care homes fees.

3. The Slovenian Long-term Care System

3.1. Residential Care

Residential care dominates the long-term care system in Slovenia today. It is dominant in terms of being a well established system, comprising more than one third of people estimated to need long term care, but also in the share of funding it receives from users, the insurance system and the state budget. Residential care is mainly a public responsibility, in terms of establishing and maintaining facilities as well as in developing the network of social care homes. The system of financing residential care is a combination of public and private responsibility: people have to cover the expenses of accommodation, food and social care services, but the state (municipality) supplements the payment up to the entire price if their income is insufficient.

Residential care is currently provided by homes for the elderly, special social care homes and centres for care and training (residential institutions for people with learning disabilities). Homes for the elderly have the longest tradition in Slovenia and operate both in the public and private domain. The centres for care and training can also be run by public and private providers while the special social care homes are always public. Public homes are usually provided by municipalities and private sector providers that need to acquire a licence or concession. In 2009, there were 83 homes for the elderly, of which 55 were public and 28 were private. Together, they offered 15,994 places which suffice for approximately 4.7% of the total population over 65 years of age. (Ministry of Labour, Family and Social Affairs 2009) There were 14 special social care homes of which 6 operated as independent institutions and 8 were special units within homes for the elderly. Out of the 71 centres for care and training, 29 public institutions existed independently, 21 were specialised units in other institutions and 21 were private ones with concessions. (Statistical Office of the Republic of Slovenia 2009) To be admitted to a social care home, a person must be over the age of 65 and incapable of independent living. Special care homes only admit people with mental health difficulties and intellectual, physical or other disabilities. If there is no place available, the person in need is added to a waiting list, but the immediacy of a need can give the application a greater priority.

In 2007, there were 13,856 residents in 69 homes for the elderly. Most of the residents were over 80 years of age (nearly 60%) and 75% of them were women. In 2007, the homes for the elderly altogether employed 6,448 persons with 90.7% of the staff being female. 53.8% were employed for health care services and 46.2% for social services. The total figure amounted to 2.1 residents per carer in a home for the elderly. (Statistical Office of the Republic of Slovenia 2009) Special social welfare institutions accommodate fewer residents, their number being 2,531 in 2007. The 14 homes had 1,462 employees, again mostly women. The 71 centres for care and training had 2,621 residents in 2007, women representing around 45% of all users. These centres employed 937 people, most of which were paid from social welfare programmes (around 80%). (Statistical Office of the Republic of Slovenia 2009)

Residents generally have to pay for residential care, but the fees are subsidized by the municipalities if necessary. Daily fees for residential care in Ljubljana varied between € 14 and € 32 per day in 2009 – depending on the specific institution and the size of the room. (Ministry of Labour, Family and Social Affairs 2009) There is no general price for a place in residential care that would be the same for all institutions in Slovenia. There are fairly strict legal regulations issued by the Ministry for Labour, Family and Social Affairs that determine in detail how the price for a place in residential care (as well as for any other social care service) may be calculated according to the set standards. (Official Journal of the Republic of Slovenia, Nos. 87/06, 127/06, 8/07, 51/08, 5/09) Just 42% of residents in care institutions pay for the stay themselves out of their income or with help from their relatives. Municipalities fully cover the expenses for 27% of the people in residential care. This data refers to accommodation and other social services, whereas health care services within institutions are financed almost entirely by the health insurance, i.e. from public sources. (Ministrstvo za delo, družino in socialne zadeve 2006) Whether and how much an individual has to pay for their residential care is determined by the Social Care Act and the Regulation on Criteria for Determining the Exemptions Regarding Payments of Social Care Services. The so-called centres for social work decide on the exemption from payments in individual cases. (Mali 2007) In principle, there are no differences between public institutions and private homes with concessions, which are also part of the public social care system. These care homes within the public social care system are run by non-profit providers, since social care services are considered not to be a for-profit sector. There is no data on for-profit-organisations offering accommodation with social services for the elderly in Slovenia.

3.2. Community Care

The provision of long-term care in Slovenia was initially based on residential care. Home care was only introduced in the late 1980s and started to develop more intensively at the end of the 1990s. Before that, help at home was provided through the community nursing service within the primary health sector, but was only available to a limited extent. In the second half of the 1990s, non-institutional forms of long-term care were increasingly facilitated. In this context, concessions were awarded to private practitioners and the activities of non-governmental organisations in the area were promoted. (Republic of Slovenia 2005) Besides home care, some other non-institutional facilities were developed, e.g. day centres, sheltered housing, life-line care and meals on wheels. However, these services can still not be provided to many users. The latest extension took place in 2006, when the network of cross-generation and self-help groups substantially expanded to 22 day care centres and six regional remote assistance centres in the country. In the same year, sheltered housing was constructed at nine locations. The Ministry of Labour, Family and Social Affairs co-financed five providers with the total capacity of over 1,300 cross-generation and self-help groups for the elderly. (Ministry of Labour, Family and Social Affairs 2006c)

Community care is a mixed public and private responsibility and responsibility is divided between the national and local level. NGOs have more impact in the field of disabilities and mental health, though third sector provision of community care is still insufficient and marginal in comparison to their share in institutional residential care (ratio approximately 30:1). The funding is almost exclusively public. In the public sector, community care is provided by the centres for social work, home help organisations, homes for the elderly, day centres and family assistants. Private institutions or individuals working in the sector require concessions or licences. Services are offered by the for-profit sector (organisers of private health care, meal delivery services) and by the non-profit sector (related to churches and other secular, specialised NGOs). There were 78 organisations providing home care in the first half of the year 2008, of which most were public. In 2006, there were 5,328 users of home care each month (on average). This number grew slightly and amounted to 5,780 in the first half of the year 2008. More than half of all home care beneficiaries (53.4%) were 80 years of age or older. (Smolej et al. 2009)

Even though home treatment and health care should be fully provided by compulsory health insurance, they are not very well regulated in Slovenia. People are provided home treatment and health care by the primary health service, when for longer periods, these can be considered to be the medical part of long-term care. Analyses of these services show that expansion and greater co-ordination is necessary at the local level. The capacities of the health visiting service and the home help service are still too small. There is an increasing number of elderly who could live independently if provided with appropriate home help and support, but otherwise need to be institutionalised. Mental health patients are often in the most underprivileged and difficult situations. Home treatment is their only true option for living independently, ensuring health care and reducing their need for frequent hospitalisation. Furthermore, the accessibility of palliative care is low. It is only provided by voluntary civil associations and mostly intended for cancer patients. It is usually only covered publicly when being provided in a hospital while the cost of palliative home care is borne by the family and civil society organisations. (Ministry of Labour, Family and Social Affairs 2006c) Home nursing is provided by community nurses, who perform preventive care, health education, health services at home and some home help services. They are one of the first professional workers to identify health and social hardship as well as the needs of individuals and their families for home help and long-term care.

Persons with disabilities who require long-term care may opt for institutional care or select one of the forms of help at home. In Slovenia, institutional care has a very long tradition, while various forms of community care have only recently been established. In some parts of the country, people with disabilities can now have personal assistants. This programme is run by persons with disabilities themselves and is financed by the state, local community and user funds. (Republic of Slovenia 2005) It was initiated and developed by a group of people with disabilities (YHD – Youth Handicapped Deprivileged) and currently employs around 100 personal assistants. Though there are other organisations providing this service now as well, YHD still employs the highest number of personal assistants. By 2007, there were 24 organisations with altogether 353 personal assistants which provided personal assistance for 705 people. Almost half of the assistants work voluntarily. (Nagode, Smolej 2007) Another option for people who would otherwise be institutionalised is the choice of a family assistant. A family assistant is a kind of personal assistant who lives with the person and provides daily assistance (Social Care Act). He or she provides support for every-day living activities and enables the person to stay at home. These services are financed through a combination of public and private sources. The concept of family assistants comprises the characteristics of service, cash benefit and informal help. (further discussion below)

3.3. Cash Benefits

As a specific tool to support people in need for long-term care, a cash-benefit for care ("supplement payment for help and support") can be provided within different social security sub-systems. This additional cash-benefit is provided as a supplement to an old-age pension, a disability pension, a disability benefit, a social benefit or a disability benefit for war disabled persons. A person is entitled to it, if he or she is not able to perform ADLs (Activities of Daily Living) without another person's support. The benefit is given directly to the person in need of care and is for free use by the recipient. Since this benefit is a supplement to a certain social right (pension, social assistance or disability benefit) a person must also meet all general criteria for the particular right.

The level of the benefit varies according to different legislations. The Pension and Disability Insurance Act and the Social Care Act distinguish between three benefit levels according to the severity of the disability. A medium benefit (€ 285) is provided for those who need support for all ADLs, the lower benefit (€ 142) for those who need support for most of the ADLs and the highest benefit (€ 407) is for special cases. The Act Concerning Social Care of Mentally and Physically Handicapped Persons only comprises two different levels of the supplement. Persons who need support for all ADLs receive € 162 per month and persons who require assistance for most of their ADLs receive € 81. There is a special, more favourable scheme for war disabled persons. It involves a higher benefit for those who need support for all ADLs (€ 1,087) with a supplement for special cases (€ 272), and a lower benefit for those, who need support for most ADLs (€ 543).

In total, there were 34,396 recipients of cash benefits in 2007. (Ministry of Labour, Family and Social Affairs 2008) The cash benefits are relatively low and not sufficient for people who have higher requirements for care (more than 30 hours of services per week). The cash benefit is mostly used by recipients to subsidise the family budget and services are rendered by family members. In general, direct payments and individualised services (home help) are usually not sufficient to fully cover a person's needs. In other words – a person who needs more than two or three hours of care per day and some effort for service coordination is usually compelled to enter institutional care.

4. Voluntary and Private Sectors

Before the transition, social services in Slovenia were almost exclusively performed by public institutions. Some indicators show that the basic structure of this network remained stable even after 1990 – the proportion of budget spent, and the number of employees in the sector remained relatively unchanged. With the new legislation of the 1990s, the state abolished legal restrictions for private individuals and organisations (NGOs or commercial service providers) to provide social services as well. In 2002, about 6.7% of employees in the health and social care sector worked in non-governmental and other private organisations (3,080 workers). (Črnak-Meglič 2006)

Slovenian NGOs attempt to cover the gap in services that are not provided by the state on a national and local level. In the social care field, these mostly include residential care in group homes and support for families and communities. The first group home care services in Slovenia developed in 1992. By 2004, there were over 25 group homes and nine day centres. (Cizelj et al. 2004) This development has mainly been promoted by the voluntary sector while the public sector has been involved in constructing community residential capacities only recently. However, these services still only represent a small share of the existing residential capacities and they are mainly offered to more able users. This was an experimental development needed to gain the experience and create the knowledge of working in the community thus providing the basis for more systematic developments and reform of the system.

National and local governments increasingly recognise the value that NGOs add to the provision of basic social services. As a consequence, there is an increasing number of programmes contracted to NGOs by government entities. The services provided by NGOs are expected to reflect the needs and priorities of their constituents and communities. NGOs with a public interest status are compelled by law to provide their service to members as well as to non-members. Besides its strengths, the NGO sector also shows some deficiencies. Firstly, it does not provide sufficient quantities of particular services (e.g. personal assistance, community residence and support, day activities, etc.). Secondly, it has developed ways of hidden commercialisation (seeking users who require less effort but create the same revenue) due to the costing strategy imposed by the government. Thirdly, while being expected to provide alternatives to institutionalisation, they often only provide complements to institutions and sustain the institution and its disciplinary nature.

5. Family and Informal Care

The role of the family in long-term care is widely debated all over Europe. Most debates are centred on the question of who is responsible and obliged to provide help to persons who cannot live without help and how far this responsibility goes. A moral principle that is often stated says that the family is obliged to take care of all their members – but this is not the practice in reality for many reasons. These involve the modification of the classical family, the increasing employment of family members and their overburdening, changes in the ratio of helpers and helped and many more. The role of the state is therefore to help and provide people in need with long-term care when their families are not able to. Slovenia as a social state (Constitution, Art. 2) guarantees – as one of the human rights – the right to social security. Therefore, every human being should be entitled to receive help from the state when they are in need and not able to help themselves. Today, the legal, moral and financial obligations and burdens of families in active long-term care can be considered too high.

Research on social support networks in the Slovenian population shows that approximately 10% of the adult Slovenian population are restricted in their everyday activities. (Nagode, Dremelj 2004) More than 16% of this group require constant help with personal hygiene and dressing, 35% with everyday domestic activities and one third with arranging different activities (going to the bank, visiting the physician and similar). People with physical disabilities have larger informal networks in case of illness than the average Slovenian population. This means that they have more people to turn to when they need help or support in health issues. The most valuable source of social support to these people is family which primarily is the domain of female family members, particularly when emotional support is provided. People with physical disabilities are satisfied with their informal social support, but are not content with the formal support they receive – meaning that there are permanent and greater needs not satisfied by informal networks. (Nagode, Dremelj 2004) The study also shows that domestic and neighbourhood care of the elderly prevails in Slovenia. One person often provides several kinds of support to others. Although the social support networks of elderly people are smaller compared to other age groups, the support is satisfying for them. Among elderly, single women are least equipped with social resources. They usually depend on their child(ren) and do not have many alternative informal resources in case of need. Older people who live in extended families in rural areas have more social support resources and their major sources are their children as well.

Providing formal social care for people in need also strongly supports their female family members. The providers of long-term care are mainly women (almost 90%), both formally as a professional occupation and informally as family carers. (Ministry of Labour, Family and Social Affairs 2006a, 2006b) Most support and help in family networks is provided by female family members who have to reconcile work and other obligations, frequently suffering from overburdening. The complementary co-operation of the informal and public sector is strongly needed and should ensure access to support for all those elderly in need, independent of material resources, extended family and other conditions. (Hlebec 2004)

A major novelty of public support for family care in Slovenia was the introduction of family assistants in 2004. (see section 3.2.) Family assistants are personal assistants who live with the user and provide daily help and support. The right to choose a family assistant pertains to an adult person with disabilities who needs help to perform everyday activities. In absence of other meaningful means of community support, it immediately became very popular. There were 253 family assistants in 2004 and their number quickly increased to 1,000 in 2005. In February 2007, there were 1,349 family assistants. (Nagode, Smolej 2007; Ministry of Labour, Family and Social Affairs 2006c) A family assistant cares for a relative with disabilities, but is not responsible for their material cost of living. She or he might have left the labour market (is not employed) or is employed only part-time in order to care for another family member. A family assistant can be someone with the same permanent residence as the person with disabilities or can be another family member. The family assistant supports the person with disabilities in accordance with the needs, the help involving nursing, nutrition, housework, medical care in co-operation with a physician, accompaniment and activity in different social activities (culture, sport, education, religion) and aids a legal representative (if there is one) to perform his or her function. A family assistant has the right to a partial payment and is covered by social insurance. The payment amounts to the minimum salary of € 597 (since 1.8.2009) or a proportional payment in the case of part-time employment. Municipalities finance the family assistant but the user is liable to refund the payment for the family assistant to the extent of his or her financial capacities. Family assistants have to attend qualifying programmes and report annually to the centres for social work. The centres for social work monitor the work of family assistants and report on it.

6. Current Challenges, Trends and Debates in Slovenia

Over the past 15 years, long-term care in Slovenia was confronted with many challenges. Criticism of the institutional system has been an issue since the 1980s as total institutions were criticised and their negative aspects were denounced. Domestic criticism along with international trends have inaugurated the initially only declarative support for transforming institutional care into community care. In 1992, the first group home was set up for people with long-term mental illness and others have followed in the third sector. However, this did not yield results in terms of reducing the number of institutional residents. The process of converting the biggest social care institution in Hrastovec began only in 2002. Soon other special care institutions were to follow and the number of institutional beds in specialised institutions was reduced by 25%. They were transformed into community residence, as set in the National Plan for Social Care 2005–2010. (Ministry of Labour, Family and Social Affairs 2006a) The deinstitutionalisation was not much of an issue in the homes for the elderly and training centres and homes (mental disabilities).

Another much debated issue in long-term care and in social care in general is the problem of coordination. This is a necessity arising from the changing long-term care system and the introduction of different actors. It was argued that there should be a monitoring process alongside the evaluation of the programmes and services provided. Local actors (authorities, service providers, users and other stakeholders) should plan and implement services for various groups of users and provide the tools for quality control of the quality of services and programmes.

Users' rights and empowerment was also put on the social and health care agenda, as well as attempts to introduce methods of individual planning and individualisation of the responses to people's distress. This was done practically, by establishing users' groups and experimenting with empowering methods, but also in terms of advocacy and public debate. (see below)

Reform Proposals

The long-term care reform was expected to give answers to the above mentioned issues and major changes are expected in the near future. A public debate about the proposed reform of the long-term care system was opened in 2006. The Draft of the Long-term Care and Long-term Insurance Act outlined the following basic principles of the proposed new model:

- the development of integrated health and social services of high quality
- special services which correspond to the special needs of individuals
- priority for home care over residential care
- individualisation of services (development of individual planning)
- sustainable financing of long-term care
- division of responsibility between the society and the family
- introduction of the new social insurance sub-system – insurance for long-term care, as a result of the reorganisation and redistribution of existing resources for long-term care
- the "single entrance point"
- development of a public-private model

According to this draft, the provision of long-term care would be based on compulsory social insurance, although supplementary voluntary insurance is also discussed. The compulsory insurance would nearly cover the whole population. A special social insurance scheme for long-term care with its own organisation has been proposed, but to avoid the cost of establishing a new insurance institution, administrative support by the national health insurance organisation has been suggested.

According to the draft concept, a person in need of care who meets the prescribed criteria could choose between receiving the cash-benefit (personal budget scheme on the basis of his or her needs) and being provided with services. A combination of both benefit and services would be possible as well. The amount of money or services granted would vary according to the person's needs. The exact manner and criteria for determining the amount and type of services needed is still under discussion. There are two trends in the debate, one stemming from health care is based on the International Classification of Functioning and the other is based on the social work tradition in Slovenia. It promotes more qualitative, biographical ways of assessing needs, goals and necessities and the individual construction of the responses required.

The idea of individual and direct funding of long-term care provision was first introduced in Slovenia in 1994. Since then there has been a process of experimentation, the development of methods and pilot studies. Methods based on the principles of normalisation (social role revalorisation) and ideas on independent service brokerage have been introduced by David Brandon (1994), further developed by Jelka Škerjanc (2006; 1997) and other professionals (Videmšek et al. 2002; Flaker 1995). Methods based on the personal account of life goals revolving around the themes of control, contacts, pain and skills, have been tried out extensively as a method of personal planning of care, but were rarely accompanied by direct funding of a personal package.

There were also pilot studies and experiments with new models of care. Besides the development of residential and day care facilities there were other innovative activities in the area of long-term care. A personal assistant profile and service was developed by the critical and radical disability group YHD (Youth Handicapped Deprivileged), which offers a personally tailored service according to the users' needs. (see section 3.2.) This service, however, has not been made a standard provision yet. It was introduced in 2004 as a temporary measure to alleviate the burden on families and to facilitate the resettlement of residents of big institutions as well as to prevent new institutionalisations. Furthermore, there were experiences of individual resettlement from long-stay institutions back into the community. Individual plans for resettlement were made, but the financial schemes were missing. Another innovation in terms of direct payment was the issue of vouchers for the deaf and hard of hearing.

Through this, major improvements in their lives were noted. The pilot studies have shown that the individualisation of services can essentially improve the quality of living and that users can both handle the money and participate in organising the service provision. The experiments have also demonstrated that changes in the system of long-term care are needed in order to allow for the direct payment of services that will really meet the needs of the users. Pilot studies had, in addition to the demonstrative effect, also a developmental one. They indicated how care services could be organised, assessed, planned and coordinated. These innovations were reflected in national policies and were planned to be explored by the National Programme of Social Care up to 2005. Long-term care and direct payments have become an issue in the Resolution on the National Programme of Social Care up to 2010.

Pilot Programmes on Personal Service Plans
In order to implement such changes, a pilot study and research were designed. (Flaker et al. 2007) Preparations started in 2003 and the first users entered the scheme at the end of 2006. A group of thirteen users with learning difficulties, physical disabilities and long-term mental health problems now receive money for a personal service package. Personal service plans express their need for support (e.g. home help, escorting, advocating etc.) but also the desire for great-er independence. Institutional residents might want to move out, to experience freedom and to reconnect with the relatives. People who live at home might wish to be independent and to organise their own lives. The average personal service package amounted to € 1,214, with values ranging between € 565 and € 1,919. Half of the amount is for living expenses while the rest should cover services (34.22%), project management and administrative support (11.35%) and other expenses like transportation (<5%). (Flaker et al. 2009) The methods employed and developed for planning the personal service plans could be termed biographical and contextual. They are based on the person's narrative and try to convey their situations accurately and with precision, which differs from the standardised methods that are more approximate. Its strength is that it can combine very contemplative parts with operational ones; it can establish the person's life visions but is very concrete regarding the first steps to be undertaken. With this method, the personal service plan becomes an important

document stating what is wanted on the one hand, and the means (services and funds) needed to achieve the goals on the other.

In establishing this project and implementing individual plans, it ran into many obstacles. Some were coincidental, some were typical for introducing innovations, but some concerned reservations, disbelief or disagreement with the conceptual propositions and the idea of direct funding. These were about the sums paid, control of the money and its use, the security and responsibility of the users. On the level of the care culture, the experiment struck the obstacles of guardianship as a basic pattern of care. Besides these difficulties, the project contains various levels of knowing and doing. It enters the concrete life worlds of the users and aims at empowering them. It develops methods and procedures and makes users its contractual partners. It evaluates the labour value, establishes prices for the services and makes deals with partners. It organises the users' transactions, connects its structures with external conditions, creates and interprets rules and laws and actively involves social policy as a means of redistributing resources. Generally, this and other pilot project attempt to pave new paths for implementing social security.

Recent Developments and Outlook

To summarise, two processes could be observed in the recent developments in the organisation of long-term care in Slovenia. There were massive changes in health care and moderate changes in social care provision. In health care, the voluntary insurance scheme was introduced alongside the compulsory and supplementary payment for health services and privatisation was very early and also quite thorough and wide. The changes did not necessarily produce favourable results and sometimes quite the contrary. Some services, e.g. prevention, public health and community nursing were downsized and became less effective. In addition, privatisation was criticised for making the services less accessible for poorer citizens. Long-term care was not a priority in health care development and deinstitutionalisation of mental health services was nonexistent within the health sector. The logic of change in the social care system, however, was different. It was more cautious, trying to improve existing services and add the missing ones (community care, home help, self-help, family assistants). In later stages, it also embarked on the deinstitutionalisation of long-stay services for people with mental illnesses and intellectual disabilities. The new services meant that the model of social care did not privatise existing services, but pluralised the provision, especially for new services. Although the cautious approach in social care seems more productive, it has not overcome its primary constitutive contradictions, namely the binary arrangement of institutional and home care. The existing system of long-term care is characterised by the discontinuity of care. There is little alternative left (except in few NGOs and family assistants) but to go to the institution for those who need more than 50 hours of services a month.

The proposed long-term care legislation is thus not only a way to provide care, but also to improve the existing services and the system as a whole. The aims were to use the resources and funding more efficiently, to provide missing services (palliative care, home help, personal assistance, community residential services, etc.), but also to offer a more adequate provision (individualised planning, personally tailored services, and support for informal care). The reform also aims at providing services to those who were previously excluded and at harmonising the requirements, accessibility and entitlements to care. In doing this, the long-term care reform should take into account and connect to the current trends in social and health care. Therefore, deinstitutionalisation, individualisation, empowerment, quality assurance and evaluation, as well as planning and the coordination of services at the local and national level will be especially important over the next years.

Long-term care requires cooperation from various sectors in planning and implementation. There is a fear that health insurance and the medical profession will perceive long-term care primarily as nursing, an extension of health and hospital care. The matter of long-term care is, however, social. It is about creating services for people who need continuous care and support to organise their lives. Social care is the main provider of long-term care in the existing system through care homes, home help, and community care, and it has developed many tools needed to stimulate the scheme. It seems plausible that the long-term care system should have distinct and separate sub-systems to perform different functions. The functions of establishing and approving plans have to be separated from *planning* itself, and planning should be separated from the implementation of measures. Separating the roles of the planner and coordinator proves to be viable since they concern two separate processes and potentially colliding interests. There is also a need for a different kind and level of expertise. Individual plans could be done by social workers, who, in Slovenia, are the most equipped for the task, but other professionals can be trained in the method at little expense as well. The possibility of including users and relatives as planners and coordinators has to be examined closely. Regarding localities, their funding should be organised centrally, assessment and planning regionally and implementation locally and individually. This division of tasks can provide a sufficient degree of universality, organisational efficiency and sensitivity to the context and needs of an individual.

A question that remains unanswered is whether the payments for care should be means-tested. It is widely agreed upon that long-term care should be based on needs and not on the status, income and assets of a person. The more the payments are seen as corrective, the more they will be used to sustain the living standard and not the services needed. Hence the introduction of the new long term care scheme has to be accompanied by viable social assistance benefits for living expenses and better housing provision. The system will have to apply a new logic and method of assessing the entitlement for services and cash benefits. Not only will they have to be based on the actual needs, but they will also have to apply a more reflexive and experimental logic to allow space and time for changing and upgrading the packages. The pilot study proved that the claim can be approved in a destigmatising manner and that it is important to organise it as empowerment. By entering the scheme, the user can achieve greater sovereignty and be included as a contractual individual. Stigmatisation and degrada-tion can and should be avoided.

The method developed in Slovenia has these effects. Moreover, it is sensitive to the specific situations and enables the response to be adequate, answering to the singular and specific needs of an individual. It thereby increases cost effectiveness, since a person gets what he or she really needs. It can encompass the complexities of the life situation of an individual, is very easy to understand for the user and still makes the quantification and calculation of costs possible. It is expected that the new system will encourage service providers to put up more diverse offers. There will probably also be a higher number of providers, among them also brokers of services. We hope that the system will encourage resettlement into the community and to independent living from big long-stay institutions, by making special provisions for doing so. The introduction of the new long-term care scheme will definitely require changes in the culture of cooperation between the different providers of long-term care. The development of ways that would ensure continuity of the provision as well as coordinated efforts for the user's wellbeing is needed. The transition from a guardian model, from the model of divided and segmented care ("our and their users") to a system of common care, where the user is not an object but an autonomous entity and care for her or him is a common project. A different division of responsibility requires a move from a "zone" to "pressing", from services that cover a real or symbolic space to the assertive action in the space, continuing follow-up and partnership.

Bibliography

Brandon, David (ed) (1994) Money for change. Cambridge: Anglia University.

Cizelj, Milka; Ferlež, Zdenka; Flaker, Vito; Lukač, Josip; Pogačar, Miha; Švab, Vesna (2004) Vizija posebnih socialnih zavodov (*Special social care platform*). Ljubljana: Skupnost socialnih zavodov Slovenije in Fakulteta za socialno delo.

Črnak-Meglič, Andreja (2006) Development of the welfare state in 1990s and at the start of the new century. In: Črnak-Meglič, Andreja (ed) Children and youth in the transitional society. Analysis of the situation in Slovenia. Ljubljana: Aristej.

Cvetko, Aleksej; Kavar Vidmar, Andreja; Kresal, Barbara (2007) Social security law – Slovenia. In: Blanpain, Roger (ed) International encyclopaedia of laws. Social security law. Haag: Kluwer Law International.

Eurostat (2009) Eurostat Database. Available from: http://epp.eurostat.ec.europa.eu (31 December 2009).

Flaker, Vito (1995) K navadnosti izjemnega (*Towards Ordinary of Uncommon*). In: Socialno delo, Vol. 34, No. 6, 361–372.

Flaker, Vito; Cuder, Maja; Nagode, Mateja; Podbevšek, Kristina; Podgornik, Nevenka; Rode, Nino; Škerjanc, Jelka; Zidar, Romana (2007) Vzpostavljanje osebnih paketov storitev (*Personal care package implementation*). Ljubljana: Fakulteta za socialno delo.

Flaker, Vito; Kresal, Barbara; Mali, Jana; Miloševič–Arnold, Vida; Rihter, Liljana; Velikonja, Ingrid (2004) Delo z dementnimi osebami – priprava modela obravnave oseb z demenco: projekt – sklepno poročilo (*Working with people with dementia – Preparation of the dementia treatment model*). Ljubljana: Fakulteta za socialno delo.

Flaker, Vito; Nagode, Mateja; Rafaelič, Andreja; Udovič, Nataša; Jakob, Polonca (2009) Individualizirano financiranje storitev socialnega varstva *(Individualised funding of social care services)*. Ljubljana: Inštitut RS za socialno varstvo.

Government PR and Media Office (2006) Slovenija jutri, Strategija razvoja Slovenije *(A modern welfare state)*. Ljubljana.

Hlebec Valentina (2004) Socialna omrežja starostnikov *(Social networks of elderly)*. In: Novak, Mojca (ed) Omrežja socialne opore prebivalstva Slovenije *(The social support networks in Slovenia)*. Ljubljana: Inštitut Republike Slovenije za socialno varstvo.

ILO Convention No. 102 (1952) Convention concerning minimum standards of social security. http://www.ilo.org/ilolex/cgi-lex/convde.pl?C102 (31 December 2009).

Javornik, Jana S. (ed) (2007) Social overview 2006. Ljubljana: Institute of Macroeconomic Analysis and Development.

Jacović Anita (2008) Sistem socialne zaščite v Sloveniji od leta 1996 do leta 2006 *(Social protection system in Slovenia from 1996 to 2006)*, Radenci, 5–7.11.2008: 17. Statistični dnevi Zmanjšanje administrativnih bremen zbiranja podatkov v statističnih raziskovanjih.

Kresal, France (1998) Zgodovina socialne in gospodarske politike v Sloveniji od liberalizma do druge svetovne vojne *(The history of social and economic policy in Slovenia from liberalism to World War II)*. Ljubljana: Cankarjeva založba.

Mali, Jana (2007) Vloga in pomen socialnega dela v razvoju institucionalnega varstva starih ljudi v Sloveniji *(The role and significance of social work in the development of institutional care of older people in Slovenia – doctoral dissertation)*. Ljubljana: Fakulteta za socialno delo.

Ministrstvo za delo, družino in socialne zadeve (2006) Predlog Zakona o dolgotrajni oskrbi in zavarovanju za dolgotrajno oskrbo *(Draft of the long-term care and long-term insurance act)*. Ljubljana.

Ministry of Labour, Family and Social Affairs (2006a) Resolucija o nacionalnem programu socialnega varstva za obdobje 2006–2010 *(Resolution on the national programme of social care for 2006–2010)*. Ljubljana.

Ministry of Labour, Family and Social Affairs (2006b) Strategy of care for elderly until 2010. Solidarity, living together and quality ageing of the population. Ljubljana.

Ministry of Labour, Family and Social Affairs (2006c) National report on strategies for social protection and social inclusion 2006–2008. Ljubljana.

Ministry of Labour, Family and Social Affairs (2008) National report on strategies for social protection and social inclusion 2008–2010. Ljubljana.

Ministry of Labour, Family and Social Affairs (2009) News on residential care. http://www.mddsz.gov.si/nc/si/splosno/cns/novica/article/12106/6181/?type=98 (18 August 2009).

Nagode, Mateja; Smolej, Simona (2007) Spremljanje izvajanja socialnovarstvenih programov, ki dopolnjujejo javno mrežo na tem področju: Analiza programov osebne asistence (*Monitoring the programmes of social care that are supplementing the public sector. Analysis of personal assistance programmes*). Ljubljana: Inštitut Republike Slovenije za socialno varstvo.

Nagode, Mateja; Dremelj, Polona (2004) Omrežja socialne opore oseb z gibalnimi težavami (*Social support networks of people with movement disabilities*). In: Novak, Mojca (ed) Omrežja socialne opore prebivalstva Slovenije (*The social support networks in Slovenia*). Ljubljana: Inštitut Republike Slovenije za socialno varstvo.

Normativni program dela Vlade RS za leto 2009. http://www.vlada.si/fileadmin/dokumenti/si/program_vlade/pdv2009_0409.pdf (31 December 2009).

Republic of Slovenia (2005) National report on health care and long-term care in the Republic of Slovenia. Ljubljana.

Smolej, Simona; Jakob, Polonca; Nagode, Mateja; Žiberna, Vid; Jerina, Petra; Kenda, Aleš (2009) Analiza izvajanja pomoči na domu (*The analysis of home help service*). Ljubljana: Inštitut Republike Slovenije za socialno varstvo.

Škerjanc, Jelka (1997) Načrtovanje neodvisnega življenja v sistemu neposrednega financiranja (*Independent life planning in the system of direct payments*). In: Uršič, Cveto; Zupan, Anton (ed) Neodvisno življenje najtežje gibalno oviranih (*Independent living of the severely handicapped*). Ljubljana: Inštitut RS za rehabilitacijo, 53–69.

Škerjanc Jelka (2006) Individualno načrtovanje z udejanjanjem ciljev (*Individual planning and goal implementation*). Ljubljana: Center za poklicno izobraževanje in usposabljanja.

Statistical Office of the Republic of Slovenia (2008) Statistical yearbook of the Republic of Slovenia 2008. Ljubljana.

Statistical Office of the Republic of Slovenia (2009) Statistical yearbook of the Republic of Slovenia 2009. Ljubljana.

Urad Republike Slovenije za makroekonomske analize in razvoj (2009) Poročilo o razvoju 2009 (*Development report 2009*). Ljubljana.

Vertot, Petronela (2007) Disabled persons, the elderly and other persons with special needs in Slovenia. Ljubljana: Statistical Office of the Republic of Slovenia.

Videmšek, Petra; Zaviršek, Darja; Zorn, Jelka (2002) Inovativne metode v socialnem delu. Opolnomočenje ljudi, ki potrebujejo podporo za samostojno življenje (*Innovative methods in social work. Empowerment of people who need support for independent living*). Ljubljana: Študentska založba (Scripta).

Zakon o socialnem varstvu (*Social care act*), Official Journal of the Republic of Slovenia, 36/04 – UPB.

10

A Comparative Analysis
of Long-term Care
in Central and South Eastern Europe

August Österle

1. Introduction

Across Europe, the organisation, provision and funding of long-term care is faced with manifold challenges. These include ageing societies and growing care needs, changes in the context of traditional family care arrangements, broader socio-economic developments, changes in expectations and perceptions towards care responsibilities and substantial pressure on public budgets. Historically, long-term care has long been widely neglected as a social risk. The bulk of care has been and in many countries still is largely organised, provided and funded within family or other informal networks. In the past two decades, however, many European countries have started to substantially extend existing programmes and to implement comprehensive social protection schemes in long-term care. (Österle, Rothgang 2010) In other countries, including those in Central and South Eastern Europe (CSEE), debates on the future of long-term care have intensified in the more recent past, even though the debates are often limited to expert groups. This is a consequence of various factors. Tradition and strong perceptions in society are placing responsibilities for long-term care in the family context. Existing welfare state approaches are fragmented and social assistance oriented, leaving help and support for older people in need of care largely to families. There is a lack of financial resources and comparatively low policy priority for long-term care. Finally, a broader debate on the future of long-term care has been hindered by a lack of data and information and large variations in the general understanding and conceptualisation of long-term care.

While there is a growing body of comparative literature on long-term care in Europe, countries in the CSEE region have often been neglected in these studies. By introducing and analysing the developments in long-term care in eight CSEE countries this book attempts to contribute to incorporate this region in the growing comparative long-term care literature. When referring to CSEE countries in this concluding chapter, it refers to those countries analysed in chapters 3 to 9 (Croatia, Czech Republic, Hungary, Romania, Serbia, Slovakia and Slovenia). Austria as the eighth country covered in this book represents one of those countries where major long-term care reforms have taken place from the early 1990s. This final chapter emphasises a comparative approach. It analyses structures, developments and trends in the region, and compares these with broader European developments. It attempts to identify and discuss commonalities, diversities and trends in CSEE long-term care systems. The chapter is organised in eight sections. In the following part, the broader welfare state context and an often lacking recognition of long-term care as a social risk in CSEE welfare states will be introduced. The third section focuses on an analysis of the family as the main actor in providing and funding long-term care. Sections four to six then discuss public sector roles in long-term care. Starting with an overview of public long-term care expenditure, these sections discuss the main features of provisions in the residential care and the community care sector, the availability of long-term care related cash benefits and the funding of these provisions. While pluralisation and privatisation have been playing an important role in the transformation debate, section seven will show that the private sector has only grown more substantially in the recent past, not least by changing funding rules and developing public-private partnership models. The concluding section discusses current trends and perspectives in developing long-term care policies and in securing the availability of long-term care for older people in need.

2. The Broader Welfare State Context in CSEE

In the past two decades, welfare systems in CSEE countries have undergone major transitions, marked by the fall of the communist regimes in Central Eastern Europe, the disintegration of the former Yugoslavia and the war period in that region. Social policy developments during the transition period have been driven by the breakdown of previous systems or the inadequacy of its provisions, the search for a new social protection model, opposing political ideologies and recommendations of international organisations, but also pressures arising from economic situations that deteriorated for large parts of the populations in the early years of the transformation. (Cook 2010; Cerami, Vanhuysse 2009; Inglot 2008; Nelson et al. 1997)

There is a growing comparative welfare state and public policy literature covering the Central Eastern European countries. Several attempts have been made in recent years to identify similarities and differences to existing models of the welfare state. (Hacker 2009; Castles, Obinger 2008; Fenger 2007; Cerami 2006; Kovács 2002) Coverage of South Eastern Europe, however, is still more limited in these research activities. (Stubbs, Zrinščak 2009) Authors disagree on whether the Central Eastern European region forms a distinctive welfare state cluster or a hybrid of other cluster characteristics. But they all emphasise the importance of the communist history, the role of social insurance as a pre-communist legacy and the impact of the socio-economic context on welfare state developments in the transition period. Social insurance orientation has generally been playing a major role in social policy transformation. But within that context countries have been developing distinct designs with important elements of the residual and liberal model, but also the universal model. International and supranational organisations such as the International Monetary Fund, the World Bank or the European Union have been important actors in the transformation process. Their emphasis on financial stability and on market development had a significant impact for welfare state development. (see e.g. Orenstein 2009; Deacon, Stubbs 2008)

During the entire period from the early 1990s, long-term care did not play a prominent role in social policy transformation in CSEE. (Österle 2010; Munday, Lane 1998) Long-term care policies have been and often remain highly fragmented up to date. In general, the needs of poor and frail older people in CSEE are addressed via social assistance and social service regulations. Provisions for specific sub-groups are made by different welfare sectors including disability policies, health policies or pension policies. The health system, in particular, often provides the only universal type service to people in need of nursing care, both in special inpatient units or in the outpatient sector.

In the transition process, debates on long-term care and more specifically on care for older people have, if at all, emerged in expert groups. Experts from governmental and non-governmental sectors made attempts to raise long-term care as a policy issue, they have developed pilot programmes but also broader policy proposals. Only in the past few years, ageing and long-term care are more specifically recognised in public policy debates. This is the case in the context of national strategy papers addressing the challenges arising from ageing societies, as in the Croatian *Development Programme of Services for the Elderly*, the Romanian *Programme of National Interest on the Development of Domiciliary Care*, in the Serbian national *Social Welfare Development Strategy* or in the Slovenian *Strategy of care for the elderly until 2010.* (see chapters 3 to 9) Beyond the national level, the Open Method of Coordination in the European Union had an important impact on raising awareness for long-term care as a social policy concern. The Open Method of Coordination requires Member States to develop national strategy reports on social protection and social inclusion that also cover health and long-term care. (European Commission 2009b; Theobald, Kern 2009)

3. Family Care: The Major Source of Long-term Care Provision

Even in countries with a longer tradition of publicly funded care services and in countries where social protection coverage in the field of long-term care has been substantially extended in the past two decades, families still provide the largest amount of care provided to people in need of regular help and support. (OECD 2005) And it is close family members, mostly women, living in the same household or living in a household in the vicinity that provide long hours of care work. (Lamura et al. 2008; Mestheneos, Triantafillou 2005) With growing recognition of the work provided in these arrangements and of the burdens involved, and with growing awareness of the increasing number of people in need of care, policies across Europe have started to react with the development of policies that intend to support and relief informal carers. At the same time, the development of more comprehensive community care or cash for care systems, explicitly or implicitly, also can work as a measure to sustain informal care resources. When benefits are targeted more strictly to the most needy population for cost containment considerations, this can even lead to a re-informalisation of care.

In CSEE, the role of the family has been and still is of central significance to long-term care provision and funding. It is mostly close family and household members that are organising, providing and funding care for their relatives. According to a Eurobarometer survey 2002, about 23% of Europeans are providing informal care. In many CSEE countries, informal long-term care provision is on slightly higher levels. These differences become more pronounced for care-giving provided within households. Compared to an average of 11% of people providing informal care inside the household, the respective proportion is beyond 14% in Hungary, Romania, the Czech Republic, Poland or Bulgaria. (Alber, Köhler 2004)

Self-reported levels of informal care-giving are influenced by different factors, including the definition and understanding of care and care-giving, the institutional and the cultural context. Variations across countries, therefore, have to be dealt with caution. There are, however, two major issues that support evidence of relatively large levels of informal care-giving in CSEE countries. First of all, there is a lack of alternatives that would allow an adequate and affordable coverage of care needs. There is a lack of social protection infrastructure which limits availability and accessibility of residential care and of community care services. Additionally, only a small proportion of the population can afford private sector provisions at market prices. (see sections 5 to 7) Secondly, as outlined in the introductory chapter, the dominance of family care-giving is deeply anchored in societal values and the perceptions of family obligations. Under state socialism, participation in the workforce provided access to social protection, which also led to high levels of employment. But, traditional patterns of the division of responsibilities within families remained predominant. While there have been well developed child care services, long-term care-giving for older people to a large extent was left to families and other informal arrangements. In the transition process, these traditional concepts were even reinforced, by cuts in social protection schemes and by ideologies drawing on traditional patterns of family responsibilities. (Klenner, Leiber 2010; Pascall, Lewis 2004; Pascall, Manning 2000).

According to a 2007 Eurobarometer survey, 45% of those living in the EU27 countries prefer to be cared for at home by a relative. In most Central and Eastern European countries preferences are beyond this average, with peak values in Hungary (66%) and in Poland (70%). (see table 10.1; European Commission 2007) Care at home by a professional service is supported by 24% in the EU27 average, while only between 8% (Hungary) and 18% (Slovakia) of the respondents in the CSEE study countries prefer this option. On the other hand, preferences for care in a long-term care institution (nursing home) are significantly above EU27 average (8%) in a couple of CSEE countries, including Slovenia (20%), the Czech Republic (16%) or Croatia (15%). Relatively larger support for this option might be explained by the fact that institutional care often is the only alternative to informal care in CSEE, while a largely underdeveloped community care system is not perceived as an option.

Similar patterns occur when people are asked about the expected rather than the preferred care arrangement. Compared to a European (EU27) average of 45% preferring care at home by a relative, this type of care arrangement is expected by between 57% (in the Czech Republic) and 70% (in Croatia) in the CSEE study countries. Slovenia (44%) is European average. In CSEE countries, the expectation to receive professional care at home is below the respective level of preferences, while expectations and preferences are on similar levels with regard to institutional care. (see table 10.1; European Commission 2007) This family orientation is confirmed by the survey in a number of additional questions. In most CSEE countries, a larger proportion regards an arrangement where an older father or mother in need of long-term care lives with one of their children as the best option. Those who regard public or private service providers visiting the home as the best option only represent about half of the European average of 27%. The statements "Children should pay for the care of their parents if their parents' income is not sufficient" and "Care should be provided by close relatives of the dependent person, even if that means that they have to sacrifice their career to some extent" are also supported by a larger proportion of the CSEE population as compared with the European average. (European Commission 2007)

Table 10.1: Long-term care provision: Preferences and expectations

	home: relative	home: care service	home: personal carer	home of family	institution	no answer
	If you needed regular help and long-term care: preferred care arrangement / expected care arrangement					
EU27	45 / 45	24 / 23	12 / 10	5 / 4	8 / 9	6 / 9
Austria	39/ 36	24 / 28	12 / 11	6 / 6	11 / 11	8 / 8
Croatia	48 / 70	13 / 4	10 / 4	10 / 7	15 /11	4 /4
Czech Rep.	54 / 57	11 / 10	9 / 6	6 / 5	16 / 14	4 / 8
Hungary	66 / 62	8 / 7	6 / 6	6 / 6	10 / 11	4 / 8
Romania	48 / 64	16 / 9	10 / 7	10 / 5	6 / 5	10 / 10
Slovakia	50 / 68	18 / 10	13 / 7	7 / 4	7 / 7	5 / 4
Slovenia	43 / 44	15 / 12	10 / 9	9 / 5	20 / 25	3 / 5
France	23 / 24	43 / 45	15 / 13	3 / 2	10 / 12	6 / 4
Germany	48 / 45	24 / 26	12 / 9	6 / 4	7 / 8	3 / 8
Italy	44 / 38	19 / 15	16 / 16	4 / 5	8 / 9	9 / 17
Sweden	34 / 31	29 / 31	20 / 12	3 / 1	12 / 21	2 / 4
UK	44 / 42	28 / 26	10 / 10	7 / 5	5 / 8	6 / 9

Definition: Agreement with the statements in %. Response categories: "In your own home by a relative (e.g. partner, nearby, etc.)", "In your own home by a professional care service", "In your own home by a personal carer hired by yourself or by your relatives", "In the home of one of your close family members", "In a long-term care institution (nursing home)".

(Source: European Commission 2007)

In-depth studies on factors that determine family arrangements, on the characteristics of these arrangements and on the burdens involved with family caregiving are relatively scarce for the CSEE region. (Holmerová 2007; Hvalič Touzery 2007; Błędowski et al. 2006; Barvíková, Bartoňová 2005; Széman 2004) Existing studies (see also the discussion in chapters 3 to 9) confirm that it is mainly women providing family care (as well as formal care). In general, it is assumed that about 80% of family members providing regular care and support are women. Women are more likely to provide personal help and help in the household and they mostly work as the main carer spending long hours on care work. Larger proportions of men being involved in long-term care work are reported for Slovakia and Romania. Though there is no systematic assessment available, a larger unemployment rate among men, and women migrating for domestic and care work to other countries (for Romania see, e.g., Dobre, Roth 2005) might to a considerable extent explain that fact.

The provision of care by close family members is determined by a mix of factors. The aforementioned perception of family responsibility and the lack of publicly (co-)funded formal care services are major determinants. What people perceive as a duty of the family or as a part of family live is in most countries also legally defined as a family obligation, at least in the context of social assistance regulations. Accordingly, means-testing not only involves the income of the user, but also considers the economic situation of the family or the household. The chapter on the Czech Republic (see chapter 4) points at experiences with institutionalisation (hospitals or nursing homes) that led people to provide informal care. Other countries, in particular Romania, Serbia or Slovakia (see chapters 6, 7 and 8), emphasise that sharing the resources in a household with a person in need of care can also be part of a survival strategy. In many CSEE countries, means-tested allowances are paid to informal carers in case they have given up employment or in case they are unemployed. (see section 6) Even if these benefits are on low levels, they can become an important part of the household income, in particular in case of unemployment. For Slovakia, it is reported that about 45% of family carers have been unemployed before they started providing informal care. (see chapter 8; Repková 2008) Another economic strategy, also reported for Slovakia, is the case where the provision of informal care is connected with inheritance procedures.

The extent to which families are able to provide long hours of care work is not least co-determined by household characteristics and employment patterns of household members. The amount of informal long-term care provision increases with vicinity between family care-giver and the person in need of care. Growing mobility within regions, from rural towards urban areas and towards other countries, trends characterising many of the CSEE countries, reduce the ability to provide long hours of care. A study on older people living on islands in Croatia has shown that for many respondents the responsibility to care for parents was among the major reasons not to leave the island in their youth. (see chapter 3; Babić et al. 2004) But, the aforementioned trends put increasing pressure on traditional informal care arrangements. And these developments make older people in the rural areas a particularly vulnerable group. While formal care services are much less developed in these areas (if available at all), older people increasingly also become deprived of informal care resources. There is some anecdotic evidence, for Bratislava for example, that this increasingly makes children bring their frail older parents to their current place of living.

With growing awareness of long-term care as a social risk, there has also been a growing focus on the role, the burdens and the needs of informal carers across Europe, including CSEE countries. (Holmerová 2007; Hvalič Touzery 2007; Błędowski et al. 2006; Barvíková, Bartoňová 2005; Széman 2004) Approaches that are developed to support and to relief informal carers are either of direct or indirect nature. Policies improving availability of and access to services or providing care allowances to care recipients (see sections 4 and 5) also can work as relief or support for informal carers. Support measures directed at family carers include allowances paid to informal carers, social security coverage related to informal care-giving, relief programmes or counselling. (Lamura et al. 2008; Mestheneos, Triantafillou 2005) The development of such measures is limited in CSEE, but there is an important tradition of paying means-tested allowances to informal carers, mostly also linked to social protection coverage. (see section 6) Relief programmes or counselling mostly exist as pilot programmes and mostly in major urban areas. Foster care, as a specific family care arrangement, plays an important role in South Eastern Europe. In the foster care system, frail older people are living with another family which is financially compensated by the state. This is particularly widespread in Croatia and became a policy issue more recently in Serbia. (see chapters 3 and 7 as well as section 5 below)

4. Public Long-term Care Policies: Measures and Expenditure Levels

In a European comparative perspective, a longer tradition of comprehensive long-term care policies only exists in the Northern European countries. In other European regions, long-term care was increasingly recognised as a major social risk in the past two decades. Earlier provisions have mostly been social assistance oriented and largely fragmented between federal levels and between welfare sectors addressing long-term care needs of people with disabilities, those of frail older or of chronically ill persons. In the past two decades, many European countries have seen extensions of earlier social care schemes or the implementation of novel more comprehensive long-term care policies. Countries have been moving from mostly social assistance oriented support to social protection schemes combining universal principles with still substantial individual responsibilities. (Österle, Rothgang 2010; Pavolini, Ranci 2008) Historically, residential care has been a major public response to long-term care needs across Europe, but in many countries with strict means- and asset-testing, often also involving family or household members. From the 1980s, policy rhetoric started to emphasise community care orientation, even if a more substantial expansion of services in many countries only started from the 1990s or even later. (Doyle, Timonen 2008; Burau et al. 2007; Anttonen et al. 2003) While the service approach has dominated long-term care policies in most countries till the 1990s, cash for care orientation became a major characteristic of policy developments in the past two decades. (Da Roit, Le Bihan, 2010; Da Roit et al. 2009; Ungerson, Yeandle 2007; Timonen et al. 2006; Glendinning, Kemp 2006) The various approaches share some common objectives (choice, autonomy, consumer-driven demand), but they differ considerably in the concrete specification and the potential impact on the development of the care sector. Approaches include those in Austria or Italy where benefits are paid to the person in need of care without predefining the use of the benefit. In the German long-term care insurance system, users can choose between a cash benefit (in this case similar to the aforementioned approach), services or a combination of the two. In the Netherlands and in France, the idea of the cash for care approach (ensuring autonomy and choice) is combined with pre-defined uses, which might include social service consumption, the employment of professional carers and helpers or even the employment of family members as live-in carers.

In CSEE, the role of the public sector in long-term care is still more limited and characterised by fragmentation and social assistance orientation. In the 1990s and the early years of this decade, long-term care was not identified as a separate social risk and did as such not play any prominent role in social policy transformation and development. (Österle 2010) There have been important changes in social assistance legislation, in health care or in disability policies that had an impact on long-term care. But, with the exception of the Czech Republic, countries have not yet approached long-term care more comprehensively. As will be shown in the following sections, historically, residential care was and often still is the major public response, even if on lower levels than in most Western European countries. Additionally, important provisions – often the only service available across countries – are made by the health sector. More recent shifts towards community care are above all developed in the urban areas, while these services often remain unavailable in rural areas. More than in Western European countries, payments made to informal family carers are an important element of the social welfare approach towards dependency in CSEE. While there are proposals for establishing long-term care as a separate branch of the welfare state in many of these countries, a more comprehensive scheme has so far only been established in the Czech Republic. (see chapter 4)

Before discussing the welfare state role in long-term care in CSEE in the following sections in more detail, an overview of public long-term care spending provides an indication of the current relative importance of the public role in long-term care. Such an approach, however, is limited by the availability and the comparability of respective data. This is caused by the fact that long-term care in most countries is not established as a separate social risk. Existing provisions can be found in the health system, in the pension system, in policies for the disabled and most importantly as part of social assistance. Apart from the frictions these overlapping responsibilities can cause, they also limit the availability of comparable data. Additionally, differences in national definitions of long-term care expenditure, differences in the range of services that are included in the respective definitions or the lack of systematically collected data on respective classifications still hinder accurate comparisons.

Table 10.2 provides an overview of existing data, using information provided by European Commission (2009a), the OECD, Eurostat, Huber et al. (2009) as well as country chapters in this book. While Eurostat covers public long-term care expenditure for the older population, other sources do not differentiate by age. According to European Commission (2009a) projections, EU countries spent an average of 1.2% of their GDP on long-term care in 2007. There are, however, huge variations across Europe. While the EU15 average is 1.3%, the EU12 average is 0.3%. Sweden is the biggest spender with 3.5% of GDP, compared to Romania with a spending level of below 0.1%. Data published by the OECD (2010) shows a variation between 3.5% in Sweden and less than 0.5% in all the CSEE countries for which data is provided. Eurostat figures, for most countries, are substantially lower, which at least partly is explained by just focusing on long-term care expenditure for those aged 65+. (Eurostat 2009) Here, public long-term care expenditure accounts for 2.4% of GDP in Sweden, and again less than 0.5% for countries in the CSEE region. Similar levels are also published for France (0.33%) and Germany (0.16%). At least for these two countries, differences between the two aforementioned sources cannot just be attributed to the 65+ focus in Eurostat statistics. Data from other national sources (Huber et al. 2009; chapters 2–9) confirms the overall picture, even if on slightly larger levels in CSEE countries where adequate national data is available.

Considering the different sources and the aforementioned limitations in data availability, three groups of countries can be identified in terms of long-term care expenditure. In Northern European countries, especially Sweden, Norway, the Netherlands and Denmark, public long-term care spending clearly is beyond European average. In a second group of countries, including Austria, Belgium, Germany, France or the United Kingdom, public long-term care spending is closer to the European average. Among the new EU member states, Slovenia is closest to the European average. Some countries, however, show quite substantial variation when using different sources, as for example Germany, Italy and Slovenia. While they would join the medium group of countries when following European Commission (2009a) or OECD (2010) figures, Eurostat (2009) figures show substantially lower levels of public expenditure for these countries. The picture for Southern European countries is somewhat inconsistent.

Table 10.2: Public long-term care expenditure as % of GDP

	European Commission[a] (year 2007)	OECD[b] (year 2007)	EUROSTAT[c] (year 2006)	National sources[d]
EU 27	1.2	:	0.48[p]	1.3**
EU 15	1.3	:	0.497[p]	:
EU 12	0.3	:	:	:
Austria	1.3	1.3	0.996	1.39* / 1.3[(i)]**
Czech Republic	0.2	0.4	0.326	0.55* / 0.3[(i)]**
Hungary	0.3	0.3	0.292	:
Romania	0.0	:	0.023	:
Slovakia	0.2	0.3	0.405[p]	0.62*
Slovenia	1.1	:	0.16[p]	1.09* / 0.8**
France	1.4	1.6	0.328[p]	0.9[(i)]**
Germany	0.9	1.3	0.156[p]	:
Italy	1.7	:	0.12[p]	1.7**
Sweden	3.5	3.5	2.393	:
United Kingdom	0.8	:	0.993[p]	1.2[(ii)]**

[a] European Commission (2009a) defines public expenditure on long-term care according to the System of Health Accounts Classification as comprised of services of long-term nursing care and social services of long term care.

[b] The OECD indicator "Total long-term care expenditure" includes expenditure on long-term nursing care and on social services of long-term care. Long-term nursing care comprises ongoing health and nursing care given to in-patients who need assistance on a continuing basis due to chronic impairments and a reduced degree of independence and activities of daily living. Social services of long-term care comprise home help and residential care services. (OECD 2010)

[c] The Eurostat indicator "Expenditure on care for elderly" is defined as the percentage share of social protection expenditure devoted to old age care in GDP. These expenditures cover care allowances, accommodation, and assistance in carrying out daily tasks. (Eurostat 2009)

[d] National data refers to measurements from the Statistical Offices or Ministries of the respective country for the most recent year. They are either drawn from the country reports* in this book or from Huber et al. (2009)**. Data marked with [(i)] refers mostly to care in old age. Note that indicators are based on different methodology and may comprise different fields of expenditure. Data marked with [(ii)] refers to England.

(Source: European Commission 2009a; Eurostat 2009; OECD 2010; Huber et al. 2009; chapters 2–9 in this book)

Some data sources place Italy or Greece in or even above the European average in terms of expenditure, while other sources would place Southern European countries on similar levels as Central and Eastern European countries. Except for Slovenia, CSEE countries studied in this book belong to a third group with low public long-term care expenditure. In the Czech Republic, Hungary, Slovakia or Romania, public long-term care spending is below 0.5% of GDP according to international sources. But even taking into account national sources that indicate a larger share of GDP, long-term care expenditure remains below European average. As outlined in chapter 1, countries in this region share all of the challenges that will increase long-term care needs in the coming decades. As a consequence, a substantial increase in long-term care expenditure is forecasted. This increase will be even more pronounced, when more comprehensive long-term care policies are implemented, as it was the case in the Czech Republic from 2007. (see chapter 4)

5. Public Long-term Care Policies: Services

In general, the provision of publicly co-funded services is characterised by the aforementioned fragmentation of long-term care policies, most importantly between health and social care. In the health sector, institutionalisation and provisions in the community are important, even if just temporarily. In the inpatient sector, older people are provided with care in special geriatric care units, in transitional units but also in general acute care units. The inpatient sector, however, is under increasing pressure as cost containment reforms in the health sector are aimed at a reduction of beds, not least of beds providing care to older people in need of long-term care, who – because of a lack of alternative social care provisions – stay in hospitals. Outpatient health services are the most widespread community care service in terms of regional coverage, but are limited in terms of what is defined as nursing care and in terms of the benefit period.

In the social care sector, residential care has long been the most important publicly co-funded service type, usually also provided by the public sector. Even if residential care provision – in terms of bed density – is on relatively lower levels than in many Western European countries, it still is the main source of care provision when family care or other informal care is not available. However, current developments show a clear shift towards community care, but respective developments have intensified only in the more recent past. In the transition process in the 1990s and the early years of this decade, major changes in service provision were linked to a decentralisation of social care. The relative importance of residential care and the dominance of the public sector as the major provider organisation did not significantly change for years. In the past decade, however, governments have intensified their efforts to strengthen community care services and to change the regulatory context and funding principles in order to facilitate the access of private providers.

The aforementioned data problems for comparative long-term care analysis also apply to services, for residential care and even more so for community care provisions. Differences in the terminology used, different ranges of service types that are offered, the division between health and social care sector responsibilities, or responsibilities split between different federal levels make a quantification of the infrastructure highly problematic. For example, different institutional types are sometimes even found within one building. Provisions in the health sector are either officially declared as beds in chronic care units, but they might also be declared as acute care beds while actually used as chronic care beds. Social care statistics only partly differentiate between long-term care needs and other needs and might be based on counting service users or service units. Also, the definition of services and the definition of boundaries between service packages differ largely between countries. Figures from different sources, therefore, point at quite some variation in service density, without changing the general picture of medium to low levels in the CSEE region when compared to other European countries.

According to national statistics presented in earlier chapters in this book, bed density in the residential care sector is beyond 35 beds per 1,000 population 65+ in Slovenia, Austria, Hungary and the Czech Republic, while it is below 12 beds in Slovakia, Serbia and Romania. According to OECD (2010) statistics, bed density (beds in nursing and residential care facilities, per 1,000 population 65+, 2007) is smaller in the Czech Republic (20.7), but similar to other Western European countries in Hungary (40.7) or Slovakia (47.4). Bed density is largest in Sweden (84.4), the Netherlands (70.8) or Belgium (70.7).

While Germany (48.7) or France (45.1) would be on similar levels as Hungary or Slovakia, Italy just provides 15.9 beds per 1,000 population 65+. A Eurobarometer survey 2007 also indicates the limitations in the availability of residential care in CSEE. A relatively larger proportion of the population in this European region finds access to residential care settings very difficult or fairly difficult. (see table 10.3) While the respective proportion is 28% in the EU 27, it is between 33% (Romania) and 65% (Czech Republic) in the CSEE study countries. Less than a quarter of the respondents find access to nursing homes easy in CSEE, compared to 40% in Austria or 48% in Germany.

The country analyses in chapters 3 to 9 indicate that the shortage experienced in accessing nursing homes is to a considerable extent due to a lack of community care services that could at least partly cover respective long-term care needs. Compared to institutional care, the availability of social services provided in the community is even more limited and fragmented. Because of the fragmentation, systematically collected information on the country level is still extremely scarce. As in the residential care sector, community services are provided by the health sector and the social sector. The availability of nursing care funded by the health sector is more broadly available in terms of regional coverage and mostly the only mobile service available across the country. But, it is limited in terms of the periods for which such services can be used and it is limited because of strict medical eligibility criteria. In the social sector, the range of services provided and the differentiation between service types varies in each country. In general, there is huge variation in service coverage. It is more extensive in the urban areas, while remote areas are partly completely deprived from such services. The village caretaker in Hungary is an example how some basic support can be guaranteed on the local level. (see chapter 6) Similar to the residential care sector, public actors also dominate social service provision in the community in most countries. But the private non-profit sector plays a growing role, both as initiator of services in previously deprived regions, as a provider of services that were initially not available and as a contracted provider in public-private partnership models. Similar to residential care, people in CSEE countries perceive access to care services for dependent older people living in their private home more difficult than in the EU27 average. (see table 10.3) While 41% of respondents in the EU27 find access to care services very easy or fairly easy, the respective proportion ranges between just 24% (Romania) and 33% (Czech Republic and Slovenia) in the CSEE study countries. Between one third and half of the respondents in CSEE find it difficult to access care services.

Table 10.3: Perceived access to nursing homes and care services

	perceived access to nursing homes		perceived access to care services	
	easy	difficult	easy	difficult
EU 27	39	28	41	25
Austria	40	41	48	35
Croatia	18	59	25	50
Czech Republic	18	65	33	47
Hungary	22	55	31	45
Romania	19	33	24	39
Slovakia	22	57	32	50
Slovenia	23	49	33	35
France	75	14	55	15
Germany	48	25	61	14
Italy	39	39	34	44
Sweden	23	17	28	10
UK	29	14	32	17

Definition: Perceived access to nursing homes and care services, agreement in %. Response categories: very easy, fairly easy (easy) / very difficult, fairly difficult (difficult) / don't know.
(Source: European Commission 2007)

In the past decade, there is a growing trend emphasising community care rhetorically, a trend which at least partly is also translated into concrete policies. The implications of the financial crisis, however, currently often put a limit to these efforts. New policy approaches include the diversification of service offers including day care centres or sheltered housing, the funding of pilot programmes, the development of public-private partnerships facilitating the entry of private providers, or the integration of existing service structures. In some countries, specific programmes attempt to combine elements of service provision in the home of the user, cash benefits and family orientation. These include personal assistance (as in Romania or Slovenia), foster care in Croatia (financial support for older people in need of care living in the private household of another family; see section 6) or the family assistant model in Slovenia (family assistants living with the person in need of care).

In terms of funding, very different principles apply for health sector and for social sector provisions. Health systems in CSEE are built on the social health insurance principle. (Waters et al. 2008; Marée, Groenewegen 1997) Services for older people in need of long-term care covered by the health sector, including chronic care beds in hospitals and outpatient health nursing, are funded from social health insurance contributions. In this case, private contributions include co-payments and payments for additional services not covered under the respective health insurance package. Additionally, informal payments are a relevant additional source of health care funding in Central Eastern Europe. (Lewis 2002) Altogether, compared to the social sector, individual financial burdens for users generally remain much lower in the health sector, creating a considerable incentive to potential users searching for health provision rather than social sector provision. More importantly, however, the use of acute health care services rather than long-term care services (where the latter would be sufficient and appropriate) is still quite common because long-term care services are simply not available.

In the social sector, service consumption is also funded by a combination of public and private sources. Different from the health sector, however, social assistance principles apply in the social sector. The public contribution is tax-funded and paid as a mix of per bed or per service unit remuneration and additional public subsidisation related to infrastructure. As a consequence of decentralisation, the state is in general only involved in subsidising infrastructure or pilot programmes, while service oriented payments are made by the regional or local level. Users have to contribute according to their economic situation. Except for those with very low income and no assets, social assistance regulations make private contributions quite substantial. New regulations apply in the Czech Republic where there is a maximum level for user contributions that are linked to the care allowance paid to the person in need of care (see section 6). Given the lack of publicly co-funded services and the social assistance orientation in the social care sector, the majority of the population regards services as not affordable. While just 7% of the Dutch or 12% of the Swedes see nursing homes as not affordable in the 2007 Eurobarometer survey (European Commission 2007), it is 64% in Slovenia, 58% in Croatia, or 52% in Slovakia. More than 40% of respondents in Hungary, Romania, Slovakia and Slovenia regard care services in the home of the dependent person as unaffordable, while it is just 9% in Sweden, 16% in the Netherlands or 32% in the EU27 average. (European Commission 2007)

6. Public Long-term Care Policies: Cash for Care

The introduction and extension of cash for care programmes is one of the major trends in European long-term care policies. The respective schemes and the underlying objectives vary widely from benefits paid to care users to benefits paid to care-givers, and from allowances without pre-defined use of the benefit to personal budgets to be used in pre-defined ways. (Da Roit, Le Bihan 2010; Da Roit et al. 2009; Ungerson, Yeandle 2007; Timonen et al. 2006; Glendinning, Kemp 2006) With the introduction of these schemes, countries have extended choices for users or have extended earlier more restrictive public long-term care responsibility. Mostly, cash for care schemes are understood as a contribution to care-related costs rather than full coverage of long-term care needs. Depending on the respective design, many cash benefit schemes are explicitly or implicitly also expected to activate (or to sustain) informal care resources. Different from community care services, cash benefits paid to care users or informal carers are an important element of long-term care policies in CSEE addressing the needs of chronically ill, disabled or frail older people. Many of these schemes are understood as income support rather than cash for care, even if eligibility is linked to care needs or the provision of care. But recent developments increasingly emphasise the link between cash for care and service provision. The different cash for care models in CSEE can be classified in three groups, payments to care users, payments to care-givers and approaches that more strictly link financial contributions with service provision.

The novel care allowance scheme in the Czech Republic introduced in 2007 is the most comprehensive example of cash for care payments directed towards care users. The scheme has significant similarities with the Austrian cash for care approach. The Czech care allowance scheme, replacing and extending earlier cash for care programmes, provides care allowances in four different levels with a benefit ranging between about € 71 in level 1 and € 400 per month in case of complete dependency. Benefit levels, however, slightly differ between those below 18 years of age (7% of recipients) and those beyond 18 years of age (93% of recipients). More than two thirds of the recipients are older people aged 65+. When recipients use social services, co-payments are calculated on the basis of the care allowance. An additional element of the scheme, directed at informal carers, is social insurance coverage. On the one hand, the main carer can become a state policy holder in the public health insurance system. Additionally, periods of informal care-giving are counted as a supplementary period in the pension insurance scheme. (see chapter 3) Another development is behind the cash for care scheme in Romania. Here, a monthly benefit originally designed for people with handicaps has been extended to older people in case they have been recipients before 65 years of age. From 2007, this benefit was replaced by a personal complementary budget with no means-testing and with no limitation to a specific age group. (see chapter 6) A similar cash compensation for older people and the disabled exists in Serbia, a system inherited from the socialist period. In Slovenia, a supplement payment for help and support provided within different social security sub-systems is also paid to the person in need. The respective level varies for different sub-systems and is mostly perceived as a subsidisation of the family budget.

Care allowances paid to informal carers are a rather common and often the only measure available to support informal carers. In the case of Hungary, the system was introduced in 1993. The so-called nursing fee is means-tested and linked to the minimum pension (about € 100 in 2006). Depending on the status of the person in need of care the benefit can be paid at a lower (80%) or a higher rate (130%). (see chapter 5) In Slovakia, a means-tested benefit is paid to informal carers with the explicit intention to provide them with a basic income. Originally not aimed at care for frail older people, it increasingly becomes a major financial support scheme for informal care provided to people of this age group. The benefit amounts to a maximum of € 206 in 2009. As also reported for other countries, for poor households the benefit is a major source of the disposable household income.

A stronger link between a cash benefit and service provision or the formalisation of service provision characterises a third group of cash for care schemes. The most important example is the foster care system in South Eastern Europe, particularly prominent in Croatia. (see chapter 3) Here, payments are made to foster families for providing accommodation, food and personal assistance to an adult person in need of care that is not a family member but is living in the same household. After a recent reform aimed at strengthening quality considerations, foster families are required to apply for a licence and to fulfil specific training requirements. A family can host a maximum of four adult persons for whom the foster family receives financial support. Additionally, families are offered professional support from outside. Similar models have recently also been promoted in Serbia. (see chapter 7)

7. Emerging Private Sector Initiatives

Decentralisation, pluralisation and privatisation are major keywords describing the transition process in CSEE in the past two decades. Social assistance and social care is one of the areas where decentralisation took place, in many countries in the very early years of the transformation. But, while competences were shifted to regional and local authorities, a lack of financial means and a lack of experience on these administrative levels have often for years hindered a systematic expansion of services and have contributed to an unequal development across countries. The process of privatisation and pluralisation in social care instead was slow. Pluralisation has been strong in rhetoric, while policies that translate this into practice only became more important in the more recent past. In terms of institutional provider background, public sector provision still dominates formal care provision in CSEE more than in most other European countries. Non-profit providers are playing an increasingly important role in long-term care provision, even if the relative importance varies largely between but also within countries. The role of for-profit actors in the provision of publicly co-funded services is almost negligible in most of the countries.

In the residential care sector, in the CSEE study countries, between 75% (in Croatia) and almost 100% (in Serbia) of beds are in public institutions, while, e.g., in Austria the public sector only accounts for about 50% of nursing beds.

About one fifth of beds in Hungary and Romania and less than 15% in the other study countries are provided by the non-profit sector, while for-profit homes account for very small shares of total publicly co-funded nursing bed infrastructure. In general, private nursing homes tend to provide smaller numbers of beds per residence compared to public sector nursing homes. With regard to social services provided in the community, the picture varies by sector and country. Health sector services are predominantly public provision. In the social care sector, public provision also plays an important role where these services have a longer tradition. Where services have been implemented more recently, non-profit organisations are playing an increasingly important role. For example, in Romania, about one third of day care centres and about two thirds of domiciliary care is provided by the non-profit sector. (see chapter 6)

Even if the role of non-profit actors is on relatively smaller levels in this region if compared to other European countries, there has been a substantial growth from the 1990s. Some actors, in particular church-related organisations, who have been active in social care before the socialist period, have renewed their activities. Other initiatives have developed in close cooperation with international counterparts providing know-how and co-funding for developing infrastructure. But there are also grassroots initiatives, or non-profit organisations that have earlier been engaged in other welfare sectors now moving into long-term care. In South Eastern European countries, for example, non-profit organisations that have been involved in help for refugees have now shifted their focus towards other areas of social work and social help. Depending on the respective roots, non-profit sector initiatives are emphasising lobbying, the provision of information or the provision of services with the latter becoming an increasingly important role of non-profit organisations.

The development of private actors in the long-term care sector in CSEE is determined by a number of factors. While the private sector development idea was strong from the early 1990s, the relationship between state, private sector and civil society was often contradictory. (Balogh 2009; Frič 2009; Jenei, Kuti 2009; Nemec 2009; Mansfeldová et al. 2004; Munday 2003; Toepler, Salamon 2003; Howard 2002) In many countries, administrative hurdles and systems of funding discriminating against private actors have hindered a larger growth of private sector provision for more than a decade. But there are also the budgetary limitations and a lack of priority of social care in public policies that made the development of new services or an extension of existing services extremely difficult, in the public and in the private sector. The low level of disposable public budgets led to situations where the modernisation of existing public provisions was prioritised over new providers making attempts to enter the market. Taken together, the situation characterised by a lack of potential public (co-) funding and a small proportion of the population that could afford privately paid services limits the entry of private providers. But efforts have been intensified in the recent past to better integrate public and private roles in provision, to stimulate the creation of private-public partnerships and to strengthen non-profit sector contracting.

Some non-profit initiatives, often on a local level, have been quite successful. Their development has been backed up by local or regional political will, by private donations, and / or the financial support from international counterparts of these non-profit organisations or from the European Union. The role these factors are playing varies largely across the region. In some countries, in particular in South Eastern Europe, non-profit organisations came into financial trouble when support from their international counterparts or from international assistance organisations was reduced while at the same time national public authorities were not willing to replace the respective budgets. Another approach that has helped the development of the non-profit sector in CSEE is a specific tax regulation allowing tax-payers to dedicate a certain amount of their annual income tax to an accredited non-profit entity. This "percentage philanthropy" legislation is more common in Central Eastern Europe than in other European regions. (Bullain 2004) In Hungary, the 1% scheme was introduced in 1997. The underlying aim was support for civil society without undermining their independence. (Jenei, Kuti 2009) In Romania a similar scheme was introduced in 2003, first at 1%, after a year at 2%. Participation of tax-payers increased from just 150,000 in 2005 to about 1.3 million in 2008. (see chapter 6)

8. Trends and Perspectives

European countries face very similar challenges with regard to ageing populations and related increases in long-term care needs, even if the extent of the
growth and the timing differ. At the same time, traditional informal care resources and arrangements are under increasing pressure. Across Europe, therefore, countries are searching for a new balance of public, private and family responsibilities to ensure the objectives of high-quality and cost-effective access
to care for all citizens, objectives laid down in European Commission documents (European Commission 2009b; 2008) and in national strategy papers.
CSEE countries share many of the challenges. But they also have to face particular contexts and local parameters, in the demographic and socio-economic
context, in the fragmentation of existing provisions, the lack of infrastructure in
community care, but also the budgetary situation and the competing demands
in the public sector.

Among the countries covered in this study, Austria is among a group of European countries, initiating a major long-term care reform in the 1990s. Since
1993, the long-term care system is built around three main pillars, the family,
a cash for care allowance and services. In CSEE countries, reform debates and
proposals for developing a more comprehensive long-term care system have
intensified only in the more recent past. The Czech Republic is the only country where these debates have led to a major comprehensive reform in 2006. At
the centre of the reform is a care allowance scheme, similar to that in Austria,
and a new law on social services regulating accreditation of and contracting
with service providers. Slovenia has put forward a detailed proposal for a long-
term care insurance scheme with important elements taken from the German
approach. The basic idea of the proposal is compulsory social insurance. A
person in need would have the opportunity either to opt for a cash benefit to
be used as a personal budget or to be provided with services instead. Despite
elaborated plans and repeated attempts for introduction, the reform has not yet
been implemented. Long-term care insurance has also been on the agenda in
Slovakia, in Romania or in Hungary (here, more strongly linked to the existing
health insurance scheme), but plans have not been developed to the same extent
as in Slovenia. Rather than implementing comprehensive reform projects, all

countries have seen social assistance reforms and regulations clarifying responsibilities in funding and provision of social care services, not least between different federal levels. More recent attempts are focusing on the relationship between public and private sector provisions and the role of the consumer of social services.

Recent reform debates in CSEE stress quite similar objectives: a clarification of responsibilities in funding and provision in health and in social care and between federal levels, the pluralisation of service provision, the development of social service provision in the community that allows older people in need of long-term care to stay in their private home, the development of alternative housing arrangements, the improvement of access to services and the effectiveness and efficiency of provisions. Difficulties in actually implementing new comprehensive long-term care systems arise from various factors. Decentralisation has led to split responsibilities. While this can help promote innovation in a competitive environment among regional and local levels, it can also hinder systematic developments of the sector, even more so in a situation of economic pressure. In fact, in the past few years, public budgets often worked as a bottleneck in implementing new or extending existing provisions, the more so as long-term care is not considered as a top priority. Long-term care debates, therefore, often remain limited to expert groups involving representatives from the public sector, practitioners and civil society, while a broader public debate is missing.

Besides the macro-level approaches, successful practices on local levels are most important for long-term care sector developments in these areas, but also as models of good practice that recognise the specific social, cultural and economic context. Such practices are rooted either in traditional approaches to provide care for older people in need of care or in more recent developments and pilot programmes. Examples include foster care in Croatia, where older people in need of care are not living with their own family, but in the household of another family. This scheme has been reinforced in 2007 becoming a more integral part of the Croatian approach to long-term care. Also in Serbia, policy documents point at foster care as an alternative to traditional residential care. In Hungary, village caretakers provide different kinds of services, including home help services, in small communities where such service provision would otherwise not be available. In Romania, as in other study countries, non-profit organisations have become important forerunners in developing social services in the community, in particular in those areas where such services were not existent before. In one Austrian province, funding and provision of qualified home care services is based on community-level associations. Individuals or families as paying members of the local association become eligible for service provision. In Slovenia, a pilot project on direct funding combines the need for support with the objective to achieve greater user independence by developing individual service planning. These are just a few examples of more traditional and more novel approaches. They have grown as a local reaction to specific deficits or as pilot programmes, recognising the particular national or local context. These programmes provide support that complements or substitutes traditional family care systems or create alternatives to institutionalisation. Taking the context into account, these approaches could also work as practice models to be considered for broader dissemination. It is, however, again not least financial considerations that often limit room for disseminating and strengthening best practices.

Current developments and debates about the future of long-term care for frail older people are driven by demographic and socio-economic challenges. To ensure high-quality and cost-effective access to long-term care services for all citizens, European countries will have to extend existing and to develop novel schemes that complement and substitute traditional care arrangements. In CSEE, the development of infrastructure in integrated and community-oriented social services, the reduction of inequalities, the focus on user needs and on quality of services, the establishment of novel governance structures and sustainable public–private relationships are key issues for the near future. Realising these objectives requires that long-term care is recognised as a major social risk, that social policies substantially increase investment in this sector and that public sector, private actors and civil society join capacities and know-how in developing and implementing accessible and high-quality long-term care provisions.

Bibliography

Alber, Jens; Köhler, Ulrich (2004) Health and care in an enlarged Europe. Luxembourg: European Foundation for the Improvement of Living and Working Conditions.

Anttonen, Anneli; Baldock, John; Sipilä, Jorma (2008) The young, the old and the state. Social care systems in five industrial nations. Cheltenham: Edward Elgar.

Babić, Dragutin; Lajić, Ivan; Podgorelec, Sonja (2004) Islands of two generations. Zagreb: Institute for Migrations and Ethnicity.

Balogh, Marton (2009) The role of Romanian NGOs in the democratization process of the society after 1990. In: Osborne (2009).

Barvíková, Jana; Bartoňová, Jitka (2005) Příběhy pečujících rodin (*The stories of caring families*). In: Problematika – generace 50 plus. II. mezinárodní konference, Třeboň 6-7 October 2005, Sborník přednášek, Třeboň, 97–107.

Błędowski, Piotr; Pędich, Wojciech; Bień, Barbara; Wojszel, Z. Beata; Czekanowski, Piotr (2006) Supporting family carers of older people in Europe. The national background report for Poland. Hamburg: LIT Verlag.

Bullain, Nilda (2004) Explaining percentage philanthropy. Legal nature, rationales, impact. In: The International Journal of Not-for-profit Law, Vol. 6, No. 4.

Burau, Viola; Theobald, Hildegard; Blank, Robert H. (2007) Governing home care. A cross-national comparison. Cheltenham: Edward Elgar.

Castles, Francis G.; Obinger, Herbert (2008) Worlds, families, regimes: Country clusters in European and OECD area public policy. In: West European Politics, Vol. 31, No. 1, 321–344.

Cerami, Alfio; Vanhuysse, Pieter (2009) Post-communist welfare pathways. Theorizing social policy transformations in Central and Eastern Europe. Basingstoke: Palgrave Macmillan.

Cerami, Alfio (2006) Social policy in Central and Eastern Europe. The emergence of a new European welfare regime. Münster: LIT Verlag.

Cook, Linda (2010) Eastern Europe and Russia. In: Castles, Francis G.; Leibfried, Stephan; Lewis, Jane; Obinger, Herbert; Pierson, Christopher (eds) The Oxford handbook of the welfare state. Oxford: Oxford University Press.

Deacon, Bob; Stubbs, Paul (2008) Social policy and international interventions in South East Europe. Cheltenham: Edward Elgar.

Da Roit, Barbara; Le Bihan, Blanche (2010) Similar and yet so different: Cash-for-care in six European countries' long-term care policies. In: Milbank Quarterly, Vol. 88, No. 3, 286–309.

Da Roit, Barbara; Le Bihan, Blanche; Österle, August (2007) Long-term care policies in Italy, Austria and France: Variations in cash-for-care schemes. In: Social Policy & Administration, Vol. 41, No. 6, 653–671.

Dobre, Suzana; Roth, Maria (2005) Emerging care services for elderly in Romania. In: Studia Universitatis Babes-Bolyai – Sociology, No. 2, 3–17

Doyle, Marta; Timonen, Virpi (2008) Home care for ageing populations: A comparative analysis of domiciliary care in Denmark, Germany and the United States. Cheltenham: Edward Elgar.

European Commission (2009a): The 2009 ageing report: Economic and budgetary projections for the EU-27 Member States (2008–2060). Joint Report prepared by European Commission (DG ECFIN) and the Economic Policy Committee (AWG). European Economy 2/2009. Brussels: European Commission.

European Commission (2009b) National strategy reports on social protection and social inclusion 2008–2010 and Joint report on social protection and social inclusion. Brussels: European Commission.

European Commission (2008) Long-term care in the European Union. Brussels: European Commission.

European Commission (2007) Health and long-term care in the European Union. Report. Special Eurobarometer 283 / Wave 67.3. Brussels: European Commission.

Eurostat (2009) Eurostat Database. http://epp.eurostat.ec.europa.eu (21 July 2010).

Fenger, H.J.M. (2007) Welfare regimes in Central and Eastern Europe: Incorporating post-communist countries in a welfare regime typology. In: Journal of Contemporary Issues in Social Sciences, Vol. 3, No. 2, 1–30.

Frič, Pavol (2009) The uneasy partnership of the state and the third sector in the Czech Republic. In: Osborne (2009).

Glendinning, Caroline; Kemp, Peter (eds) (2006), Cash and care: Policy challenges in the welfare state. Bristol: The Policy Press.

Hacker, Björn (2009) Hybridization instead of clustering: Transformation processes of welfare policies in Central and Eastern Europe. In: Social Policy & Administration, Vol. 43, No. 2, 152–169.

Holmerová, Iva (2007) Supporting family carers of older people in Europe. The national background report for the Czech Republic. Hamburg: LIT Verlag.

Howard, Marc Morje (2002) The weakness of postcommunist civil society. In: Journal of Democracy, Vol. 13, No. 1, 157–169.

Hvalič Touzery, Simona (2007) Supporting family carers of older people in Europe. The national background report for Slovenia. Hamburg: LIT Verlag.

Inglot, Tomasz (2008) Welfare states in East Central Europe, 1919–2004. Cambridge: Cambridge University Press.

Jenei, György; Kuti, Éva (2009) The third sector and civil society. In: Osborne (2009).

Klenner, Christina; Leiber, Simone (eds) (2010) Welfare states and gender inequality in Central and Eastern Europe. Brussels: etui.

Kovács, János Mátyás (2002) Approaching the EU and reaching the US? Rival narratives on transforming welfare regimes in East-Central Europe. In: West European Politics, Vol. 25, No. 2, 175–204.

Lamura, Giovanni; Döhner, Hanneli; Kofahl, Christopher (eds) (2008) Family carers of older people in Europe. Münster: LIT Verlag.

Lewis, Maureen (2002) Informal health payments in Central and Eastern Europe and the former Soviet Union: Issues, trends and policy implications. In: Mossialos, Elias; Dixon, Anna; Figueras, Josep; Kutzin, Joe (eds) Funding health care. Options for Europe. Buckingham: Open University Press.

Manning, Nick (2004) Diversity and change in pre-accession Central and Eastern Europe since 1989. In: Journal of European Social Policy, Vol. 14, No. 3, 211–232.

Mansfeldová, Zdenka; Nałęcz, Slawomir; Priller, Eckhard; Zimmer, Annette (2004) Civil society in transition: Civic engagement and nonprofit organizations in Central and Eastern Europe after 1989. In: Zimmer, Annette; Priller, Eckhard (eds) Future of civil society. Making Central European nonprofit-organisations work. Wiesbaden: VS Verlag für Sozialwissenschaften.

Marée, Jörgen; Groenewegen, Peter P. (1997) Back to Bismarck: Eastern European health care systems in transition. Aldershot: Avebury.

Mestheneos, Elizabeth; Triantafillou, Judy (2005) Supporting family carers of older people in Europe. The pan-European background report. Münster: LIT Verlag.

Munday, Brian (2003) State or civil society? Social care in Central and Eastern Europe. Canterbury: European Institute of Social Services.

Munday, Brian; Lane, George (1998) The old and the new. Changes in social care in Central and Eastern Europe. Canterbury: European Institute of Social Services.

Nelson, Joan M.; Tilly, Charles; Walker, Lee (1997) Transforming post-communist political economies. Washington: National Academy Press.

Nemec, Juraj (2009) The third sector and the provision of public services in Slovakia. In: Osborne (2009).

OECD (2010) OECD Health Data 2010. Paris: OECD.

Orenstein, Mitchell A. (2009) Transnational actors in Central and East European pension reforms. In: Cerami, Vanhuysse (2009).

Osborne, Stephen P. (ed) (2009) The third sector in Europe. Prospects and challenges. London: Routledge.

Österle, August (2010) Long-term care in Central and South Eastern Europe: Challenges and perspectives in addressing a 'new' social risk. In: Social Policy & Administration, Vol. 44, No. 4, pp. 461–480.

Österle, August; Rothgang, Heinz (2010) Long-term care. In: Castles, Francis G.; Leibfried, Stephan; Lewis, Jane; Obinger, Herbert; Pierson, Christopher (eds) The Oxford handbook of the welfare state. Oxford: Oxford University Press.

Pascall, Gillian; Lewis, Jane (2004) Emerging gender regimes and policies for gender equality in a wider Europe. In: Journal of Social Policy, Vol. 33, No. 3, 373–394.

Pascall, Gillian; Manning, Nick (2000) Gender and social policy: Comparing welfare states in Central and Eastern Europe and the former Soviet Union. In: Journal of European Social Policy, Vol. 10, No. 3, 240–266.

Pavolini, Emmanuele; Ranci, Costanzo (2008) Restructuring the welfare state: reforms in long-term care in Western European countries. In: Journal of European Social Policy, Vol. 18, No. 3, 246–259.

Repková, Kvetoslava (2008) Situácia rodinných opatrovateľov/liek vo svetle sociálnych štatistík (*The situation of family carers in the light of social statistics*). Bratislava: Institute for Labour and Family Research.

Schubert, Klaus; Hegelich, Simon; Bazant, Ursula (eds) (2009) The handbook of European welfare systems. London: Routledge.

Stubbs, Paul; Zrinščak, Siniša (2009) Croatian social policy: The legacies of war, state-building and late Europeanization. In: Social Policy and Administration, Vol. 43, No. 2, 121-135.

Széman, Zsuzsa (2004) Eurofamcare. National background report for Hungary. Hamburg: University of Hamburg.

Széman, Zsuzsa (2003) The welfare mix in Hungary as a new phenomenon. In: Social Policy & Society, Vol. 2, No. 2, 101–108.

Theobald, Hildegard; Kern, Kristine (2009) Elder care systems. Policy transfer and Europeanization. In: Cerami, Vanhuysse (2009).

Timonen, Virpi; Convery, Janet; Cahill, Zusanne (2006) Care revolutions in the making. A comparison of cash-for-care programmes in four European countries. In: Ageing & Society, Vol. 26, No. 3, 455–474.

Toepler, Stefan; Salamon, Lester M. (2003) NGO development in Central and Eastern Europe: An empirical overview. In: East European Quarterly, Vol. XXXVII, No. 3, 365–378.

Toth, Georgiana; Tufiş, Paula; Păun, Georgiana; Şerban, Monica; Mihai, Ioana-Alexandra (2007) Efectele migratiei. Copiii ramasi acasa (*Effects of migration. Children left alone at home*). Bucureşti: Fundaţia Soros România.

Ungerson, Clare; Yeandle, Sue (eds) (2007) Cash for care in developed welfare states. Basingstoke: Palgrave Macmillan.

Waters, Hugh R.; Hobart, Jessica; Forrest, Christopher B.; Siemens, Karen Kinder; Pittman, Patricia M.; Murthy, Ananthram; Vanderver, Glenn Bruce; Anderson, Gerard F.; Morlock, Laura L. (2008) Health insurance coverage in Central and Eastern Europe: Trends and challenges. In: Health Affairs, Vol. 27, No. 2, 478–486.